Critical Geographies of Sp

Sport is a geographic phenomenon. The physical and organizational infra-structure of sport occupies a prominent place in many societies. This important book takes an explicitly spatial approach to sport, bringing together research in geography, sport studies, and related disciplines to articulate a critical approach to 'sports geography'. *Critical Geographies of Sport* illustrates this approach by engaging directly with a variety of theoretical traditions as well as the latest research methods.

Each chapter showcases the merits of a geographic approach to the study of sport, ranging from football to running, horseracing, and profes-sional wrestling. Including cases from Asia, Africa, the Middle East, Europe, and the Americas, the book highlights the ways that space and power are produced through sport and its concomitant infrastructures, agencies, and networks. Holding these power relations at the center of its analysis, it considers sport as a unique lens onto our understanding of space.

Truly global in its perspective, it is fascinating reading for any student or scholar with an interest in sport and politics, sport and society, or human geography.

Natalie Koch is Assistant Professor in the Department of Geography, The Maxwell School of Citizenship and Public Affairs, Syracuse University, USA. Her current research focuses on state-making, nationalism, geopoli-tics, and authoritarianism, with a special interest in spectacle – both in urban landscapes and in events like national celebrations and sports. An elite cyclist herself, she has a long interest in the intersection between polit-ical geography and sport, and has published numerous articles in journals such as *Political Geography*, *Urban Geography*, *Geoforum*, *Social and Cultural Geography*, and *Transactions of the Institute of British Geographers*.

Routledge Critical Studies in Sport
Series Editors
Jennifer Hargreaves and Ian McDonald
University of Brighton

The Routledge Critical Studies in Sport series aims to lead the way in developing the multidisciplinary field of Sport Studies by producing books that are interrogative, interventionist and innovative. By providing theoretically sophisticated and empirically grounded texts, the series will make sense of the changes and challenges facing sport globally. The series aspires to maintain the commitment and promise of the critical paradigm by contributing to a more inclusive and less exploitative culture of sport.

Also available in this series:

Critical Geographies of Sport

Space, power and sport in global perspective

Edited by Natalie Koch

Routledge
Taylor & Francis Group
LONDON AND NEW YORK

First published 2017
by Routledge
2 Park Square, Milton Park, Abingdon, Oxon OX14 4RN

and by Routledge
711 Third Avenue, New York, NY 10017

First issued in paperback 2018

Routledge is an imprint of the Taylor & Francis Group, an informa business

British Library Cataloguing-in-Publication Data
A catalogue record for this book is available from the British Library

Library of Congress Cataloging in Publication Data
Names: Koch, Natalie, editor.
Title: Critical geographies of sport : space, power and sport in global perspective / edited by Natalie Koch.
Description: Abingdon, Oxon ; New York, NY : Routledge is an imprint of the Taylor & Francis Group, an Informa Business, [2016] |
Series: Routledge critical studies in sport | Includes bibliographical references and index.
Identifiers: LCCN 2016018277| ISBN 9781138927124 (hardback) | ISBN 9781315682815 (ebook)
Subjects: LCSH: Sports–Anthropological aspects. | Sports–Social aspects. | Human geography.
Classification: LCC GV706.2 .C75 2016 | DDC 306.4/83–dc23
LC record available at https://lccn.loc.gov/2016018277

ISBN 13: 978-1-138-54145-0 (pbk)
ISBN 13: 978-1-138-92712-4 (hbk)

Typeset in Sabon
by Wearset Ltd, Boldon, Tyne and Wear

In memory of Doug Foster

Contents

Figures

Tables

Contributors

Jon D. Bohland is Associate Professor of Political Science and International Studies at Hollins University in Roanoke, Virginia, USA. His research interests are focused primarily on the intersections between geopolitics and popular forms of culture including sports, visual science fiction, and public practices of collective memory. His published work has appeared in journals such as *Southeastern Geographer, Dialogues in Human Geography,* and *Southwestern Geographer,* and in collected volumes including *Neo-Confederacy: A Critical Introduction; Battlestar Galactica and International Relations;* and *Football and the Boundaries of History: Critical Studies in Soccer.*

Neil Conner is Assistant Professor of Geography and Social Science Education at Delta State University. He received his Ph.D. in Geography at the University of Tennessee studying the intersections of political and cultural geography. His dissertation research explores the politics of national identity, migration, and religion in Dublin, Ireland. His publications on sports include "Global cultural flows and the routes of identity: the imagined worlds of Celtic FC" (*Social and Cultural Geography* 2014) and "Geography of Sports" (*Oxford Bibliographies in Geography* 2014). In 2015, he received the K. Patricia Cross Future Leaders Award from the Association of American Colleges and Universities.

Simon Cook is a human geographer based in the Department of Geography at Royal Holloway, University of London, UK. His research concerns the everyday practices of everyday life: the ways in which they happen, in which they change, and what they can tell us about societies and spaces. He is currently exploring this interest in a project on the practice of running and his doctoral research considers the emergence and potential of run-commuting as an urban mode of mobility. More information about his work and geographical perspectives on running is available at: jographies.wordpress.com

Arlene Crampsie is a Teaching Fellow in the School of Geography, University College Dublin, Republic of Ireland. A historical geographer with interests in social and cultural change, her doctoral research examined the operation of local government in nineteenth- and early-twentieth-century Ireland. This interest in locally based democracy and power was expanded over the course of a four-year postdoctoral research position on the GAA Oral History Project, where she assisted with the publication of *The GAA: A People's History* and *The GAA: County by County* (The Collins Press, 2009, 2011). Her current research is in the realm of sports geography, utilizing the GAA and the detailed empirical archive of the GAA Oral History Project to examine issues around power and identity.

Michael Friedman is Assistant Research Professor in the Physical Cultural Studies Program in the Department of Kinesiology at the University of Maryland, College Park, USA. His research focuses on the relationship between public policy, urban design, and professional sports in the postindustrial city with a perspective informed by cultural studies and cultural geography. By examining sports facilities such as stadiums and arenas, he is concerned with the ways in which space expresses and (re) produces power relationships, social identities, and societal structures. He has published research in the *Sociology of Sport Journal, International Review for the Sociology of Sport, Journal of Urban Affairs, Journal of Sport History, Economic Development Quarterly*, and *City, Culture & Society*.

Bradley S. Gardener is a GIS Teaching Fellow at Middlebury College, Vermont, USA. His research addresses how patriarchy and racism are articulated and reproduced at various geographical scales. More specifically, he examines the intersections between space, race, gender, and identity. His other research interests include sport, migration, critical applications of GIS, and gentrification. Bradley is also a co-editor of the volume, *Geographies of Privilege*. He currently co-hosts a monthly podcast about the business of professional wrestling.

Slavomír Horák is Academic Fellow at the Department of Russian and East European Studies, in the Institute of International Studies, Faculty of Social Sciences, Charles University, in Prague, Czech Republic. He focuses on social and political development in Central Asia, with particular attention to Turkmenistan. He is interested in the problems of state- and nation-building, authoritarian regime ideology, and the formation of elites. He has published numerous articles and books. Among his monographs are, in Czech, *Afghan Conflict* (Public History 2005) and *Russia and Central Asia After 1991* (Karolinum 2008), and, in English, *Dismantling Totalitarianism? Turkmenistan Under Berdimuhamedow* (co-authored with Jan Šír, Central Asia and the Caucasus Institute 2009).

David Jansson is Associate Professor of Human Geography at Uppsala University, Sweden. He previously taught at Vassar College in Poughkeepsie, New York, USA. His work focuses on the geographic aspects of identity. He has published widely on American nationalism and representations of the US South, employing the perspective of internal orientalism. His current research project investigates the role of automobility in the construction of the Swedish *folkhem* as well as a modern Swedish national identity. Other interests include sports geography, placebranding, and the cultural politics of visuality.

Natalie Koch is Assistant Professor in the Department of Geography at Syracuse University's Maxwell School of Citizenship and Public Affairs, New York, USA. She specializes in political geography, with a focus on geopolitics, nationalism, and authoritarian state-making. Her regional expertise is in the resource-rich countries of the Arabian Peninsula and post-Soviet Central Asia, where she examines statist spectacles and development agendas – both in urban landscapes and in events such as nationalist celebrations and sports. She has authored numerous articles in journals, such as *Political Geography, Urban Geography, Geoforum, Area,* and *Transactions of the Institute of British Geographers.* In addition to her interest in the geography of sport, Dr. Koch is an athlete herself, races for Team NovoNordisk, the world's first all-Type 1 diabetes cycling team.

Jung Woo Lee is Lecturer in Sport and Leisure Policy at the University of Edinburgh, UK, and received his PhD in the sociology of sport from Loughborough University, UK. He is an editorial board member of *International Review for the Sociology of Sport* and is also an associate editor of *Asia Pacific Journal of Sport and Social Science.* His research interests include sport media and communication, semiotics, sports mega-events, and globalization of sport. He has published articles in various peer-reviewed journals including *Sociology, International Review for the Sociology of Sport, Journal of Sport and Social Issue, International Journal of Sport Communication,* and *Communication and Sport.* Dr. Lee is also currently co-editing the forthcoming *Routledge Handbook of Sport and Politics.*

Lise Nelson is Associate Professor in the Department of Women's, Gender, and Sexuality Studies and in the Department of Geography at Penn State University, USA. Drawing on research based in Mexico and the United States, her work focuses on labor, social reproduction, identity, and citizenship in the context of globalization. She has published her research in the *Annals of the Association of American Geographers, Progress in Human Geography* and *Environment and Planning D: Society and Space* among other journals, and is co-editor (with Joni Seager) of *A Companion to Feminist* Geography (Blackwell 2005).

Pauliina Raento is Professor of Human Geography at the University of Helsinki, Finland. She is Principal Investigator of "The Horse in Finland" research project, funded by the Kone Foundation (2014–18). Her research focuses on political and cultural geography and the geographies of leisure in Europe, North America, and the Caribbean. She is particularly fond of interdisciplinarity, visual and field methodologies, and teaching science writing and editing. Her edited work includes over a dozen books and special issues, including *Gambling in Finland: Data and Methods for Qualitative Research* (Gaudeamus Helsinki University Press 2014) and *Gambling, Space, and Time: Shifting Boundaries and Cultures* (with David G. Schwartz, University of Nevada Press 2011). She received her PhD in Basque Studies at the University of Nevada, Reno, and holds a degree in Stable Management from the Ypäjä Equine College, Finland.

Jon Shaw is Professor and Head of Geography at Plymouth University, UK. He has been Associate Editor of the *Journal of Transport Geography* and a Specialist Adviser to the Transport Committee of the House of Commons, and is currently a member of the Great Western Railway Advisory Board. He researches issues associated with mobility, transport policy, and governance. He is author and editor of eight books, the most recent of which, *The Transport Debate* (Policy Press 2014), explores mobility and related issues from the perspective of different family members making a series of journeys in a variety of circumstances.

Magid Shihade is a faculty member at the Institute of International Studies at Birzeit University, Palestine, and is currently Lecturer in the Middle East/South Asia Studies Program at the University of California-Davis, USA. His research focuses on settler colonialism, decolonization, modernity, violence, identity, and the anthropology and politics of knowledge, and he has published several articles and book chapters on these topics. He is the author of *Not Just a Soccer Game: Colonialism and Conflict among Palestinians in Israel* (Syracuse University Press, 2011), and is currently working on a second book project tentatively titled, *Global Israel: Settler Colonialism and Rupture*.

Paul Simpson is Lecturer of Human Geography in the School of Geography, Earth and Environmental Sciences, Plymouth University, UK. His research focuses on the social and cultural geographies of everyday, artistic, and mobile practices and explores the complex situatedness of such practices in the environments in which they take place. Most recently he has pursued these interests through a collaborative project funded by L'Agence National de la Recherché, considering the imbrications of ambiances, atmospheres, and security in spaces of urban mobilities. He has published on these themes in *Area, Cultural Geographies, Environment and Planning A, Geoforum, Social and Cultural Geography*, amongst other outlets.

Veli-Pekka Tynkkynen is Professor in Russian Energy Policy at the University of Helsinki, Finland. He has focused on conflicts and power analytics related to natural resource use and spatial planning and development in Russia. He leads several research projects on energy and environmental policies, energy security, and societal power and culture in Russia. He has published widely on these topics in journals such as *European Planning Studies, Slavic Review, Journal of Environmental Planning and Management*, and *Polar Geography*. He is also co-editor (with Susanne Oxenstierna) of *Russian Energy and Security up to 2030* (Routledge, 2013).

Nicholas Wise is an independent researcher in the fields of geography, sport, events, and tourism. He has numerous publications focusing on sports geography addressing sense of place, community and identity, and social regeneration, in outlets such as the *International Review for the Sociology of Sport, Geographical Research, Journal of Sport & Tourism* and *Soccer & Society*. He has conducted research in the Dominican Republic, Croatia, and Serbia. His current research focuses on social regeneration linked to community change and local impact in Croatia.

Chapter 1

Introduction

Critical geographies of sport in global perspective

Natalie Koch [1]

Introduction

"The world of play," geographer Yi-Fu Tuan (1984: 3) has noted, "has an air of innocence." But this innocence is deceptive, he argues, since power and domination are always at work in the world of play and in what he terms the "cultural-aesthetic realm." Because of play's unique ability to delight, power and domination are easily dissociated from it and other aesthetic activities. Writing over 30 years ago, Tuan's work has played a key role in shaping contemporary critical geography, which foregrounds questions of power in theoretical and empirical research. Like social science more generally, geography's recent emphasis on power has been brought to bear on a wide range of subjects. Sport, however, has not been fore among these. To be sure, geographers have been undertaking critical studies of sport in recent years, but this has been more sporadic than coherent; scholars are often more in conversation with their primary subfield than one another, or even the field of sports studies more widely.

Critical Geographies of Sport thus arises from two broad trends in contemporary geographic scholarship: the first is the institutional weakness of "sports geography" as a disciplinary subfield, and the second is an opportunity to advance existing work through directly engaging critical theoretical approaches, both within geography and beyond. United by a common research interest in sport and power, this volume brings together geographers and sports studies scholars to showcase the merits of a deeply geographic approach to the study of sport, as well as the synergies and new avenues of inquiry opened up when geographers work toward a more substantive engagement with the wider body of sports studies scholarship. By holding power relations at the center of our analyses, the aim of this volume is to take up sport as a lens for considering how scale, space, and identity come to life in a grounded fashion in diverse settings around the world. And this is a project that cannot – and should not – be confined to a disciplinary silo. Including chapters from both geography and other fields, this book aims to stimulate geographers' interest in the wider field of sports studies and to challenge the status quo of sports geography's institutional weakness. *Critical Geographies of Sport* thus provides a concrete illustration of what a reinvigorated field of sports geography might look like.

Sports geography as a subfield

John Bale's seminal book, *Sports Geography* (first published in 1989, and again in 2003), initiated an ambitious agenda to define a geographic approach to studying sport. Though the author himself was nothing short of prolific in advancing this agenda, his efforts never quite coalesced into a robust subfield within geography. This notwithstanding, John Bale's writing on sports geography has spurred many scholars to consider sport more seriously and accorded a certain name recognition to geographic research on sport outside the discipline. As with any academic leader, Bale's contribution also consists of the way scholars work with his ideas – pushing and pulling them into new terrains – as do the contributors of this book. However, such scholarship is only sporadically articulated under the explicit rubric of "sports geography," despite the large body of research considering the connection between sport and politics (for a recent review, see Gaffney 2014).

It is still rare to find academic geographers today who would claim the identity of "sports geographer," despite it being commonplace to otherwise identify by subfield, such as "political geographer," "urban geographer," or even "Marxist geographer." In large part responding to the stigmatization of studying sport as unprofessional or insufficiently serious (for one such critique, see Dear 1988), geographers have instead tended to frame their study of sports through their other subfield associations. Internal to geography, one effect of this dynamic is that the excellent existing work on sports geography is diffuse and lacks a clear center. Of course, such a center may not be imperative, but the lack of coherence has meant that geographers interested in sport are often not engaging in direct discussion. Externally, this lack of coherence has also meant that geography as a discipline has had a relatively small impact on the broader interdisciplinary field of sports studies. So, despite the proliferation of critical research on sport in ancillary fields, such as sociology, cultural studies, and international affairs, there is rather limited interdisciplinary learning between these disciplines and geography.

This collection revisits the question of what it means to study sport spatially, aiming to bring together some of the diffuse conversations in geography to discover our commonalities, and to make it clear to those in ancillary fields what a critical geographic approach can offer to the study of sport. Acknowledging the limitations to disciplinary Balkanization, it is nonetheless important to consider what geographers mean today when they seek to conduct research or teach on the topic of "sports geography," and to highlight the potential for future directions and engagements with existing research in other fields. Through their diverse case studies, the contributors here collectively set the agenda for a new generation of scholars to advance a critical geography of sport. Nowhere do we seek to circumscribe the meaning of "sport," and instead embrace its variation to promote an international perspective. Chapters therefore draw cases from a wide range of sports and sporting discourses – from football to falconry, running, horseracing, and professional wrestling – in Eurasia, the Middle East, and the Americas.

Of course, in a collection such as this, it is not possible to exhaustively capture the tremendous diversity of sports and sporting practices around the world. This is not simply because of the sheer volume of pages such a task would demand, but largely because of our own limitations as scholars. For example, the larger number of case studies drawn from Europe and the Americas reflects the comparative ease with which scholars are able to conduct research at or near home, with little financial and institutional support. Due to the prevailing stigma attached to sports geography as lacking rigor and relevance, which crops up in the ranking of grant applications for competitive funding sources, geographers seldom receive research funds to develop more substantive research agendas. It may also be the case that researchers are simply not applying for funding – either discouraged by mentors or advisers or convincing themselves that reviewers will not take seriously an application with sports geography as its focus.

In any case, the result is that for many geographers, studying sport has been treated as something of a "side project," undertaken as an addendum to larger projects positioned within their respective fields of political, urban, or cultural geography, and often shaped by their personal sporting interests or a chance encounter or discovery in their fieldwork (see for example my own work on the Astana cycling team and falconry in the Gulf states: Koch 2013, 2015). As a result, this volume includes some overlapping coverage of certain mainstream sports such as soccer/football, as well as accounts of some lesser known and studied sports such as professional wrestling or everyday urban running. It is also a struggle to find geographers working on sports-related issues in non-English speaking settings. Although aiming to achieve as much geographic diversity as possible, the chapters do not cover any case studies from Africa, for instance. While this is an admitted shortcoming, it points to the need and opportunity for geographers to expand their analyses to consider a broader range of field sites and bolster their efforts to get funding for more ambitious research projects beyond their backyard. Of course, academic disciplines can be slow to change, but overcoming the stigmatization of sports geography will require that we take our research seriously and seek the funding resources to do so.

Critical theory and the study of sport

Sports studies scholars have long approached sport as a lens through which to illuminate the political dimensions of key social challenges of the day, such as authoritarianism, international migration, under/development, and inequalities around race, gender, and class. With the exception of a recent flurry of work on mega-events, geographers have been absent from many of these discussions – despite making individually important interventions. With a two-pronged focus on sport and the politics of space at the state and sub-state scales, *Critical Geographies of Sport* illustrates the critical and innovative research currently underway in geography and among sports studies scholars interested in the spatial dimensions of sport. Hoping to promote a wider interdisciplinary discussion that may lay the groundwork for developing unique perspectives on sport and politics, the book encompasses a range of theoretical approaches to incorporating and foregrounding questions of power in the use – and abuse – of sport, sporting rhetoric, and athletic spectacles.

As the social sciences increasingly coalesce around critical theory, an exceptional opportunity to broaden geography's engagement with scholars in other fields presents itself. So, while geography is an enormously diverse field, it has also begun to unite around the umbrella concept of "critical geography" – indexing theoretical inclinations as diverse as Marxism, postcolonialism, feminism, postmodernism, Foucauldian-inspired poststructuralism, and actor-network theory. So dominant is this approach today that it is hard to imagine any current geographic scholarship that is not "critical." While a number of these frameworks have ossified into solid subfields (e.g., "critical geopolitics," "critical race studies," and "critical cartography"), the field of geography has not yet systematically analyzed the subject of sport from this critical vantage point. Treating this situation as an opportunity to push beyond the early work of John Bale and others, *Critical Geographies of Sport* builds upon the diverse theoretical traditions encapsulated by the "critical turn" to envision a more critical sports geography that foregrounds *power* and the *production of space*.

The spatial lens that geographers typically emphasize in their work forms the foundation of what the discipline can offer to the wider study of sport. Additionally, critical social theory's emphasis on theorizing power as produced and performed at multiple scales – especially Michel Foucault's (1980, 1982) "capillary" understanding of power, and Bruno Latour's (2005) network-based approach to power – has increasingly led other disciplines to undergo their own "spatial turn." Central to this volume's focus, these advances have together radically transformed academic treatments of politics by giving impetus to the serious study of key cultural institutions (Dittmer 2010) – such as sport. By decentering traditional approaches to politics as an elite phenomenon, critical theory has enabled scholars to consider the unique ways that sport is bound up with the production of power relations. Take, for example, the issue of how gender is engaged by scholars in this volume. The effort that geographers make to foreground the *political production of space* means that the role of sporting spaces in (re)producing gender hierarchies are woven into the varied analyses here – with nearly all of the chapters addressing the issue in some manner. This is a seemingly small but important difference from the central place gender or female sports are given in gender in sports sociology (e.g., Burstyn 1999; Hargreaves 1994, 2000; Hargreaves and Anderson 2014; Messner 2007).

Adopting a resolutely spatial lens, this volume does not just assert the merits of such an approach, but the individual chapters serve as solid examples of the diverse manner in which this research might actually be conducted. The basic assumption running through every chapter is that sport is inherently political – an approach that has been well established in the critical work on the sociology of sport (Hallinen and Jackson 2008; Giulianotti 2015; Marjoribanks and Farquharson 2012; Sugden and Tomlinson 2002). While much of the existing geographic research on sport has centered on questions of space and place (e.g., Bale 1993; Eichberg *et al.* 1998; Vertinsky and Bale 2004), this work has not always foregrounded critical questions of power. Or, in other words, instead of making key arguments about the working of power and the politicized production of space, sports geographers have tended to make empirical and theoretical contributions about the nature of sport itself. While this approach is not necessarily problematic in and of itself, it has meant that sport-focused researchers have not always been able to assert the wider relevance of their work to those who are not interested in sport or who fail to see its sociopolitical importance. In this volume, we demonstrate that by highlighting the relationship between sport and power, sports geographers are better positioned to answer the key question constantly posed to all scholars: "so what?" In justifying the significance of critical geographies of sport, we are also pressed to answer the question: "for whom?" Discussed at length in my conclusion with David Jansson, suffice it to say here that, in answering these questions, power must necessarily be at the heart of our concerns if we are to properly account for our own positionality as researchers, our relationship to those with whom we work, and our audiences (Pryke *et al.* 2003).

As approached in this volume, power relationships are generally understood to be both enabling and constraining, and to have both "positive" and "negative" expressions (Foucault 1980). As noted already, holding in focus these more positive expressions of power is especially important in the study of sport because of the impression of innocence and delight that Tuan (1984) attributes to the "world of play." It is fair to say that the academic dismissal of sport is often rooted in some of the same dichotomies between work/play or politics/aesthetics which Tuan challenges in his radical search for power and domination beyond the oft-studied spaces of politics and economics. Although many of our colleagues may still hold onto this dualistic worldview, scholars of sport have long since moved beyond the deceptive innocence of play and illustrated the many injustices and subtle political agendas that infuse our favorite pastimes, "installed in the territory of our pleasure" (Billig 1995: 125). But rather than being accorded an a priori normative status, the chapters in this collection show that power relationships always have the potential for both "positive" and "negative" outcomes, depending on different individuals' positionality and socio-political context.

Beyond the basic assumption that power is not only "repressive," our aim is not to pin down any one definition of power or political agenda for the future of critical geographies of sport; the aim of this volume is to preserve the theoretical plurality that each of the contributors brings to bear on their individual research questions. This is especially important because sports geography has historically tended toward a rigid dogmatism that has resulted in the field being generally considered a site of "importing" theory. By instead embracing diversity and innovation, it is possible to open up sports geography's potential as a place for developing and "exporting" theoretical insights to wider academic debates, social theory, and practical challenges around inequality and social justice. Working with the adage that "your theory is your method" (see Pryke *et al.* 2003), the individual chapters also employ a wide array of research methods and the authors all draw upon materials from many disciplinary and theoretical traditions. By bringing together this varied set of chapters, we hope to illustrate and advance a *pluralized* critical approach to the spatial politics of sport from a global, but empirically grounded, perspective.

Chapter overviews

The primary goal of *Critical Geographies of Sport* is to advance a critical geographic approach to sport, while spotlighting the intellectual confluence around questions of power and space in the already interdisciplinary field of research on sport. With cases spanning Eurasia and the Americas, the individual chapters illustrate how space and power relations are produced, contested, and reimagined through sport and its various infrastructures, agencies, networks, and opportunities. The book is structured around two seven-chapter sections, with a loose focus on state space and geopolitics in Part I, and urban space and sub-state communities in Part II. Geographers have long stressed the political construction of scale (Marston 2000), so this two-pronged focus should not be interpreted as reflecting any "natural" divisions in the spatiality of sport. Rather, this separation is partly a gesture to the strengths of existing literature on sport and space, but is primarily out of recognition that states and cities are the two most dominant modes of organizing political space today.

In Part I, Sports, geopolitics, and state space, the authors focus on power and the production of space globally and within states and regions. Pauliina Raento (Chapter 2) explains how both geopolitics and identity politics have shaped horse sports in Finland. Seeking to advance beyond human-centered identity narratives, Raento puts the political geographic literature on geopolitics, nationalism, and borders in conversation with interdisciplinary animal scholarship in the social sciences and humanities to highlight the role of the horse as a co-producer of political and cultural processes.

Jon Bohland (Chapter 3) analyzes the regional geopolitics of women's football in the Western Hemisphere. As the most popular sport in the world, football has been widely studied due to its massive and variable political, cultural, social, and economic impacts, but with far less attention given to the women's game. Noting the significant gap between the growth and relative importance of the women's game between North America and the rest of the Americas, he examines the political implications of the United States' "pull" for regional women's players, the rise of dual nationals, and embedded sexism within footballing federations.

Slavomír Horák (Chapter 4) examines how mega-events can be used as a tool for bolstering the domestic stability and international image of authoritarian regimes. Considering the case of the 2017 Asian Indoor and Martial Arts Games ("Aziada-2017"), to be held in Ashgabat, Turkmenistan, his chapter explores the dual nation-building and regime-legitimating role of this event. In addition to showing how the authoritarian regime of Gurbanguly Berdimukhamedov has used sport in both these capacities, he demonstrates how construction and infrastructure development for spectacular events such as Aziada-2017 can also entrench prevailing power structures and negatively impact the local population.

Magid Shihade (Chapter 5) takes a detailed look at how a supposedly small incident – in this case a soccer game between two teams from two Palestinian villages in Galilee and the violence that took place during and after the game – can reveal a larger story about territory in a contested region. Situating the incident within the history of the Palestinian community and its relationship to the Israeli settler-colonial state, Shihade shows how sport can offer a lens to explore how a native community navigates between its own mechanisms of conflict resolution and reliance on colonial state structures.

Veli-Pekka Tynkkynen (Chapter 6) examines the all-Russian "gasification" program of Russia's state-controlled gas company Gazprom and, specifically, its "corporate social responsibility" programs that have focused on sports and the construction of stadiums. He shows that, as a parastatal organization, Gazprom works in close cooperation with the government of Vladimir Putin to materialize a form of "energopower" that aims at advancing the Great Power ambitions of Putin's regime. Tynkkynen argues that, through this amalgamation of energy and sports, the "presence" of the state is made concrete via gas pipelines and spatially extensive sport facilities.

Natalie Koch (Chapter 7) asks why certain autocrats are frequently portrayed as athletes. Stressing wider political and contextual factors to explain the phenomenon of "athletic autocrats," the chapter takes a cross-regional approach to examine three leaders: Russian President Vladimir Putin, Sheikh Zayed of the UAE, and Chinese Communist Party Chairman Mao Zedong. The cases demonstrate how the depiction of autocrats as sportsmen both reflects and entrenches prevailing power structures of authoritarian regimes that stake governmental legitimacy in personalistic rule, nationalism, and paternalism.

Arlene Crampsie's (Chapter 8) study of the Gaelic Athletic Association (GAA), an Irish amateur sporting organization, offers a unique account of the impact of post-colonial identity formation and reconstitution in a national, yet non-state, context. Founded in 1884, the GAA was formed with, and has retained, a dual mandate as a sporting and cultural nationalist organization. The recent removal of the organization's overtly nationalist rules, she shows, has forced it to refocus its identity around modern cultural and local values. This process has required careful mediation to ensure the agreement of all members, and Crampsie's *longue durée* approach indicates how identity narratives are co-constituted with geopolitical contexts, and are constantly in flux.

The chapters in Part II, Sports, community, and urban space, take a finer-grained approach than in Part I, with a focus on power and the production of space at the sub-state scale. Lise Nelson (Chapter 9) explores efforts by low-wage, mostly undocumented, Latino immigrants to find a space to play soccer in their adopted home in rural Georgia. Having been recruited to Rabun County in the 1990s and early 2000s to work in construction, landscaping, and other service industries linked to rural gentrification, these immigrant men have been explicitly excluded from publicly maintained sports fields in the area. Nelson shows how their exclusion provides insight into the profound tensions between the economic recruitment of, and dependence on, immigrant workers and spatial processes of social–civic exclusion shaped by class, race, and "illegality."

Jung Woo Lee (Chapter 10) explains the recent demolition of South Korea's long-revered Dongdaemun Baseball Stadium, which was the country's first modern baseball field and hosted many historically important baseball matches. Despite citizen protests and the stadium's central place in national identity narratives, the Seoul Metropolitan Government demolished the old stadium and replaced it with a new iconic building, the Dongdaemun Design Plaza. Aimed at reconfiguring the city's identity for a global audience, this project shows how the logic of neoliberal development led planners to undervalue the cultural meaning of the Dongdaemun stadium and erase it from Seoul's rapidly changing urban landscape.

Simon Cook, Jon Shaw, and Paul Simpson (Chapter 11) investigate how runners encounter pedestrians "on the go" in public spaces in Plymouth, England. By paying particular attention to the everyday mundanity of these mobile encounters, they draw out ideas of belonging, transgression, and citizenship to gauge where running fits into contemporary cities. Employing innovative mobile ethnographic methods, they consider several ways that these encounters happen to suggest that pedestrians hold a primacy on the streets, and that, despite its ubiquity, running is often seen as "out of place" in the public urban realm in the United Kingdom.

Michael Friedman (Chapter 12) examines the rise of "mallparks" in the symbolic reconstruction of urban space in the United States. Using Henri Lefebvre's theories on spatial production and George Ritzer's theories on the enchantment of consumption space, he shows how baseball stadiums built since the 1990s combine diverse amenities with thematic veneers. In so doing, he shows, they create increasingly homogenized consumption environments that follow the principles of both shopping mall and theme park design. In many places around the US, local governments have sought to use these new stadiums to transform once-industrial, urban cores into postindustrial, consumption landscapes.

Neil Conner (Chapter 13) analyzes the place of popular sports in the social integration process of migrants in South Dublin, Ireland. Historically a country of emigrants, Ireland has recently become one of immigrants, receiving large numbers since the mid-1990s. Based on surveys and other qualitative methods, Conner examines identity narratives around three everyday sports – Gaelic football, rugby football, and Association football – and the degree to which migrants and non-migrants perceive each to be a "bridge" or "barrier" to social integration. He demonstrates how each of these sports and sporting cultures are bound up with narratives and performances of "Irishness," but highlights their different degrees of inclusiveness, as perceived by both foreign- and non-foreign-born residents of the country.

Bradley Gardener (Chapter 14) examines the evolution of professional wrestling in North America during the mid to late twentieth century. In particular, he traces the history of the National Wrestling Alliance, a cartel of wrestling promoters, that developed a spatial system to exploit and control the labor of performers. Drawing on the narratives of wrestlers in "shoot interviews," Gardener unpacks the geographic strategies implemented by promoters in wrestling's territorial system and explores how wrestlers survived, and in some cases succeeded, in spite of these strategies. He also traces the technological and political transformations that led to the demise of the territorial system at the end of the twentieth century.

Nicholas Wise (Chapter 15) advocates incorporating more ethnographic research in sports geography, especially in communities increasingly marginalized by the "shadow of mega-events." After reviewing the utility of ethnographic methods, he reflects on the insights gained through his research with Haitian soccer players in the Dominican Republic. He then shows how the deeply contextualized insights of an ethnographic approach can be productively applied to the growing literature on sporting mega-events, much of which tends to obscure local voices, despite stressing issues of social justice. More geographically informed ethnographic research, he suggests, is an important methodological imperative to advance this agenda and promote a more critical sports geography in the future.

In the conclusion, David Jansson and Natalie Koch (Chapter 16) explore precisely this potential of critical sports geography to advance a locally informed research agenda committed to exposing unequal power dynamics and contemporary challenges surrounding social justice. While *Critical Geographies of Sport* aims to reinvigorate the subfield of sports geography, and to set an agenda for future research in sports studies that takes space seriously, the aim of this book is not to reinforce disciplinary boundaries. Rather, by embracing an interdisciplinary approach to sports geography, this book serves as an example of how geographers and other social scientists might productively come together to explore the multi-scalar connections between sport, space, and power. Part of a field with a long history of embracing multidisciplinary research, geographers are ideally suited to promote the methodologically plural and deeply contextual approach to the study of sport which characterizes the contributions to this book. Our hope is that promoting a sustained dialogue between geographers and the field of sports studies will inspire scholars in a range of disciplines to take up the challenges and questions raised here to further advance this literature and develop their own critical geographies of sport.

Note

1 This project arose out of many conversations with colleagues around the world in the past few years, as well as several sessions organized at the annual meetings of the Association of American Geographers in 2014 and 2015. In addition to all the participants there, I would like to thank Ingrid Nelson, Tina Catania, and Julian Georg for their support in the process of bringing this book to life.

References

Bale, J. (1989). *Sports Geography*. New York: E. & F.N. Spon.
Bale, J. (1993). *Sport, Space, and the City*. New York: Routledge.
Bale, J. (2003). *Sports Geography*. New York: Routledge.
Billig, M. (1995). *Banal Nationalism*. Thousand Oaks: Sage.

Burstyn, V. (1999). *The Rites of Men: Manhood, Politics, and the Culture of Sport.* Toronto: University of Toronto Press.

Dear, M. (1988). The Postmodern Challenge: Reconstructing Human Geography. *Transactions of the Institute of British Geographers* 13(3): 262–74.

Dittmer, J. (2010). *Popular Culture, Geopolitics, and Identity.* Lanham: Rowman & Littlefield Publishers.

Eichberg, H., J. Bale, C. Philo, and S. Brownell (1998). *Body Cultures: Essays on Sport, Space, and Identity.* New York: Routledge.

Foucault, M. (1980). *Power/Knowledge: Selected Interviews and Other Writings, 1972–1977.* New York: Pantheon Books.

Foucault, M. (1982). The Subject and Power. *Critical Inquiry* 8(4): 777–95.

Gaffney, C. (2014). Geography of Sport. In *Social Sciences in Sport* ed. J. Maguire. Leeds: Human Kinetics, 109–34.

Giulianotti, R. (2015). *Routledge Handbook of the Sociology of Sport.* New York: Routledge.

Hallinan, C., and S. Jackson. (2008). *Social and Cultural Diversity in a Sporting World.* Bingley: Emerald.

Hargreaves, J. (1994). *Sporting Females: Critical Issues in the History and Sociology of Women's Sports.* New York: Routledge.

Hargreaves, J. (2000). *Heroines of Sport: The Politics of Difference and Identity.* New York: Routledge.

Hargreaves, J., and E. Anderson. (2014). *Routledge Handbook of Sport, Gender and Sexuality.* New York: Routledge.

Koch, N. (2013). Sport and Soft Authoritarian Nation-Building. *Political Geography* 32: 42–51.

Koch, N. (2015). Gulf Nationalism and the Geopolitics of Constructing Falconry as a "Heritage Sport." *Studies in Ethnicity and Nationalism* 15(3): 522–39.

Latour, B. (2005). *Reassembling the Social: An Introduction to Actor-Network-Theory.* Oxford: Oxford University Press.

Marjoribanks, T., and K. Farquharson. (2012). *Sport and Society in the Global Age.* New York: Palgrave Macmillan.

Marston, S. (2000). The Social Construction of Scale. *Progress in Human Geography* 24(2): 219–42.

Messner, M. (2007). *Out of Play: Critical Essays on Gender and Sport.* Albany: State University of New York Press.

Pryke, M., G. Rose, and S. Whatmore. (2003). *Using Social Theory: Thinking through Research.* London: Sage.

Sugden, J., and A. Tomlinson. (2002). *Power Games: A Critical Sociology of Sport.* New York: Routledge.

Tuan, Y.-F. (1984). *Dominance and Affection: The Making of Pets.* New Haven: Yale University Press.

Vertinsky, P., and J. Bale. (2004). *Sites of Sport: Space, Place and Experience.* New York: Routledge.

Part I

Sports, geopolitics, and state space

Chapter 2

Geopolitics, identity, and horse sports in Finland

Pauliina Raento

This chapter explores the relationship between sporting bodies, subjectivity, and the nation by tracing how geopolitics and nation-building have steered horse sports and identity in Finland. The examination highlights interdependency between identity and boundaries by relating horse sports to Finnish national, urban–rural, and socio-economic class affiliations in changing international contexts. The case study thus sheds light on a society's ideological framework within which certain sports evolve and shows how time- and place-sensitive attention to human identity politics about animal sports can expand insight in sports research.

Finland illustrates the interplay between geopolitics, identity, and horse sports well due to the prominent role of the horse in the country's socio-economic and military history, regional development, and the strong identity-political turns in Finnish geopolitics. The relationship between the state, horses, and the sports system is historically intimate, and even before independence from the Russian Empire in 1917, sports served Finnish nation builders as a source of pride (Raento 2006: 620–2; Tervo 2003). Not surprisingly, then, public figures have been a common sight at racetracks and are involved in the equine economy and the politics surrounding trotter racing and wagering. Hobby groups in parliament include an equine society with high-profile trotter racing and charity activities. The chair of board of the national trotting and breeding association Suomen Hippos is a center-conservative member of parliament. An influential figure in Finland's national independence process and, later, president and marshal, Gustav Mannerheim (1867–1951), was a cavalryman, horse trader, and keen recreational rider. Finns, in many ways then, have been, and are, led by horsemen.

Adding to the intimacy between the state, horses, and sports is the historical importance of the Finnhorse as an export resource and an agricultural and a military asset, the quality of which was tested by racing. The Finnhorse is an all-purpose coldblood horse breed, for which a national studbook was created in 1907 during the heat of nation-building and resistance against imperial Russia. The studbook marked the nation's boundaries by defining the Finnhorse as a purebred horse which originates only from Finland. The strategic importance of the breed for national defense and food production became outdated after World War II, but the Finnhorse still carries powerful identity-political meaning and symbolic value (e.g., Schuurman and Nyman 2014).

Statistics reveal the role of horses today in this country of 5.5 million people. About 170,000 Finns are regular leisure riders, and the number of enthusiasts grows – especially in the urban south where most horses and people live. Riding clubs have 50,000 members and the number of riding stables and schools exceeds 1,000. Some 7,600 riding horses are licensed to compete and over 500 national or regional competitions are organized each year in the Olympic sports dressage, show jumping, and eventing (Raento 2015; SRL 2015). Trotter racing, with 200,000 active followers and accounting for 670,000 visits to the tracks in 2015, is the second most popular spectator sport in the country. Of the 74,200 horses in Finland in 2015, 34 percent were Standardbred trotters, 26 percent were Finnhorses (most of which are bred for trotting), another 26 percent were warmblood riding horses, and 14 percent were ponies, some of which serve as trotters. Turnover from wagering (€230 million in 2015), prize money (€17 million), and the number of posts (5,000) and licensed trotters (6,900) make Finland a medium-size trotter-racing country in Europe, where France, Sweden, and Italy lead the way (Suomen Hippos 2016; UET 2016).

These numbers hide complex affiliations, sport-specific lifestyles and values, and identity-political and socio-cultural tension with long historical roots. All this is embodied in the type and breed of sports horses, which, in addition to the sport itself, are molded by economic and geopolitical circumstances, human ideologies, and fashion and image. The Finnish case shows clearly how wars and their aftermath steer the fate of particular breeds and sports. Individual horse sports and their structures also relate to strong affiliations which sustain particular sports cultures and underscore the interdependent and contested nature of identities and boundaries.

This discussion contributes to the political study of sports, nation, and identity from the perspective of political geography (see Bale 2003; Koch 2013; Tervo 2003). By focusing on animal sports, this chapter reaches beyond the emphasis on the politics of national human team sports and mega-events (e.g., Dichter and Johns 2014), bridging sports studies with the study of animal geographies and the human–animal relationship (Hobson 2007; Urbanik 2012). It expands the focus on the gallop racing industry in the study of animal sports structures and introduces geopolitics to the discussion (Cassidy 2002, 2007; McManus *et al.* 2013; Raento and Härmälä 2014). Building on the Finnish-language popular horse sports literature, which describes the history of a particular sport, organization, or venue (Erola 2010; Jalkanen and Saarinen 1986; Mahlamäki 2003;

Vasara 1987), this examination also draws on a long-term personal interest and varied involvement in trotter racing, gambling and wagering, equine education, and their research (Karekallas *et al.* 2014; Raento 2015; Raento and Härmälä 2014; for an anthropological ethnography in the gallop-racing industry, see Cassidy 2002, 2007).

Socio-economic exclusivity

Riding in late-nineteenth- and early-twentieth-century Finland was a military sport and fashionable among upper-class urbanites and land-owning gentry in the south. These people introduced foreign novelties to Finland, as they had close economic, cultural, and political-ideological connections to Central and Western Europe. For this Western-minded, national-independence-oriented, and mostly Swedish-speaking elite, riding was one way to confirm their modern outlook and sophistication. Imports of thoroughbreds and warmblood riding horses from Britain, Germany, the Benelux, and Sweden fostered these bonds and image in a context where Finland was an aspiring nation keen on demonstrating its worth to more mature nations (see Karekallas *et al.* 2014: 35; Raento 2006: 604–5, 2015).

At home, riding was important for political networking and community building. The first riding clubs were created in southern cities, mostly in the capital city Helsinki, and the elite used their power to build sports facilities. In a poor country, major funding was channeled to urban stables, manèges, and racetracks. Helsinki received a gallop track and Olympic-level riding facilities where presidents, professors, and bankers were a common sight (see photographs in Erola 2010; Jalkanen and Saarinen 1986; Vasara 1987). The scene was ideologically and identity-politically homogeneous, as the property- and land-owning elite had united behind the government-supporting White troops against the revolutionary Reds in the 1918 Civil War. Ideological Whiteness meant strong patriotic, Lutheran, right-wing nationalist, and even fascist tendencies, and supported the close association between civilian elite riders and cavalry officers in the 1920s and the 1930s. Not surprisingly, then, the military sport eventing (a combination of dressage, show jumping, and endurance) was popular in this era. Personal networks, shared outlook, and the search for international legitimacy also go a long way toward explaining the state, the young society, and the Finnish national sports system evolved together and why international success in any sport evoked national pride (see Koch 2013).

Riders, however, were relatively "isolated" and held a "particular" position in the emerging sports system (Vasara 1987: 163). The Equestrian Federation of Finland (SRL) was founded as early as in 1920, but it focused on promoting competitive sports and cultivating international contacts. The urban, wealthy, and Swedish-speaking profile of the riders contributed to the social distance in a country where most people were poor, rural Finnish-speakers. This contrast gave riding an "aristocratic" image and annoyed those who instead prioritized physical education of the masses in the name of national defense. As Finnish-speaking nationalism grew stronger and the fitness of the majority population gained ground as an ideal of the sports system, riding was denied the status of a "proper sport" with funding from public sources (Vasara 1987: 158–63). It is common that advocates of individual sports and their competitive and hobby branches wrestle over status and support (McManus *et al.* 2013: 59–72). In the case of Finnish riding sports, socio-cultural, linguistic, and urban–rural affiliations fueled this contest in an ideologically divided country.

The Finnish sports elites, however, largely agreed about geopolitics by acknowledging the importance of national defense, international prestige, and visibility. Riding was important to the young nation because of its military and competitive emphases, and one Finnish officer was sent to ride in the Antwerp Olympics in 1920. SRL's prompt joining in the international equestrian federation (FEI) in 1923 was deemed of utmost importance, and riders raised funds for the construction of the 1940 (1952) summer Olympic stadium in Helsinki (Vasara 1987: 163). Both the pragmatic and propagandistic motives of these efforts helped reduce the social distance between SRL and the other national sports federations.

Socio-economic exclusivity and the limited size of the riding elite, however, were evident in club membership. In the 1930s – a decade of structural and international progress in Finnish riding sports – membership reached an all-time high of just over 1,000 individuals (Vasara 1987: 177). Although riding was now promoted to the masses in the name of national defense, "class hygiene" was maintained through certain rules and practices. The most important model was English riding sports, so gallop and steeplechase racing and leisurely fox hunting were popular in upper-class Helsinki. The so-called gentlemen's rule limited the selection of horses, competitions, and club membership available to petty and police officers (Figure 2.1), and it was even claimed that lower-rank riders would wear out the best horses (these, invariably, were warmblood or thoroughbred sports horses that represented a tiny fracture of the equine population, which mostly consisted of Finnhorses in agricultural labor). Women, however, were equal competitors, as long as they were of the same social category (Erola 2010; Vasara 1987: 81), and some upper-class women from land-owning families were also central in the creation of the Finnish warmblood riding horse, the FWB (Jalkanen 1984). Domestic breeding, too, was to support national defense, for it would ensure the availability of good-quality riding horses for officers in the case of a crisis – after all, these image-conscious officers could not ride just *any thing* (Ojala 2007: 19–22).

Figure 2.1 Petty and police officers on Finnhorses in a 1,200-meter steeple-chase race at the Tali race track in Helsinki in the 1930s (source: Aili and Eino Nevalainen Collection at the Equestrian Sports Museum of Finland, courtesy of Juha Erola).

A world apart

In the meantime, trotter racing – one of the first competitive sports in Finland – developed in its own, predominantly rural, Finnish-speaking realm, which was isolated from European trends. The first record of organized trotting in Finland is from the southwestern city of Turku, where horsemen from the surrounding region tested the quality of their horses by racing them on river ice in 1817. A fast runner was prestigious and served transportation in a sparsely settled country. A good horse also generated income through prizes, covering fees, and foals. Indeed, for a long time, the purpose of racing was to support breeding, which motivated the autonomous state's involvement in trotting since the mid-1800s. In order to improve the quality of horses and promote their appropriate care, the autonomous senate launched "state races" in 1865 and funded their prizes. These popular races guarded the national interest by improving the speed, size, and treatment of horses and by reducing the interest in selling the most valuable individuals abroad (Mahlamäki 2003: 11–17).

An unwanted side effect, however, was cross-breeding: the local horse was mixed with Central European and Russian warmbloods in order to improve racing speed. The senate therefore excluded from state races those horses that had not been accepted to the newly founded Finnhorse studbook as purebreds. This reduced the value of racing as a competitive sport and the shifting emphasis on breeding toward the draft-horse type because of motorized transportation created an enduring divide in the interests of sportsmen and breeders (Mahlamäki 2003; Raento and Härmälä 2014). The organization and regulation of trotting progressed in the 1920s, however, with the creation of new events and the legalization of totalizator (pari-mutuel wagering) in 1927. Sensational record times were reached on the track. Meanwhile, the state's role diminished, because prizes in its races failed to match the declining value of Finnish currency in the late 1920s and because several organizations offered opportunities to race horses. By World War II, competitive trotter racing in Finland was largely in the hands of local and regional organizers, for whom the popular sport offered a way to fund the equine economy and other activities (Mahlamäki 2003: 44).

In many ways, the evolution of Finnish trotting deviated from developments in such leading racing countries as the USA, France, Germany, and the other Nordic countries (Mahlamäki 2003: 22–3). By and large, Finnish trotting still lacked modern facilities, and many races were run on lake or sea ice or local roads. The only breed used for racing was the Finnhorse and all trainers were amateurs. Rules, regulations, and tote games were modeled on those in Germany, Denmark, and Sweden, but competing abroad was difficult. After a few trials it was clear that the Finnhorse was much faster than the Swedish and Norwegian coldbloods, but slower than the warmblood racer. Therefore the Finnhorse faced either restrictions on participation or a clear disadvantage (Mahlamäki 2003: 21). For these reasons trotting in Finland was primarily "a hobby for the rural population" (Mahlamäki 2003: 23) and urban working-class wagerers, who also liked gallop races.

The impact of war

World War II and the following decades transformed Finnish national identity, geopolitical status, and horse sports. The war erased ideological and identity-political boundaries by damaging everyone. It destroyed infrastructure and killed animal and human athletes in two conflicts against the Soviet Union (1939–40 and 1941–44) and, in the end, against the former ally Germany (1944–45). During the war years, "riding survived only in Helsinki and in the front during trench warfare," where officers organized competitions (Vasara 1987: 327). Small-scale trotter races were organized locally in rural areas. A brief revival of horse sports during the peace of 1940–41 suffered from transportation problems and from the rationing of fodder, which made it difficult to keep horses in the required condition. The ceding of Finland's second-largest city, Vyborg, to the Soviets and the evacuation of 420,000 people from the surrounding Karelia region meant giving up a thriving sports center, but spread know-how and quality animals within the remaining territory. The war also advanced sports betting, as sports organizations were allowed to create their own betting monopoly company in 1940 (see Karekallas *et al.* 2014; Matilainen 2010).

New technologies, industrialization, and urbanization began to reduce the total number of horses in the country from an all-time high of 409,000 in 1950 to a mere 35,000 by the early 1980s. Cavalry and draft animals were old technology. The end of rural paramilitary mounted troops following the Moscow Armistice of 1944 severed the thin contact riding sports had with the countryside. Riding also suffered from the unmounting of the Finnish cavalry and the closure of the army's own breeding program, which limited the availability of high-quality riding horses (Vasara 1987: 414–15). National reconciliation and geopolitical circumstances changed the atmosphere in domestic politics and strengthened the ideological Left. Emphasis on equal opportunity and hard work fueled suspicion about the perceived elitism of horseback riding and the leisure class, the image of which was now severely out of fashion.

Riding thus lost strength during the 15 years following the war and started to transform into a fully civilian sport. Emphasis shifted from adult to junior riders and the proportion of women among leisure riders grew. The socio-economic profile remained largely intact, but many new juniors spoke Finnish and the sports had begun to spread across the country. The national equestrian federation SRL was in economic ruin, which, together with general transportation difficulties after the war, complicated the organization of competitions. On the other hand, the economic trouble fostered contacts between clubs and encouraged SRL to collaborate with other national sports federations (Vasara 1987: 328–434). The international equestrian federation FEI also abolished the gentlemen's rule from international competitions, which made them more accessible to Finnish competitors – who themselves had erased this class and rank restriction right after the war in the new context of national unity fostered by the war experience (Vasara 1987: 339). One significant victim of the postwar situation was gallop racing in Helsinki (and, gradually, in Finland), which never recovered from the war and its aftermath, despite its popularity among the public (Erola 2010).

Embodying the nation

In the context of Finland's new, delicate relationship with the victorious Soviet Union, sports built trust and self-esteem. This approach also suited the new superpower, which had begun to test its athletic might against the West. From the mid-1950s onward the annual "Friendship Races" in trotting made horses embodiments of the nation (Koch 2013) and contributed to the politicization of sports in the Cold War era (Dichter and Johns 2014). The equine assets of state propaganda fostered an amicable relationship between the wartime enemies, but made it clear that the Soviet warmblood racers were faster than their Finnhorse counterparts. These races nevertheless qualify as a prime example of "sports diplomacy" on the animal front, not least because they were massive media events and the exchange sought to promote bilateral trade between the two countries. The states confirmed their interest by the joint appearance of Finland's Secretary of State Johannes Virolainen and the Soviet Ambassador Viktor Lebedev in the audience of the first tour in 1955 (Mahlamäki 2003: 99).

The appearance of the Orlov breed and other Russian racers on Finnish tracks led to a "warmblood fever" (Mahlamäki 2003: 113), which split the Finnish horsemen into two camps in an ideologically charged dispute over the right of warmblood trotters to compete in Finland. Those who wanted to open Finnish borders, tracks, and racing business to foreign imports flagged for higher-quality competitive sports, increased wagering and media visibility, and better economic sustainability of trotting and trotter breeding. These business and international arguments were countered by stressing national identity and values, particularity of the Finnhorse, and the threat of cross-breeding the "national" purebred horse with foreign (ideologically undesirable eastern) blood. Indicative of the social distance between racing and riding – and, perhaps, the relative acceptability of Western influences – was that few fears had been expressed over cross-breeding of the Finnhorse with warmblood riding horses (Mahlamäki 2003: 114; Ojala 2007: 19–22).

The debate echoed the old division between sportsmen and breeders. The boundary also ran between city and country – and modernity (perceived progress) and tradition (stagnation) – as the most vocal promoters of warmblood trotting were in Helsinki and the opponents centered in the rural western and central parts of the country. As the conflict spilled from the equine media to national headlines, it evolved from an internal matter among the horsemen to reflect identity-political boundaries and related turmoil in Finnish society in the context of urbanization, industrialization, and opening up to the West (Mahlamäki 2003: 116–19). Again, innovation and tradition collided, fueling "a debate that almost all sports and activities have to address … on a continual basis" (McManus et al. 2013: 73).

Geopolitics and bilateral trade interests played a key role in the resolution of the matter in favor of warmblood racing. The Soviets knew that President Urho Kekkonen (in office 1956–82) was a prominent sportsman and sports politician whose roots were in the countryside and in the center-conservative rural party. When the Soviet leader Nikita Khrushchev gave two pregnant Orlov mares as a gift to Kekkonen in 1957, trotter racing rose to international limelight and put pressure on the Finns to begin exchanging horses for cows like the Soviets wanted. The two foals' name-giving ceremony at the Ypäjä state stud was a high-profile media event, and when the Soviets added an Orlov stallion to the President's stable, during his visit to their country, the long monopoly of Finnhorses in Finnish trotter racing was about to end. In a speech at the national trotting organization in 1958, Kekkonen expressed his opinion that "the success of trotter racing, like that of other sports, requires international competitive activity. Therefore we, too, should perhaps consider the changing of rules so that warmblood horses owned by Finns could also compete in our country" (cited in Saranpää 2012: 48).

The first race arranged exclusively for Finnish-owned warmblood trotters was run in 1960, and their first national championships a year later. During the 1960s, more than half of the imported warmblood racers came from the Soviet Union. Most of them, however, were Russian trotters rather than Orlovs, which were already an outdated breed in trotting. By 1968, 610 warmblood trotters had been licensed to compete in Finland, and 230 foals had been born (Mahlamäki 2003: 125). The numbers were still minuscule compared to the Finnhorse population (which now stood around 100,000), but their impact on both Finnish trotting and breeding was critical. The transition also turned Finnhorse breeding toward the light racer and all-purpose sports horse types, which had developed in the shadow of draft performance requirements determined by field and forest. The change was now unavoidable, as the draft horse was outdated, and the warmblood trotter was a superior performer on the track. The transition also began to create professions in the training, driving, breeding, care, and trade of trotters.

In a society that was more united ideologically and culturally than it had been before the war, trotting offered opportunities for social mobility. As individual skill and merit increasingly determined one's socio-economic status in Finnish society, a good trotter and training expertise were tickets to visibility, peer respect, leadership, and international contacts. This mattered because many trotter-racing people still came from modest rural backgrounds.

From East to West in a new sports culture

Urbanization, the nascent Nordic welfare state, and transition toward a service-based economy contributed to a structural change in Finnish work life, affording people more leisure time and disposable income. By the 1970s, increased international contacts and cooperation transmitted influential ideals about citizens' health and participation. These developments resulted in a new, popular sports and physical education culture in Finland. The Finnish national sports organizations continued to be ideologically, socially, and structurally divided between Left and Right because of the legacy of the 1918 Civil War, but the state's renewed interest in both competitive sports and the physical education of the masses began to mend this polarization into "Red working-class" and "White bourgeois" sports federations. The state's active role meant subsidies and attention to infrastructure, which, together with novel private funding interests, led to vigorous construction of both riding and racing facilities across the country. Regulation of sports and wagering progressed and both fields began to play a more prominent role in socio-political considerations and policies concerning Finnish political and cultural life.

Most importantly, competitive sports were one geopolitically acceptable way to cherish Western connections, and riders' competition experience and training contacts gradually expanded from the Nordic and Olympic realms (Vasara 1987: 510). An example of the new thinking and organizational collaboration was the development of riding for the disabled (RFD), from the first experiments in the early 1970s to participation in international RFD competitions by the end of the decade – with joint support from the Rehabilitation Foundation and SRL (Vasara 1987: 567–8). The expansion in international activity and selection of sports in the following decades directed attention to the equine population and put pressure on both imports and domestic breeding. The development of skills gained significant support from the formal inclusion of SRL's riding college at Ypäjä (founded in 1972) in the state-subsidized national sports college network in 1986.

Finnish warmblood trotting operators also turned to the West earlier and more openly than most of the nation's leaders, who were blamed in the West in the 1970s and 1980s for Finlandization, or letting the Soviets influence their decision-making. By the 1970s, it was clear that the Russian racer was a poor match for the French and, especially, the American Standardbred trotter. The emphasis in imports turned to these breeds, first from Denmark and Sweden and then directly from the USA (Mahlamäki 2003: 22). Standardbred bloodlines soon became dominant in the Finnish warmblood trotting business. The capital needed for the imports came from wealthy entrepreneurs and landowners who had a Western outlook and contact networks along with the language and business skills needed for the exchange.

The transition from East to West and the subsequent growth of domestic warmblood trotter breeding were visible in the racing program sheets from the late 1970s and, especially, the 1980s onward, as Russian bloodlines and foreign-born competitors gradually disappeared from sight. Success of Finnish horses, trainers, and drivers in European top competitions made media headlines and provoked public celebrations of national excellence. These developments commercialized and politicized Finnish horse sports further – and brought them closer to mainstream society.

The number of riders was on the rise, too, and the trend toward the predominance of Finnish-speaking young women in riding sports grew stronger. By the mid-1980s, active riders numbered 20,000 and riding was a popular hobby nationwide, even if over three-quarters of riders were urbanites and a quarter of all still resided in metropolitan Helsinki. Riding was now a "proper sport," and its relative position among the most popular leisure sports strengthened rapidly (Vasara 1987: 435, 448, 572). The growth, however, renewed internal tensions between leisure riding and competitive sports, as their advocates competed with one another over money and influence.

Following the end of the Cold War and the Soviet Union at the turn of the 1990s, and Finland joining the European Union in 1995, the borders to the West were wide open. This encouraged the international mobility of Finnish riders, drivers, trainers, and their horses. Riders headed primarily to Central Europe and many opted for a professional career in riding. Trainers of trotters favored neighboring Sweden, where purse money and economic sustainability of racing and breeding were better than in Finland. Wagering was in turmoil in the context of an economic depression in Finland (1991–94) and the development of online technologies, which were about to upheave the global gambling and wagering industries. The effects in Finland included the rapid expansion of human sports betting products since 1993, and the legalization of off-track horse betting in 1995. Revenue from wagering was generally on the rise, but its management and allocation split opinions. The tracks were in trouble as attendance began to drop from the 1.5 million annual visits reached in the years preceding off-track betting (Karekallas *et al.* 2014; Mahlamäki 2003: 304–35).

By the end of the millennium, Finnish horse sports were international and dependent on global trends. The selection of sports under SRL had expanded to include combined driving, Western riding, and equestrian vaulting, and monté (also known as trot monté, trotter racing under saddle) was about to increase the number of young female drivers in trotting. The activities were more professional, commodified, and business-oriented – and individualistic, like the rest of society. These processes supported standardization, goal-orientedness, and quality, but also worked toward fragmenting identities and practices. As traditionalist defenders of national, regional, and local interests resisted the developments in trotting, the scene was also increasingly politicized and polarized. In riding and other horse sports, too, new fragmentation was on its way.

Division and unity in the 2000s

Two boundary-related global phenomena have significantly shaped Finnish horse sports in the new millennium. They relate to postmodern consumption practices and neoliberalism and are, to some extent, interconnected. One phenomenon is the globalization of the gambling industry and related progress of online wagering. This new operative environment and cut-throat worldwide market competition over gamblers' money has challenged Finland's national gambling monopoly, borders, and sense of sovereignty. The structural and regulatory responses at the national level include the founding of Fintoto Limited as a subsidiary of the trotting and breeding association in 2001, the fast development of online wagering services by this company in the 2000s, the transfer of all available horse games to Fintoto in 2012 (Raento and Härmälä 2014), and the rewriting of national gambling legislation in defense of the monopoly within the European Union (2001, 2010–12; and 2015–17). The global market change and the national response are ideologically controversial, not least because the fortification of the Finnish national gambling monopoly counters the predominant European trend toward liberalization and limits competitive product development, but simultaneously protects the domestic market.

In this setting, Fintoto competes with international online betting companies which cannot operate in Finland, but which Finnish gamblers can legally access online. Domestic competition comes from other forms of gambling and, more generally, from other sports and entertainment (Karekallas et al. 2014). This matters because horse sports, and the equine economy as a whole, depend on wagering revenue, which is earmarked for "the promotion of horse breeding and equestrian sports," prizes, expenses, and state subsidies of the equine economy (Lotteries Act 2001, §17), as is generally typical of the horse industry (McManus et al. 2013: 59–78). Predictably, the downturn of revenue since the general recession in 2008 has caused turmoil in Finnish trotting because views differ on how to generate revenue, how it should be allocated, and whose interests racing should serve.

These disagreements follow the old identity-political boundaries between regionally and nationally oriented rural traditionalists and the more international and urban business outlook (Mahlamäki 2003: 116). The setting has, however, become increasingly complex since the 2000s as postmodern consumer culture, internationalization, the rise of new horse sports and professions, and related lifestyles and values have diversified identities and blurred their boundaries (Raento and Härmälä 2014: 144). Individual sports also differ increasingly in their gender profiles, which are imbalanced internally; riding, for example, is now the number one leisure sport among Finnish females, but men are disproportionately represented in competitions (Raento 2015; SRL 2015; see Butler and Charles 2012). Lack of money and insecurity about future prospects complicate things further, and no simple solution is in sight as the costs of racing (and all horse keeping) are up, numbers of covering and foaling are down, and the gambling monopoly faces yet another restructuring in a difficult market situation. The structures, decision-making practices, and management of Finnish horse sports organizations have also proven to be outdated and are having a hard time responding to the change.

On the other hand, there is evidence of a new kind of community building around horse sports in Finland today. Fans gather around particular sports and breeds, and horse people are active defending their economic and cultural interests in Finnish society. One example is the recent promotion of trotting through open mass syndication (group funding and ownership) of young racers under the loose umbrella of the "Trotting League," formed by ten racetracks and SRL in 2013–14 for the duration of about three years (see www.raviliiga.fi). The activities organized around each syndicated horse (Figure 2.2), combined with racing events promoted to the several thousand first-time racehorse owners, have created media visibility, eased access to the specialized sport, and overcome some of the socio-cultural distance between trotting and other horse sports, as well as between horse people and other Finns.

The Trotting League courts the thrill- and emotion-seeking postmodern, individualistic, but conservative consumers who wish to push their personal boundaries in a safe, leisurely manner. They are willing to try new things and spend quite generously on (perceived) authenticity, personalized service, and unique products, but balance their individualism with a desire to belong and share their stories with others. The campaign has successfully engaged "feelings, emotions, imaginations, and knowledge" (McIntosh and Prentice 1999: 607), narrating an image of excitement, novelty, entertainment, and speed. Purchasing one share (of the 700–800 shares per horse) was designed to be convenient, carefree, and tailor-made in a sense

Figure 2.2 The Equestrian Federation of Finland SRL crosses boundaries within horse sports by participating in the Trotting League. New racehorse owners pose with their young Finnhorse trotter, his trainer, and the SRL league coordinator (source: Viivi Huuskonen/SHKL).

that the new owner could choose from well-known trainers, multiple locations, and two breeds. This mass syndication concept is a prime example of "the experience economy" (Pine and Gilmore 1999), a global postmodern business trend which generates value by commodifying experiences and which now shapes Finnish horse sports and related consumer behaviors and identities.

The Finnhorse reflects place-specific tensions generated by the two global trends because its utility and image as a sports horse continue to split opinions and the breed carries a historical and identity-political charge. Some Finns see the breed as peripheral, old-fashioned, and clumsy, whereas others cherish its suitability for all competitive horse sports and find the "national" and "traditional" image to be empowering rather than negative. The popularity of the Finnhorse as a riding horse is growing, and its expanding use for purposes such as riding therapy connect to more general processes in postmodern society. Riding or racing a Finnhorse can thus embody a territorial bond, a sense of place, a lifestyle choice, and resistance to globalization, neoliberal standardization, and loss of biodiversity (see Koch 2015; Schuurman and Nyman 2014). The Finnhorse also has its own sense of time. The slowly maturing breed starts its competition career older than the Standardbred (but can also continue it longer), and trots about ten seconds slower per kilometer. Training and racing a coldblood, therefore, requires patience and builds on broader motives than speed and immediate cost efficiency, central in the global horseracing industry (Cassidy 2002, 2007; McManus *et al.* 2013). That some urban Finnhorse trotter owners explicitly appreciate the breed's "local" origin(ality) and time span as motives for their choice exemplifies the new blurring of identity-political boundaries and affiliations in Finnish trotting (Raento and Härmälä 2014).

The Finnhorse makes an equine contribution to national culture and image by participating in all horse sports, by bridging equine themes with broader socio-political and identity-related issues in Finnish society, and by profiling Finland as a horse (sports) country (see Hobson 2007). For example, the Finnhorse co-produces one of the country's largest popular gatherings: about 50,000 tickets are sold each year to the crown of the Finnish racing calendar in which the breed's best 12 stallions and 12 mares trot in a two-day contest for prestigious titles and sizeable purses in front of nationwide media audiences (see www.kuninkuusravit.fi). This event brands the Finnhorse as a territorial icon which embodies affect for a particular nation's endurance, adaptability, and originality (Schuurman and Nyman 2014). Both the event (organized since 1924) and the branding campaign (designed in the late 2000s) exploit narration and nostalgia, two key constituents of postmodernism, and thus illustrate "consuming cultural heritage" (McIntosh and Prentice 1999). In so doing, the brand harnesses everyday nationalism in defense of the "national" breed – and simultaneously promotes it as a modern all-purpose sports horse in the neoliberal contexts of globalization.

One clever move in the promotion of the Finnhorse has been to bring Finnish Presidents back into horse business, which was thoroughly transformed by President Kekkonen's horse ownership and participation in racing. Instead of being exotic geopolitically and trade-politcally motivated gifts from a foreign country, the Finnhorse mares owned by presidents Tarja Halonen (in office 2000–12) and Sauli Niinistö (since 2012) were given to them by the Equine College at Ypäjä, a former state stud which houses an internationally acknowledged equine school with a fine sports competition record of its own (see www.hevosopisto.fi). The two mares are of celebrated descent bred at the state stud, and their public appearances attract positive attention. Politicians and other defenders of Finnish national peculiarity have thus been eager to vocalize their support for the Finnhorse, stress the importance of the equine economy and horse sports in Finnish society, and show up in those major events where Finnhorses play a prominent role, stimulating desired media visibility for "our own" breed and horse sports.

Conclusion

This chapter has demonstrated how the evolution of Finnish horse sports has depended on geopolitical transitions at multiple scales, and how the space- and time-sensitive concepts of identity and boundary offer one way to understand the process. The Finnish case study shows that horses as sporting bodies, and the activities and structures around them, are important constituents of territorial and place-specific human subjectivity. Human identities shape the fate of these animals as breeds deemed suitable for particular purposes and as sentient individuals, not least because of the related human power contests over image, money, and influence. Human needs and changing circumstances also affect the physical shape of the equine bodies through utility- and fashion-motivated breeding. But, as any horse sport event shows, the equines themselves are crucial co-producers of these structures and stories and their subjectivity, too, merits attention. These intersections encourage further exploration into the place of animals in the political study of sports and to the connections between (broadly defined) geopolitics, animals, and the animal sports business. Students of geopolitics and political geography might find some of the discussion in animal geography about agency, subjectivity, and biopolitics to be of interest. Controversial boundary management issues of the global sports horse industry – such as equine biosecurity and the global trade of sentient beings, their semen, and embryos – could also expand the horizons of political geographers.

References

Bale, J. (2003). *Sports Geography*, 2nd edition. London: Routledge.

Butler, D., and N. Charles (2012). Exaggerated Femininity and Tortured Masculinity: Embodying Gender in the Horseracing Industry. *The Sociological Review* 60(4): 676–95.

Cassidy, R. (2002). *The Sport of Kings*. Cambridge: Cambridge University Press.

Cassidy, R. (2007). *Horse People*. Baltimore: The Johns Hopkins University Press.

Dichter, H. L., and A. L. Johns, eds. (2014). *Diplomatic Games*. Lexington: University of Kentucky Press.

Erola, J. (2010). *Muistoja Talin laukkaradoilta* [Memories from the Tali Race Track]. Helsinki and Ypäjä: SRL and Equestrian Sports Museum of Finland.

Hobson, K. (2007). Political Animals? On Animals as Subjects in an Enlarged Political Geography. *Political Geography* 26(3): 250–67.

Jalkanen, L. (1984). *Suomen ratsujalostus* [The Breeding of Riding Horses in Finland]. Hämeenlinna: Arvi A. Karisto.

Jalkanen, L., and A. Saarinen. (1986). *Vuosisata ratsain* [A Century on Horseback]. Ratsastuskustannus.

Karekallas, M., P. Raento, and T. Renkonen (2014). Diffusion and Learning: Twenty Years of Sports Betting Culture in Finland. *UNLV Gambling Research and Review Journal* 18(1): 25–50.

Koch, N. (2013). Sport and Soft Authoritarian Nation-Building. *Political Geography* 32: 41–52.

Koch, N. (2015). Gulf Nationalism and the Geopolitics of Constructing Falconry as a "Heritage Sport." *Studies in Ethnicity and Nationalism* 15(3): 522–39.

Lotteries Act (2001). November 23, 2001/1047. *Ministry of the Interior*. Available at: www.finlex.fi (accessed August 4, 2016).

McIntosh, A., and R. Prentice. (1999). Affirming Authenticity: Consuming Cultural Heritage. *Annals of Tourism Research* 26(3): 589–612.

McManus, P., G. Albrecht, and R. Graham. (2013). *The Global Horseracing Industry*. London: Routledge.

Mahlamäki, M. (2003). *Pellolta paanalle ja pussihousumiehistä patiinipoikiin* [From Field to Track]. Espoo: Suomen Hippos.

Matilainen, R. (2010). A Question of Money? The Founding of Two Finnish Monopolies. In *Global Gambling* ed. S. Kingma. London: Routledge, 21–37.

Ojala, I. (2007). Suomalainen hevonen ja suomenhevonen sotilashevosena [Finnish horse and Finnhorse as a military horse]. In *Suomenhevonen* [The Finnhorse] ed. M. Saastamoinen (Espoo: Suomen Hippos 2007), 17–32.

Pine, J., and J. Gilmore (1999). *The Experience Economy*. Boston: Harvard Business School Press.

Raento, P. (2006). Communicating Geopolitics through Postage Stamps: The Case of Finland. *Geopolitics* 11(4): 601–29.

Raento, P. (2015). Role and Functioning of Clubs within the Finnish Sport and Horse Riding Training System. Paper presented at Horse Industry – Vocational Education Project Seminar, March 18–19, in Warsaw, Poland. Available at: www.youtube.com/watch?v=I_SigV7k_8Y (accessed August 4, 2016).

Raento, P., and L. Härmälä (2014). The Contested Structural Change in Finnish Trotter Racing and Betting in the 2000s. In *Gambling in Finland* ed. P. Raento. Helsinki: Gaudeamus Helsinki University Press, 125–52.

Saranpää, K. (2012). Kekkosen perintö raviurheilulle [Kekkonen's Legacy to Trotter Racing]. In *Presidenttien hevoset Ypäjällä* [The Presidents' Horses at Ypäjä] ed. J. Erola. Ypäjä: Equestrian Sports Museum of Finland, 42–59.

Schuurman, N., and J. Nyman (2014). Eco-National Discourse and the Case of the Finnhorse. *Sociologia Ruralis* 54(3): 285–302.

SRL (2015). Suomen Ratsastajainliitto [The Equestrian Federation of Finland]. Available at: www.ratsastus.fi (accessed June 15, 2015).

Suomen Hippos (2016). Annual Report 2015. [The Finnish Breeding and Trotting Association.] Available at: www.hippos.fi (accessed August 4, 2016).

Tervo, M. (2003). Geographies in the Making: Reflections on Sports, the Media, and National Identity in Finland. *Nordia Geographical Publications* 32:1.

UET (2016). L'Union Européenne du Trot [European Trotting Union] Annual Report 2014. Available at: www.uet-trot.eu (accessed August 4, 2016).

Urbanik, J. (2012). *Placing Animals*. Lanham: Rowman and Littlefield.

Vasara, E. (1987). *Suomen ratsastusurheilun historia* [The History of Finnish Riding Sports]. Helsinki: SRL.

Chapter 3

Spreading the game or reproducing hegemony?

The United States and the regional geopolitics of women's football in the Americas

Jon D. Bohland[1]

Introduction

For the first time in its history, the 2015 FIFA Women's World Cup (WWC) included 24 teams in the final round, expanded by 6 teams from previous tournaments. Seven of the teams had qualified for every tournament since the WWC began in 1991, including perennial favorites and former champions Germany, Norway, Japan, and the eventual winner the United States of America. The popularity of women's football in the United States exploded in the 1980s and 1990s, as youth clubs began producing an increasing number of women's players in order to keep up with the massive post-Title IX growth of women's college soccer during the same period (Williams 2007: 62).[2] As Markovits and Hellerman (2003: 14) argue, successful US Women's National Team (USWNT) players such as Mia Hamm, Brandy Chastain, Julie Foudy, Alex Morgan, and Abby Wambach are as widely known publically as their equivalent stars on the men's team. As they suggest, "Nowhere else is women's soccer the cultural equivalent of – or even superior to – the men's game, as it is in the United States." The World Cup final versus Japan, for example, set the record as the most watched soccer match (men's or women's) in American history. One week after the match, tens of thousands of fans lined the streets of Manhattan for the first ticker tape parade held in honor of a women's sports team in American history. *Sports Illustrated* issued 23 different commemorative covers of its magazine featuring all the members of the team holding the World Cup trophy in individual poses.

While the 2015 Women's World Cup reaffirmed the US as a dominant force in women's soccer, the event proved a fairly dismal failure for the teams from the rest of the Western Hemisphere. Apart from Canada and the USA, no other team from the region advanced to the final eight of the tournament. Additionally, Brazil and Colombia were the only teams from Latin America or the Caribbean to make it out of the group stage, culminating in losses for both teams to Australia and the United States respectively. The teams from Costa Rica, Mexico, and Ecuador all failed to record a single victory in the tournament, with the Ecuadorian team suffering the ignominy of exiting the tournament with a goal difference of one goal scored against 17 goals conceded. In a part of the world where women's soccer suffers from a lack of funding and woeful support from their own soccer federations, the failure of the Latin American teams was predictable – but there is more to the story than first meets the eye. Though there continues to be some growth in the women's game across northern and western Europe, Canada, East Asia, and Australia, the relative stagnation and underfunding of the women's game throughout the rest of the Americas means the United States has very few regional rivals to challenge their hemispheric hegemony. The embarrassing performances by the teams of CONMEBOL (the South American Football Confederation) and CONCACAF (Confederation of North, Central American, and Caribbean Association Football) at the 2015 World Cup illustrated just how far many of these programs have to go to even become competitive at international events.

This chapter examines this clear discrepancy in the growth and quality of women's soccer across the Western Hemisphere, examining the role the United States plays in engendering the growth of the women's game within the region.[3] Women's soccer has a long history in Latin America, well predating the passage of Title IX in the United States. Nonetheless, it remains massively underdeveloped and underfunded in comparison to the men's game, with much of the blame resting with national and local federations, which have historically viewed the women's game with a mixture of indifference, sexism, and contempt (Nadal 2014). As such, aspiring women footballers from the Americas have left their home countries in large numbers to hone their craft at a higher level abroad – and many of them end up playing collegiately or professionally in the United States.

The idea of leveraging the success of the women's game in the US to grow women's soccer across the region is a major talking point for FIFA Administrators and general advocates of the women's game in the US. In a purely sporting sense, it would certainly be in the best interest of US women's soccer to have strong competition regionally. From a purely nationalist sporting perspective, a stronger region would actually benefit US women's soccer in the long run. Their games against stronger regional rivals would theoretically produce more seasoned and confident US women's teams, placing them at an even stronger position during World Cup and Olympic events. Additionally, US collegiate and professional teams could benefit from an additional pool of stronger international players, some of whom would most likely come from soccer-crazed Latin American countries with large minority populations in the United States. This has not happened, however, and this chapter asks why. Or, more specifically, why has the explosive and unparalleled growth of the women's game in the US failed to ignite a similar dynamic movement for the vast majority their regional neighbors?

Building on the research of Booth and Liston (2014) on the rising demand for players within NCAA and NAIA women's soccer programs, I trace the growing internationalization of university women's soccer programs in the United States, which has opened opportunities for young women's players across the Americas to play at high levels. But many of the same programs and sporting structures that seem to promote and strengthen women's soccer across the region also simultaneously serve to reproduce the position of the United States as the regional "soccer hegemon." For example, the current lack of racial and class diversity within the women's game in the United States at every level of competition severely limits the size and quality of the dual national player pool available for "export." Additionally, I discuss how NCAA, NAIA, and even professional teams tend to favor domestic players and internationals from Europe and Canada over those from the rest of the Americas, thereby limiting the labor opportunities for regional players. This chapter, thus, illustrates the need for a geopolitical lens to highlight regional power dynamics and explain the relationship between the women's soccer programs of the US and the rest of the Americas.

Geopolitics and women's soccer in the Americas

Within the fields of geography and international relations (IR), sport and its connection to politics remains a marginalized subject of research (Grix 2013). But, as John Bale (2003: 2) argues,

> The traditional neglect of sport by geographers is paradoxical for several reasons ... sport is a major aspect of economic, social and political life. Second, space and place – regarded by many as the two geographical fundamentals – are central to both geography and sport.

Similarly, Levermore and Budd (2004: 5) emphasize the shared connections between sport and IR in their focus on the interconnectedness of local and regional spaces within a globalized world. This chapter, therefore, works to advance the geographic literature on sport in general, and the geopolitics literature in particular, through a regionalized case study of women's soccer. As part of their defense of contemporary regional geography, Murphy and O'Loughlin (2009: 245) contend that despite the trend in critical geopolitics emphasizing localized and "micro-scales" of study, there are many geopolitical issues that remain ideally suited for regional, "meso-scale" forms of geographic analysis. In the spirit of this regionally focused geographic research, this study analyzes women's soccer across the Americas to illustrate how the rapid development of the sport in one country, the United States, impacts the relative strength of the women's game throughout the rest of the continent.

Through its focus on women's soccer, this chapter contributes to the relatively small, albeit growing, subset of studies within a larger field of scholarship dominated by studies on the men's game – a challenge that reflects the sexism present in the women's game on the pitch (see Doyle 2014). Though the focus of research on women's soccer is nearly as wide ranging and dynamic as work on the men's game, there has been a major emphasis on archival work documenting the history of women's soccer around the world (e.g., Agergaard and Tiesler 2014; Botelho and Agergaard 2011; Nadal 2014; Perets *et al.* 2011; Williams 2003, 2007, 2011). Regarding the United States, this work reveals that the roots of the women's game are far older than the passage of American Title IX legislation in the 1970s. Indeed, as these scholars suggest, the history of the women's game is largely a story of how its early- and mid-twentieth-century growth led to active suppression of the sport by both national footballing federations and state government legislation (Williams 2007). Internationally, there has been a major growth of women's sports as part of the so-called "women in sport movement" since the 1990s. However, this movement did not target developing countries and thus "had a rather elitist and European and North American character" (Meier 2005: 6–7).

Female footballers in the Global South face many barriers that limit their participation in the sport. Institutionally, a 2015 FIFA survey of 177 member federations revealed that only 25 percent of national federations had a staff dedicated to women's soccer (all in Europe, East Asia, or North America); 50 percent had no youth development for girls and 20 percent of those federations did not even field a women's national team (Waldron 2015). Additionally, women footballers from the Global South are rarely glorified by members of their own national sporting media, meaning that there are few local role models for young players. The ambivalence to the women's game by local and national soccer federations further contributes to its marginalization (Meier 2005), while the global regulatory body, FIFA, refuses to mandate federations to develop women's footballing programs. Sepp Blatter, the infamous, long-standing head of FIFA, once famously recommended that if women only "wore tighter shorts," women's soccer would grow in popularity (Christenson and Kelso 2004). Despite these difficulties, women around the world continue to find ways to play the game and participate in the joy of sport, even as they might be consciously or unconsciously rebelling against normative values within sexist societies (Williams 2007: 18–19).

Despite a history of organized competition stretching back to the early twentieth century, women's soccer in Latin America and the Caribbean exemplifies the gendered inequities plaguing female players globally. Soccer is the most popular sport in the Americas, though it is regionally coded as a "man's game," and remains a bastion of *machismo* masculinity and a crucial underpinning of regional patriarchy (Alabarces and Rodriguez

1999; Archetti *et al.* 1994; Bar-On 1997; Biram 2012; Elsey 2011; Mason 1995; Nadal 2014). Consequently, Latin American and Caribbean women playing soccer are viewed by a large percentage of the population (both men and women) as threats to traditional gender norms, which must be actively suppressed (Nadal 2014: 210). For example, female footballers face social, economic, and cultural obstacles including arguments that soccer is too strenuous for women and encourages homosexuality (Harris and Humberstone 2014). In Brazil, often considered the "home of football" due to its success in men's World Cups and a wide fan base, women's soccer was actually illegal until 1979, and young female players are often threatened and bullied with homophobic stereotypes (Biram 2002; Garcia-Navarro 2015). In such contexts, the simple act of women playing soccer can be viewed as a subversive and radical act.

In stark contrast to the millions of dollars spent by national federations on men's programs and professional leagues, women's soccer teams throughout Latin America and the Caribbean receive scarce financial and logistical support. As Costa Rican national team player Raquel Rodriguez suggests: "It is hard [for women] because there is no structure ... the conditions in which teams play and train, it is just not the best. There's no material to practice with or just the fields are awful" (quoted in Hays 2014). The women's national teams from both Trinidad and Tobago and Jamaica had to publically crowd-source funding online to continue their World Cup qualifying campaign. Trinidad and Tobago's coach Randy Waldrum received only US$500 total from his federation to mount a month-long campaign of games and practices for qualification (Waldron 2015). Like their counterparts all around the Global South, female footballers in Latin America and the Caribbean are faced with immense societal, cultural, and economic barriers that limit their development as players and the popularity of women's game in their home countries.

Title IX and the growth of women's soccer in the United States

The 2015 WWC victory of the USWNT, the third world title for the national team since 1991, capped a 30-year period of massive growth in the domestic women's game. National team players from the 2015 team, such as Carli Lloyd, became sporting celebrities, creating a new generation of players for young American girls to idolize and emulate, just as Mia Hamm and Julie Foudy were for the current generation of players. Certainly, the massive growth of women's soccer in the United States is due in no small part to the long-term success of the national team. American soccer hegemony has also been achieved largely as a result of an impressive infrastructure for the women's game that is unrivaled outside of some western and northern European countries. This infrastructure is in large part a direct result of federal government legislation. Though historians have documented the existence of organized women's soccer in the United States beginning in the early decades of the twentieth century, the landmark passage of Title IX legislation in 1972 was a critical moment for the growth of women's soccer in the country (Markovits and Hellerman 2003; Williams 2007). Title IX outlawed any exclusion or limitation of participation based on sex within educational programs or activities receiving federal funding or assistance. Title IX was only marginally enforced until the early 1990s, when a series of actions by Congress and the decision of the United States Supreme Court in the 1992 case *Franklin* v. *Gwinnett County Schools* radically altered the gender landscape of youth and university athletics.

Since the introduction of Title IX, soccer has become one of the largest team sports for young women in the United States, with nearly 1.5 million youth players officially registered with US Youth Soccer and an estimated two million more players participating at a recreational level. At high school level, soccer is the third highest participatory sport among young women, with an estimated 375,000 registered players (Morris 2015). As a direct result of Title IX legislation, university athletic programs within the NCAA are required by law to have equal numbers of athletic scholarships for female athletics as their male counterparts. The growth of NCAA women's university soccer was meteoric, increasing 910 percent during a 32-year period from 1982 to 2014.[4] Today 81 percent of all NCAA universities have a women's soccer team, including 88 percent of the scholarship-granting institutions at the Division I and II level (NCAA 2015).

In terms of financial support for the game and professional opportunities for players, the United States ranks among the world leaders in both categories. The US Soccer Federation (USSF) funds youth national programs, Olympic development talent recognition programs, and advanced training opportunities for women's players from age 12 to adulthood. Though FIFA does not offer equal prize money for men and women's World Cup winners, the USSF is one of the few soccer federations globally where women players collectively bargain with their national federation for compensation that rivals the men's program. This is in large part a result of the financial and sporting successes of the USWNT, as women's national team friendly matches regularly feature crowds of 25,000 to 40,000 fans. USWNT players receive annual salaries from the federation and women's players also have professional options in the National Women's Soccer League (NWSL). The average attendance at NWSL matches is the highest of any women's professional soccer league in the world, at just over 4,000 viewers per match. This number is sometimes even higher; for example, the Portland Oregon Thorns Club averages over 13,000 for their matches (Dundas 2015). Additionally, the NWSL is primarily funded with money from the USSF, and smaller subsidies from the Canadian Soccer Association and the Mexican Football Federation.

The United States as a footballing destination

Given the massive disparity in the relative health of the women's game across the Americas, it is not surprising that many women footballers look for opportunities in the United States. As a women's soccer powerhouse, the "magnetic pull" of the United States to foreign players is strong. The facilities and funding available in the United States for female players are far superior to those found across the rest of the Americas. In describing her desire to play professionally in the United States in two separate interviews, Brazilian superstar Marta explained:

> The home of women's football.... In the US I was able to understand why the main players never leave the country. They get support from their club and local confederations to stay. It is very different from what happens in Brazil.
>
> (quoted in Gray 2009)

International players who come to the United States also receive a four-year college education and most likely an undergraduate degree, as the most recent graduation success rate for women's soccer players is close to 90 percent (Grasgreen 2012).

As the demand for players to fill NCAA women's soccer programs has risen, college coaches now recruit heavily internationally, which they see as a way to quickly improve their teams within an increasingly competitive soccer landscape. And they are not going far: fully 65 percent of the international players playing for NCAA Division I teams now come from Central American and Caribbean countries (Booth and Liston 2012). For example, McCree (2014: 76) documents how American coaches recruit female Trinidadian players through both informal and formal player networks, leading to over 40 players from that country coming to play university-level soccer since the mid-1980s. These opportunities have translated to a marked increase in the number of youth soccer clubs for women across the country, from a total of only five in 1985 to 19 by 2012. These advances notwithstanding, Trinidadian players must continue to travel to the US if they want to compete at higher levels in the sport.

At the professional level, the United States offers international players both the opportunity to get paid playing the game and to further develop their talent in a highly competitive environment – opportunities that are largely absent in their home countries. There are numerous summer semi-professional leagues that provide further opportunities for player development. For example, the club FC Indiana, based in Indianapolis and South Bend, Indiana, is dedicated to providing international players an opportunity to train and play in the United States. The 2015 roster features two assistant coaches from Ecuador and is largely comprised of players from

Haiti. In describing why he had the players come to the United States, Coach Shek Borkowski commented that, "Being in the United States, [it] kind of opened up their eyes to other ways of interacting. Being in the United States, the culture opened up their eyes and maybe their minds to 'Hey, there's a different way'" (quoted in Lewis 2014).

These limited (semi) professional opportunities, while positive in terms of providing higher-level post-university training for regional players, are a far inferior professional environment than found in the National Women's Soccer League (NWSL). The third professional league for women founded in the USA since 1999, the NWSL is home to the majority of players from the US and Canadian national teams. Along with Division I Feminine (France), the Frauen Bundesliga (Germany), and the Damallsvensken (Sweden), the NWSL is one of the premier women's professional leagues in the world. NWSL rules limit each team to only 4 international players on a 20-player roster (defined as non-US green card holders), making these international spots highly competitive and sought after. Though the NWSL is partially funded with money from the Mexican Football Federation (in addition to the USSF and CSA), few Mexican national team players (four) are on current 2015 rosters. Additionally, only one Caribbean player has ever played for a NWSL team (in 2013) while no Central American players have. Among CONMEBOL players on 2015 NWSL rosters, the only representatives are four Brazilians, one Colombian, and one Argentine. With such limited access to the top tier of women's professional soccer in the Americas, the top Latin American and Caribbean players must either try to find a team in one of the highly competitive northern European leagues or continue to train in relative obscurity in one of the poorly funded, semi-professional leagues in their home countries.

Dual nationals and US women's soccer

The issues of dual nationality footballers and their eligibility for FIFA-approved national team competitions have received a great deal of public media scrutiny, particularly as it relates to the men's game (Bohland 2016). Within women's soccer, by contrast, the phenomenon of dual national players has received little or no media attention, despite the fact that some national teams feature as many prominent players from transnational backgrounds as their male counterparts. Furthermore, there has been little recognition of the changing regional role of the United States, an immigrant nation with a huge population of female footballers, as an "exporter" of women's soccer talent. In opposition to the men's team as talent importers, the US women's national team programs are primarily *suppliers* of dual nationals to foreign-national team programs. In fact, the USWNT has brought in only one major dual national player to the national team program over the past 20 years: Canadian-American Sydney Leroux.

As the United States continues to produce a large pool of American players through its youth programs and the college system, there are many good female players in the country who may never appear for the highly competitive USWNT programs.

For those players with access to a second passport, playing for another country in the region offers a chance to participate in soccer competitions at the prestigious international level. For example, Mexican-American Bianca Sierra describes how she "grew up watching Mia Hamm, Brandi Chastain, and the US National Team. I loved them so much and wanted to be like them. To be playing against that team is unbelievable" (quoted in Auburn University 2013). In turn, these more developed players instantly become leaders for their new national teams and generally elevate the level of play within the program. As noted by Mexican national team manager Leo Cuellar,

> The way the level of competition is going, you just look for the best talent. It happens that in the [United] States there are millions of Mexicans. And it happens that more and more of the girls like to play this sport.
>
> (quoted in Baxter 2011)

Table 3.1 indicates the number of US eligible dual women's national players who have attended a national team camp from another country in the Americas since 2010. The vast majority of these players went on to

Table 3.1 Dual women's national players from the United States since 2010

Country represented (all from CONCACAF and CONMEBOL)	Number of players since 2010
Argentina	1
Brazil	2
Canada	11
Cayman Islands	1
Chile	2
Colombia	8
Costa Rica	3
Ecuador	2
El Salvador	6
Guatemala	9
Haiti	12
Honduras	1
Jamaica	21
Mexico	66
Panama	2
Trinidad and Tobago	13

Source: bigsoccer.com (2012).

appear in an official match for the countries, either as a youth or a full international. Not surprisingly, the data reveals Mexico as the country benefitting most in this exchange, with over 60 players with US citizenship joining the Mexican national team program. The 1999 team from Mexico that qualified for the World Cup featured 12 players with US citizenship: one reason why the Mexican government has chosen to regularly hold sporting festivals in Los Angeles to identify potential dual athletes from seven sports, including women's soccer (Baxter 2011). Many of the dual national players who have represented Mexico speak little or no Spanish, but dream of becoming the first Mexican female players to become celebrities. Veronica Perez and her sister Amanda have both been chosen to represent Mexico, leading Veronica to state that, "We have to speak Spanish fluently in, like, a year because, if we're going to be famous, they're going to want to do stories on us and we have to communicate with the Mexican press" (quoted in Baxter 2011).

Though the presence of dual nationals has certainly improved the player pool for some regional teams, significant factors limit just how substantially this trend might lessen the gap between the US and other regional teams. The US has yet to lose a dual national player to a regional rival who would have been a starter or key member of the USWNT program. Because of the success of the USWNT program, elite players with US passports hold out most of their hope to play for the USA, even if they have opportunities elsewhere. As such, the players being "exported" tend to be second tier in terms of quality. Though this is also true in regard to dual nationals in the men's game, the sheer number of well-trained professional male players means that the gap between the elite and second tier is much smaller than within women's soccer.

Furthermore, given the large Central American community in the United States, the number of dual national team members playing for countries in that region is relatively small. This is largely due to two main factors. First, with the notable exception of Costa Rica, women's soccer in the region remains underdeveloped and extremely underfunded. Unlike Mexico, these Central American federations – the majority of which are at best ambivalent about the women's game – tend to not actively scout the United States for female dual national team players in hotbeds of Central American populations such as southern California, Washington DC, or Chicago as they do with the men's program. In truth, most of the dual nationals currently choosing to play for Guatemala, El Salvador, or Honduras must contact the federations themselves to make them aware of their eligibility and/or fly themselves down for personal tryouts with national team coaches. Additionally, these teams rarely play friendlies in the United States that might raise their visibility within the Central American community.

Additionally, it is important to note that in the "home of women's football," the game remains largely dominated by middle- and upper-class white women. Put simply, US women's soccer has a "diversity problem." For example, the 2015 USWNT winning team included only four players of color, with Cuban-American Amy Rodriguez representing the only Latina on the roster. Similarly, only 3.9 percent of the players found on current NWSL rosters are Latinas (Finn 2011). As noted by Dionne Koller, the whiteness of women's soccer is "right out of the feminist movement [as a whole]. To some extent, the sports piece of the feminist equality movement stayed stuck in a 1970s version of the axis of oppression, especially experienced by women and girls of color" (quoted in Rhoden 2012). According to a 2007 study of high school sophomores undertaken by the US Department of Education, Latinas had a participation rate in high school sports of only 32 percent compared to 51 percent for white girls and 40 percent for African-Americans. The same study revealed that girls of color participated in women's soccer at a rate of only 5.3 percent (Rhoden 2012). Similarly, 2009–10 data from the NCAA reveals that Latinas comprise only 5.2 percent of all Division I women's soccer players (Hays 2011).

Apart from southern California, youth soccer clubs in the United States remain largely devoid of a sizable Latina presence. Much of this is financial, as US elite girls' club soccer utilizes a "pay to play" model, commonly practiced within US youth sports, where families pay thousands of dollars for their daughters to participate (Tapia 2011). The need to move away from this model is one of the major discussion points within youth soccer, though most of the clubs that have actually been able to do so financially are those youth teams affiliated with MLS, the top tier men's professional league. Despite many clubs offering scholarships for working-class families, most families must pay for their daughters to participate. As Yang (2015) notes: "This is not to suggest that US Soccer is consciously racist. But it is suggesting that based on a variety of factors, women of color are systematically excluded from soccer as they increase in competition level."

Conclusion

As the findings in this chapter suggest, there have been some positive spillovers from the impressive development of the women's game in the US to countries in Latin America and the Caribbean. But these impacts have done little to change the balance of footballing power in the region. The United States remains the clear hegemon of the women's game and there is little evidence to suggest that this is likely to change any time soon. It is important to note that the impact of regional underdevelopment of women's soccer in the Americas is not limited to the sporting arena. There are also significant societal impacts, as an increasing amount of research documents the positive physical and social impacts achieved by increasing the rate of sporting participation for young women (Kirk 2012). Simply put, growing the women's game across the region helps not only the quality of women's soccer: it can help improve the quality of life for women. Actually doing so, however, requires a degree of financial and legislative commitment that most Latin American and Caribbean federations and state governments continue to be unwilling to undertake.

The US Soccer Federation, particularly through its most visible star players, could take on a vocal and public leadership role to support the growth of the women's game across the region, but domestic battles to stabilize and diversify the game often seem to take priority over international challenges.[5] And, even then, the position of the United States as the dominant power in women's soccer is not without its criticism and challenges. Despite the pull of the country for female players throughout CONCACAF and CONMEBOL seeking better opportunities, there is now an increasingly vocal undercurrent of criticism of America's privileged and sheltered position within the women's game. During the 2015 Women's World Cup, prior to Colombia's knock-out round game versus the United States, their captain Lady Andrade asserted that the American team,

> belittle[s] us. They think we're a team they're going to walk over and it will be an easy game for them ... there would be huge repercussions [if we win] because of what the U.S. symbolizes and what has been said about us there ... they play very physically, taking a lot of shots and kicking out at you all the time.
>
> (quoted in Logothetis 2015)

Similarly, Canadian commentators Kristen Jack and former player Gilles Blondeau both suggested that the USWNT "complain too much," receive unfair preference from the referees, and are the most spoiled and entitled women's footballers (quoted in Rogers 2015).

Though such public criticism could be dismissed as isolated acts of jealousy, such comments reflect a widespread tension regarding the US position as the dominant force in women's soccer. For players and fans of women's soccer outside of the US, particularly for those from the Global South, the American team is perceived as having all of the advantages – a strong infrastructure, a large fan base, a seemingly unlimited player pool, a federation that values women's soccer, and a media that covers and televises every USWNT match. So when USWNT players take public positions, such as criticizing the 2015 tournament's artificial turf, despite often being quite legitimate, their concerns are dismissed by many players from the region as elitist and American-centric. The regional geographic case study approach to women's soccer in the Americas practiced in this chapter reveals that, until there is a more level playing field across the Americas for women's footballers, such regional divisions and relatively petty forms of infighting are likely to continue.

Notes

1 I would like to thank Pavithra Suresh and Taylor Walker for their help in compiling the data used in this study.
2 As it is known as soccer in the US, I will use soccer when specifically referencing the sport in the United States. In all other cases, I use football.
3 I largely exclude Canada from my analysis, as the women's game in Canada is at a much more developed level than the rest of the non-US CONCACAF countries.
4 There were 103 NCAA women's soccer programs in 1982 (Markovits and Hellerman 2003), and 1,041 in 2014 (NCAA 2015). There are currently 202 teams playing women's soccer at NAIA university programs (NAIA 2015). There are 252 total NAIA college programs, meaning a total of 80 percent of NAIA schools sponsor women's soccer.
5 Illustrating the lack of stability for women's professional and semi-professional football in the United States, the Pro-Am W-League announced on November 6, 2015, that it was ceasing operations after 20 years.

References

Agergaard, S., and N. Tiesler. (2014). Introduction: Globalization, Sports Labor Migration and Women's Mobilities. In *Women, Soccer and Transnational Migration* eds. S. Agergaard and N. Tiesler. Abingdon: Routledge, 15–31.

Alabarces, P., and M. Rodriguez. (1999). Football and Fatherland: The Crisis of National Representation in Argentinian Football. *Culture, Sport, Society* 2(3): 118–33.

Archetti, E., R. Giulianotti, and J. Williams (1994). Masculinity and Football: The Formation of National Identity in Argentina. In *Game Without Frontiers: Football, Identity, and Modernity* eds. R. Giulianotti and J. Williams. London: Ashgate, 225–43.

Auburn University (2013). Sierra Set to Face US National Team. *Auburn Tigers. com*, 3 September. Available at: www.auburntigers.com/sports/w-soccer/spec-rel/090313aac.html (accessed April 5, 2015).

Bale, J. (2003). *Sports Geography*. London: Routledge.

Bar-On, T. (1997). The Ambiguities of Football, Politics, Culture, and Social Transformation in Latin America. *Sociological Research Online* 2(4): Available at: http://socresonline.org.uk/2/4/2.html (accessed June 27, 2016).

Baxter, K. (2011). A Chance at Soccer South of the Border. *Los Angeles Times*, 2 January. Available at: http://articles.latimes.com/2011/jan/02/sports/la-sp-womens-soccer-20110103 (accessed April 9, 2015).

Bigsoccer.com. (2012). Yank Women on Foreign WNT or YWNT: Compiled by Boston Red. Available at: http://forums.bigsoccer.com/threads/yank-women-on-foreign-wnt-wynt.1943490/ (accessed August 21, 2015).

Biram, M. (2012). Marta and the Revolution. *In Bed with Maradona*, May 13. Available at: http://inbedwithmaradona.com/journal/2012/5/13/marta-and-the-revolution.html (accessed December 6, 2015).

Bohland, J. (2017). Who Counts As a Real American? Dual Citizenship, Hybridity, and the Internationalization of the U.S. Men's National Team. In *Soccer and the Boundaries of History: Politics, Social Change, and Social Theory* eds. B. Elsey and S. Pugliese. New York: Palgrave Macmillan.

Booth, S., and K. Liston (2014). The Continental Drift to a Zone of Prestige: Women's Soccer Migration to the US NCAA Division I 2000–2010. In *Women, Soccer and Transnational Migration* eds. S. Agergaard and N. Tiesler. Abingdon: Routledge, 65–84.

Botelho, V., and S. Agergaard (2011). Moving for the Love of the Game? International Migration of Female Footballers into Scandinavian Countries. *Soccer and Society* 12(6): 806–19.

Brake, D. (2010). *Getting in the Game: Title IX and the Women's Sports Revolution.* New York: New York University Press.

Christenson, M., and P. Kelso. (2004). Soccer Chief's Plan to Boost Women's Game? Hotpants. *Guardian Online*, 15 January. Available at: www.theguardian.com/uk/2004/jan/16/football.gender (accessed November 7, 2015).

Doyle, J. (2014). On the Sexism of Football Scholars and Sports Critics. *The Sport Spectacle*, 12 May. Available at: http://thesportspectacle.com/2014/05/12/on-the-sexism-of-football-scholars-and-sports-critics/ (accessed March 2, 2015).

Dundas, Z. (2015). Are the Portland Thorns the First "Real Club" in Women's Football? *Guardian Online*, April 10. Available at: www.theguardian.com/football/blog/2015/apr/10/are-portland-thorns-the-first-real-club-in-womens-football (accessed April 13, 2015).

Elsey, B. (2011). *Citizens and Sportsmen: Fútbol and Politics in Twentieth Century Chile.* Austin: University of Texas Press.

Elsey, B., and J. Nadal (2014). Marimachos: On Women's Football in Latin America. *Soccer in Latin America*, 8 December. Available at: http://football-scholars.org/uncategorized/marimachos-on-womens-football-in-latin-america/ (accessed April 6, 2015).

Finn, E. (2011). Commentary: Women's Soccer in the US Lacks Diversity. *Dominica News Online*, September 25. Available at: http://dominicanewsonline.com/news/homepage/features/commentary/commentary-womens-soccer-in-us-lacks-diversity/ (accessed April 13, 2015).

Garcia-Navarro, L. (2015). Mean Boys Can't Keep Girls Off The Soccer Field. *NPR Online*, October 13. Available at: www.npr.org/sections/goatsand-soda/2015/10/13/446873862/girls-of-brazil-face-slurs-and-taunts-if-they-play-soccer-15girls-source-abtest2 (accessed November 7, 2015).

Grainey, T. (2013). Early Days, but Borkowski Has Big Ideas for Caribbean Subsidized NWSL Team. *The Equalizer*, September 11. Available at: http://equalizersoccer.com/2013/09/11/shek-borkowski-carribean-nwsl-team-idea-fc-indiana/ (accessed April 11, 2015).

Grasgreen, A. (2012). Trade-Off in NCAA Grad Rates. *Inside Higher Ed*, 26 October. Available at: www.insidehighered.com/news/2012/10/26/ncaa-athlete-graduation-rates-football-and-mens-basketball-down-over-all (accessed March 14, 2015).

Gray, A. (2009). I Have the Skill to Play in the Men's Game-People Say I'm Like Ronaldinho, Says World No 1 Woman Marta. *Daily Mail Online*, March 30. Available at: www.dailymail.co.uk/sport/football/article-1163931/I-skill-play-mens-game-people-say-Im-like-Ronaldinho-says-world-No-1-woman-Marta.html (accessed March 18, 2015).

Grix, J. (2013). Sports Politics and the Olympics. *Political Studies Review* 11(1): 15–25.

Hall, M. (2003). The Game of Choice: Girls and Women's Soccer in Canada. *Soccer and Society* 4(2–3): 30–46.

Harris, J., and B. Humberstone (2014). Sport, Gender, and International Relations. In *Sport and International Relations: An Emerging Relationship* eds. R. Levermore and A. Budd. Abingdon: Routledge, 48–61.

Hays, G. (2011). Natalie Lagunas fulfills parents' dream. *ESPN.com*. Available at: http://espn.go.com/college-sports/story/_/id/6993991/ncaa-women-soccer-child-immigrants-natalie-lagunas-fulfills-parents-dream-northwestern-wildcats (accessed July 6, 2016).

Hays, G. (2014). Penn State's Rocky Rodriguez a Champion for Costa Rican Girls. *ESPNw.com*, September 4. Available at: http://espn.go.com/espnw/news-commentary/article/11464118/penn-state-rocky-rodriguez-champion-costa-rican-girls (accessed April 2, 2015).

Kirk, D. (2012). *Empowering Girls and Women through Physical Education and Sport: Advocacy Brief* ed. C. Wing. Bangkok: UNESCO Asia and Pacific Regional Bureau for Education. Available at: http://unesdoc.unesco.org/images/0021/002157/215707E.pdf (accessed January 18, 2016).

Levermore, R. (2008). Sport in International Development: Time to Treat it Seriously? *Brown Journal of World Affairs* 14(2): 121–30.

Levermore, R., and A. Budd (2014). *Sport and International Relations: An Emerging Relationship*. Abingdon: Routledge.

Lewis, M. (2014). Trying to Climb a Steep Mountain: Haitians, who Play as FC Indiana in WPSL, Faces USA in WWC Qualifiers. *Big Apple Soccer*, October 20. Available at: www.bigapplesoccer.com/us/wnt.php?article_id=39044 (accessed March 27, 2015).

Logothetis, P. (2015). Colombia Star Predicts Win Over U.S. Because "They Like to Talk so Much." *USA Today*, June 20. Available at: www.usatoday.com/story/sports/soccer/2015/06/19/colombia-lady-andrade-abby-wambach-world-cup/28999129/ (accessed July 28, 2015).

McCree, R. (2014). Student Athletic Migration from Trinidad and Tobago: The Case of Women's Soccer. In *Women, Soccer and Transnational Migration* eds. S. Agergaard and N. Tiesler. Abingdon: Routledge, 85–98.

McIntyre, D. (2015). Red, White, and Green: Dual Citizens Suit Up for Mexico's National Team. *ESPNw.com*, June 6. Available at: http://espn.go.com/espnw/news-commentary/2015worldcup/article/12962975/dual citizens-help-comprise-mexico-women-world-cup-roster (accessed July 28, 2015).

Malliris, C. (2013). The Female Pele and the Growing Pains of Women's Soccer. *Soccer Politics*, October 30. Available at: https://sites.duke.edu/wcwp/2013/10/30/the-female-pele-and-the-growing-pains-of-womens-soccer/ (accessed April 10, 2015).

Markovits, A., and S. Hellerman. (2003). Women's Soccer in the United States: Yet Another American "Exceptionalism." *Soccer and Society* 4(2): 14–29.

Mason, T. (1995). *The Passion of the People: Football in South America*. London: Verso.

Meier, M. (2005). Working Paper: Gender Equity, Sport and Development. Swiss Academy for Development. Available at: http://assets.sportanddev.org/downloads/59__gender_equity__sport_and_development.pdf (accessed July 6, 2016).

Morris, B. (2015). Why is the US so Good at Women's Soccer? *Five Thirty Eight Sports*, June 30. Available at: http://fivethirtyeight.com/datalab/why-is-the-u-s-so-good-at-womens-soccer/ (accessed November 5, 2015).

Murphy, A., and J. O'Loughlin (2009). New Horizons for Regional Geography. *Eurasia Geography and Economics* 50(3): 241–51.

Nadal, J. (2014). Left Out: Women's Soccer. In J. Nadal, *Fútbol! Why Soccer Matters in Latin America*. Gainesville: University of Florida Press, 208–38.

NAIA (2015). Participating Schools NAIA Women's Soccer 2015–16. Available at: www.naia.org/ViewArticle.dbml?ATCLID=205334034 (accessed August 21, 2015).

NCAA (2015). NCAA Sports Sponsorship Database. Available at: http://web1. ncaa.org/onlineDir/exec2/sponsorship? (accessed August 21, 2015).

Perets, S., M. Levy, and Y. Galily (2011). National and Gender Identity Perceptions Among Female Football Players in Israel. *Soccer and Society* 12(2): 228–48.

Rial, C. (2014). New Frontiers: The Transnational Circulation of Brazil's Women Soccer Players. In *Women, Soccer and Transnational Migration* eds. S. Agergaard and N. Tiesler. Abingdon: Routledge, 99–114.

Rhoden, W. (2012). Black and White Women Far from Equal under Title IX. *New York Times*, June 10. Available at: www.nytimes.com/2012/06/11/sports/title-ix-has-not-given-black-female-athletes-equal-opportunity.html?_r=0 (accessed April 9, 2015).

Rogers, M. (2015). Canadians Criticize U.S. Team: Focus on Play, not Drama. *USA Today*, June 25. Available at: www.usatoday.com/story/sports/soccer/2015/ 06/24/canadians-criticize-us-womens-world-cup-drama/29240279/ (accessed July 28, 2015).

Tapia, A. (2011). US Women's Soccer: Not Quite America's Team. *New American Media*, July 17. Available at: http://newamericamedia.org/2011/07/us-womens-soccer-not-quite-americas-team.php (accessed April 2, 2015).

Votre, S., and L. Mourao (2003). Women's Football in Brazil: Progress and Problems. *Soccer and Society* 4(2): 254–67.

Waldron, T. (2015). World Cup Champion Julie Foudy: Women's Soccer is a Major Untapped Market. *Think Progress*, March 5. Available at: http://thinkprogress. org/sports/2015/03/05/3628410/wheres-funding-womens-soccer/ (accessed April 8, 2015).

Williams, J. (2003). *A Rough Game for Rough Girls? A History of Women's Football in Britain*. London: Routledge.

Williams, J. (2007). *A Beautiful Game: International Perspectives on Women's Football*. Oxford: Berg.

Williams, J. (2011). *Globalising Women's Football: Europe, Migration, and Professionalization*. Bern: Peter Lang.

Williams, J. (2014). "Soccer Matters Very Much, Every Day": Player Migration and Motivation in Women's Soccer. In *Women, Soccer and Transnational Migration* eds. S. Agergaard and N. Tiesler. Abingdon: Routledge, 32–44.

Yang, S. (2015). Pay to Play Damages USWNT Diversity. *SB Nation: The Bent Musket*, March 30. Available at: www.thebentmusket.com/2015/3/30/8213245/ usa-womens-national-soccer-team-diversity-pay-play-youth-financial (accessed April 4, 2015).

Chapter 4

Nation-building and sporting spectacles in authoritarian regimes

Turkmenistan's Aziada-2017

Slavomír Horák

Introduction

Since gaining independence after the dissolution of the Soviet Union in 1991, Turkmenistan has been governed by two presidents: Saparmyrat Niyazov, or "Turkmenbashi," (r. 1986–2006) and Gurbanguly Berdimukhamedov (r. 2006–). Both men emphasized sport and healthy living as foundational in the country's post-Soviet state- and nation-building. Turkmenbashi mostly emphasized healthy lifestyles rhetorically, through official state speeches; however, he was rarely an active participant himself. He initiated the development of several sporting facilities and complexes in the reconstruction of the capital city, Ashgabat, in the 1990s and early 2000s, including his eponymous Olympic stadium and the "Leader's Health Path" (*Serdaryn Saglyk Ýoly*). The latter, a 30-kilometer system of trails on the slopes of Ashgabat's Köpet Dagi mountains, was where government representatives, public workers, and students were often forced to participate in mass walking exercises, or "ascents" (Šír 2008).

In contrast to his predecessor, Turkmenistan's second president, Berdimukhamedov, promoted sport with more than words and public ceremonies. For him, healthy living and sport were not only foundations of state- and nation-building, but one of the main triumphs of his so-called "Great Renaissance" period. Berdimukhamedov introduced this official designation, essentially demarcating his reign as a special period in Turkmen history (Polese and Horák 2015). In presiding over this "epoch" or era, his slogan, "The health of the nation – the wealth of the homeland!" (*Il saglygy – yurt baýlygy!*), quickly became the central tenet of the country's nation-building propaganda.

Celebrated today as the founder of sport and physical education reforms in the early 2000s, Berdimukhamedov portrays himself as an example of living a healthy lifestyle. His demonstrative involvement in various sporting activities serves as both a form of self-adulation and the regime's effort to reinforce his wide-reaching personality cult (on this theme more generally, see Koch, Chapter 7 this volume). And, yet, looking beyond the rhetoric, we find that public access to sports is actually extremely limited in Turkmenistan: people lack access to proper fields, clubs, coaches, and other basic infrastructure. The neglect of small and less visible projects is symptomatic of the political dynamics in authoritarian regimes, which typically prioritize spectacular events, buildings, and one-man-centered sport (Grix 2008). Nonetheless, according to official state propaganda, the president is personally committed to improving sports infrastructure and the overall health of the country's citizens.

Since coming to power in 2006, Berdimukhamedov has eclipsed his predecessor, Turkmenbashi, by intensifying and expanding the construction of monumental sporting facilities – ostensibly to project Turkmenistan's modernity, both domestically and internationally. The centerpiece of this effort has been Turkmenistan's bid for the 2017 Asian Indoor and Martial Art Games (hereafter "Aziada-2017"). Although the government has tried to rally the public around this event and use it to promote national development, it is not targeted at the "masses" in the same way that they have previously been forced to participate in sports-oriented rallies. As this chapter illustrates, the event marks a new form of mass participation in sport in Turkmenistan; the drive for Aziada-2017 has impacted not only the living conditions and organization of daily life, but has also forced the population to participate financially in the event for the first time and on a massive scale.

Considering the case of Turkmenistan's preparations for Aziada-2017, I analyze the connection between sporting events and ceremonies alongside nation-building projects in authoritarian states. While the connection between sport and authoritarianism has a long history, the case of Turkmenistan is exemplary of a personalistic regime, characterized by a strong personality cult around the leader (Kunysz 2012). As this chapter illustrates, this political configuration permeates into the realm of sport insofar as the president's interests are key determining factors in the country's sports-related policies. Sporting programs and facilities result primarily from top-down governmental initiatives, which are highly dependent on the personal preferences of the president. In Turkmenistan's post-Soviet era, developing new sporting facilities has been part of a massive reconstruction of the capital. Defined by spectacular, monumental stadiums, Ashgabat's new sports infrastructure has been developed primarily for one-time international events. Like many other new buildings around the city, they stand mostly empty.

Why, then, has the government invested so much in these stadiums? Apart from their discursive role in nation-building, authoritarian regimes utilize massive construction projects to generate financial profits for the elite (Koch and Valiyev 2015; Müller 2011; Trubina 2014). In Turkmenistan, the president controls the building industry by awarding bids only to family-owned companies or those with strong connections to the regime.

The architectural transformation of the capital geared toward the Aziada-2017 event provides Berdimukhamedov the opportunity to further entrench his financial interests by aligning them with his health-focused ideology. His government has thus used the games to promote and increase support for his personalistic rule by fusing it with broader state- and nation-building narratives and ideals, while simultaneously forcing the population to participate in regime-dictated – and largely elitist – development agendas. Since independent research in Turkmenistan is severely restricted, data for this chapter is drawn primarily from official and opposition sources. This textual data is supplemented by official and unofficial interview material, collected outside Turkmenistan, and during two short-term visits in 2013.

International sporting events, infrastructure, and authoritarian governance

In democratic and nondemocratic contexts alike, governments consider sport as more than a tool for promoting the health and well-being of their respective societies. The success of sports teams is considered a part of the affirmative process with the state and/or nations within more liberal, open societies and established states (Bishop and Jaworski 2003). Often seen as a way to unite states and nations, sports mega-events are frequently seen as an opportunity for general development. Using events as a way to improve infrastructure or social services in the public interest was best exemplified in the 2010 Vancouver Olympic Games, but the Tokyo 1964 and London 2012 Olympic Games are also notable cases (Lehrer and Laidley 2008; Shimizu 2014).

   More authoritarian states also organize sports mega-events and seek to establish successful sports teams. In this case, though, their aims are primarily to cement the loyalty of their citizens to the system, as well as to present themselves as modern and rapidly emerging nations – seen most recently in the examples of China, Kazakhstan, and Russia (Gorokhov 2015; Koch 2013; Müller 2011; Xu 2006).[1] Historically, there has been a strong connection between sports and ideology-building in places such as the Soviet Union, North Korea, and East Germany (Grix 2008; Riordan 1980). Part of the Soviet Union until 1991, Turkmenistan has adopted some of the same sport propaganda traditions for ideology-building around Aziada-2017. However, there are some important differences with respect to how Turkmenistan engages with international sport today. In part, this is because Turkmenistan's regime is not focused on political parties or narrow oligarchies as in the former USSR or present-day Russia. Instead, political culture is centered on the presidential person, which makes organizing such an event both a national development and a personal success for the leader.[2]

Whereas Soviet or East Germany sports politics were primarily targeted at globally significant events (Hazan 1982; Wagg and Andrews 2007; Witt 1984), Turkmenistan has focused on a more regional or specifically Asian context: Aziada-2017, which does not rank among the world's first-tier mega-events – such as the Olympic Games or the European and World Championships in football, which are truly global in their scope and reach. However, as a lower-tier regional sporting event, Aziada-2017 does represent one of the highest achievable events for some countries (Gorokhov 2015; Müller and Pickles 2015). As Koch and Valiyev (2015) note, such events are often treated as a "stepping stone" toward hosting first-tier events. Indeed, officials in Turkmenistan do not hide the president's ambition for hosting Olympic Games in the future (Tétrauld-Farber 2015). Treated as an element of state- and nation-building discourses, a successful international sporting event is also seen as a way to enhance the prestige of the leader while cementing his unquestioned supremacy at the top of Turkmenistan's political hierarchy.

Harnessing Aziada-2017 to promote state- and nation-building

When news broke that Turkmenistan had been awarded the Aziada-2017 bid, the event was regarded as the highest achievement of Gurbanguly Berdimukhamedov's sport and health policy (NT 2010b, 2011c). The event was immediately celebrated with spectacular festivities that included a parade headed by the president, together with government officials and young students, and accompanied by "living images" representing Aziada-2017. The government also organized an ascent on the "Healthy Path" above Ashgabat to celebrate the event (NT 2010c). Even though the Aziada-2017 bid was filed before Berdimukhamedov became president in 2006, official news outlets attributed the success to him – for he was a key figure in the Olympic Council of Asia Executive Committee at the time (NT 2006). Still serving on this committee, the Turkmen sports media typically refer to Berdimukhamedov with the titles "director of National Olympic Committee" or "the holder of the highest Olympic Council of Asia Award" (in addition to other honorary monikers, such as "the holder of the sixth *dan* of the black belt" awarded by the World Karate Federation, or "convinced supporter of healthy life") (NT 2011b). Overall, the regime has widely broadcasted all advances related to Aziada-2017 as the result of presidential effort (NT 2014b).

Looking to broader state- and nation-building narratives, Turkmenistan's leadership has focused on two principal ideological threads in organizing Aziada-2017. First, they have justified the event on the grounds that it will project an image of Turkmenistan as a "modern" and developed nation to the outside world. Immediately after being selected to host the event, the domestic press launched a massive publicity campaign to present the successful bid as a profound achievement for modern Turkmenistan (NT 2014b). They underlined the event's exclusivity within the region, ultimately overstating the importance of the games themselves. Since the Olympic Council of Asia organizes various other international regional games (the Asian Winter Games, Asian Beach Games, Asian Youth Games, and the most prestigious all-Asian Games), the event hardly seems to be a sign of exclusivity, let alone signaling Turkmenistan's primacy. Nonetheless, these claims form an important part of the state's nationalist narratives about its success in achieving positive international attention for Turkmenistan, and being taken seriously as a "modern" state on the world stage.

The second ideological narrative guiding the official rhetoric is the idea that the success of Turkmenistan's athletes at the Aziada-2017 event is a top nationalist goal. As a result, the government has made a strong effort to recruit elite athletes. Authoritarian regimes usually do this in one of two ways. The first tactic is to "purchase" or otherwise entice athletes from abroad. This strategy has already been used for some intra-Turkmenistan tournaments, but has not yet been intensively applied to global sporting events (KT 2013).[3] The second tactic is to create a specialized training center with the best coaches and conditions to develop domestic talent. Lacking coaches and human resources at all levels and age categories, such top-down efforts have had an extremely limited impact on sport culture in Turkmenistan – resulting instead in an exodus of athletes from the country (KT 2012).

The prevailing ideological narratives around Aziada-2017 suggest that the government is pushing to achieve parity with its regional competitors, and Kazakhstan in particular. Despite achieving a handful of top positions at previous Asian regional championships, Turkmenistan remains the only former Soviet state whose athletes have never received an Olympic medal (IWPR 2011). One therefore cannot assume that the country will demonstrate its athletic superiority during Aziada-2017, as was the case with China at the 2008 Beijing Olympic Games, Kazakhstan at the 2011 Asian Winter Games, or even Azerbaijan at 2015 European Games. In all these cases, host countries employed all possible tactics to emerge first in medal rankings. For example, in the case of Kazakhstan, the popular local sports of bandy and ski-orienteering were added to the program with the hope that Kazakhstani athletes would dominate these events (Müller and Pickles 2015). Given Berdimukhamedov's push to add Turkmen national wrestling (*göre*) to the Aziada-2017 agenda (NT 2014a), it seems the government is trying to adopt similar measures to obtain the highest medal ranking possible. However, the fact remains that, on the whole, Turkmenistan's sporting system is as yet unable to produce top-quality athletes in many categories.

Beyond this ideological and realist approach of seeking regional parity, Berdimukhamedov's government is increasingly demonstrating a desire to become a global sporting hub or, at the very least, a center of all-Asian sports within the region. Apart from national interests, the regime clearly aspires to have the world community view present-day Turkmenistan as a developed country. While these themes are all essential to understanding the politics behind Turkmenistan's top-down effort to promote sport through international events, beyond the ideological rhetoric one cannot miss the exceptional political and economic implications of hosting the Aziada-2017, as the following section explores.

Building for Aziada-2017: sports infrastructure and the construction industry

Gurbanguly Berdimukhamedov's term in office is known for being a period of massive construction, including sport facilities (NT 2011a). Almost every month, the media announces an opening ceremony for some new sports school, playground, stadium, or athletic complex. The "National Program of the Turkmenistan President for the Reform of Social and Living Conditions of the Population," meant to last until 2020, anticipated building 200 sport schools around the country. Furthermore, the program also expected to build more than 100 sports complexes, while reconstructing and refurbishing another 70. Usually, official sources do not report on athletic conditions once the project has been inaugurated; just a few locations in Ashgabat are mentioned further as being managed by the State Committee for Sport and Tourism.

As explained in the press, these sports facilities are designed to grow future Turkmen champions (NT 2012). At the most elite level, the new and modern Institute of Sport and Tourism, which is part of Ashgabat's new Olympic complex, is to become the country's central institution for developing and supporting top athletes. The institute plans to attract more than 1,500 students, which corresponds to about 300 student vacancies for the first grade (NT 2013a). It resembles, among others, the Korean government's efforts in the 1960s to 1980s to promote elite athletes; although in that case, coaches were provided with the appropriate assistance and resources needed to achieve their goals (Nam-Gil and Mangan 2010: 220–3). Turkmen coaches and athletes, by contrast, lack the required training and other resources to reach peak athletic performance. Perhaps most importantly, such elite sport agendas require long-term investments and often have uncertain results, inherent to human capital. By contrast, focusing on iconic architecture to symbolize sporting aspirations, despite having less sustainable effects, is appealing to government officials because it seems an easier method for rapid self-promotion.[4]

In developed countries, preparing for top sporting events mostly focuses on improving already existing infrastructural networks, and sometimes creating new urban facilities for longer-term use (Horne and Whannel 2012). Many rapidly developing countries, however, tend to stress the symbolic dimensions of such events and seek to advertise or "brand" their countries through their monumental sport architecture, such as in the recent case of China's "Bird's Nest" Olympic Stadium, which was part of a wider effort to restructure Beijing's urban space (Broudehoux 2007; Ren 2008; Zhang and Silk 2006). In such contexts, urban planners often try to attract famous foreign architects so as to be included in the global architecture market while maintaining some elements of local traditions intact, as witnessed in the example of Khan Shatyr in Astana (Koch 2012: 2456–8; on similar issues in Seoul, see Lee, Chapter 10 this volume). Compared to the global ambitions of places such as Beijing, Astana, or Seoul, however, the architecture in Ashgabat is not designed to import Western architectural norms or achieve "world city" status. On the contrary, planners assert their desire to use it as a vehicle to spread native Turkmen traditions and architecture to the outside world. This desire corresponds to Turkmen-centered ideology, in which "Turkmenness" occupies the central position in state and national narratives (Polese and Horák 2015).

Seemingly inspired by regional neighbors such as Azerbaijan and Kazakhstan, Berdimukhamedov pragmatically realized that the country lacks the know-how to organize the event relying solely on its own resources. The resulting policies thus signaled a shift from an isolationist, "do-it-yourself" approach, which prevailed under President Niyazov until his death in 2006, toward a more engaged, global approach of organizing elite sporting events. Foreign advisers began consulting with Turkmenistan's government, and several high-profile international firms were eventually hired. For example, the JTA Consulting company – well-known for its work on the 2014 Sochi Winter Olympic Games bid, the 2015 Baku European Games bid, and other sport diplomacy and lobbying – became the principal partner of the National Olympic Committee of Turkmenistan. The company is responsible for public relations, sport event marketing and management, media training, and seminars (NT 2013b). The government has also enlisted CSM Strategic, a "major events" planning firm that helped formulate the London 2012 Olympic Games, the Baku 2015 European Games, and a host of other top-level sport bids (CSM Strategic 2014).

For facilities development, a British design and construction firm, Arup, was hired for technical assistance with constructing the new Olympic City complex (Arup 2015). General construction for this US\$2 billion project was entrusted to "certified" companies in the country. President Berdimukhamedov usually prefers one of three firms for key projects in Ashgabat: Çalyk Holding (Turkey), Polimeks (Turkey), and Bouygues (France).

Final selection and contract assignments depend on personal connections to the president and, ultimately, payoff amounts. In this case, Polimeks was selected as the "winner" for the Olympic complex (Polimeks 2015). Knowing how to satisfy Berdimukhamedov's economic wishes, the head of the company, Erol Tabanca, has a better relationship with the president than his competitors (Garcia 2015). Whereas Çalyk would have been more likely to win such a prestigious and pricey contract under the first president, the fact that Polimeks was accorded the Olympic City is yet another indication of changing power dynamics under Berdimukhamedov. Indeed, whereas the president typically gives very specific guidance, or "recommendations," for major architectural projects, these have been unusually circumscribed in the case of Aziada-2017 constructions.

As the primary venue for Aziada-2017, the site for the Olympic City complex was chosen within the wider Ashgabat city center, close to the existing Olympic stadium named after the first Turkmenistan president, Saparmyrat Turkmenbashi (NT 2010a). Its foundations were laid in October 2010 and total expenditures have increased from initial estimates of US$2 billion, up to $5 billion – in a country with an estimated total GDP of $48 billion. The complex's first phase of development included building a 6,000-seat indoor velodrome (projected to be the world's largest), a basketball stadium, and an indoor athletic hall. The second stage, launched in May 2012, added a water-sports complex, a tennis complex, an open cycling and jogging path, and a host of other features. The Turkmenbashi Olympic Stadium, built on the order of the first president, was gutted and replaced with a practically new stadium with a capacity of 45,000 to serve as the complex's central venue.[5]

The architecture of the entire complex replicates the white marble style characteristic of the newly developed areas of Ashgabat (even putting Turkmenistan's capital in the Guinness World Records as the city with the highest density of white marble-clad buildings in the world). This stylistic dimension effectively marks the complex as a prestige project and one of Berdimukhamedov's personal priorities. Although this enormous project has already reached Olympic capacity, the president remains ambitious enough to continue building even bigger sporting arenas (Tétrauld-Farber 2015). Planned facility additions in the future include a media center, hotels, and an Olympic village for athletes, with the entire complex connected by a circular monorail. Reflecting the government's broader policy of limiting foreign visitors, and the free movement of those who do come, the Olympic complex creates a comprehensive sporting space. By limiting the movement of foreign guests to this clearly delineated space, trips outside can be more easily controlled by the organizers.

In sum, Turkmenistan's infrastructural preparation for Aziada-2017 demonstrates the leadership's willingness to construct necessary sport venues and organize a large-scale event for the self-presentation and affirmation of its place in Asian, Eurasian, or even the global sport map. Hiring professionals from abroad for the organization of elite sports games should secure the organizational success, while marking a significant new step in Turkmenistan's foreign policy by declaring its openness to the world. However, plans to further utilize the Olympic complex after the end of Aziada-2017 remain unclear. The mass construction projects related to the event are likely to remain unused in future years – unless Turkmenistan's sport diplomacy eventually wins a bid for some other significant regional or international sporting event in the future. While the likelihood that Turkmenistan would be chosen to host the Olympic Games would appear extremely slim, the colossal resources that are spent on mega-events are coming under increasing criticism in more developed cities and countries. In this geopolitical context, Ashgabat's hosting chances may only be improved if these places are unwilling to bid (IWPR 2009; Witcher 2014).

Assessing the social impact of Aziada-2017

While official rhetoric has stressed the state- and nation-building dimensions of Aziada-2017, hosting the event has had several significant social impacts that reach far beyond ideology. First, direct involvement is based on the forced participation of society in mass events like sports. Second, although further development of mass sports was proclaimed one of the main ideological and internal aims of Aziada-2017, the enormous resources invested have not gone toward improving public mass sports facilities. Third, the massive reconstruction of Ashgabat has and will continue to involve the demolition of thousands of homes and communities or, at best, the refurbishment of older buildings, while many of the athletic facilities remain inaccessible to residents. Finally, the economic crisis in Turkmenistan in 2015 has resulted in financial contributions being extorted from citizens for the Aziada-2017 spectacle and the construction of Ashgabat's major new Olympic City complex.

Differing internal and external portrayals of mass participation by the population is not uncommon in authoritarian regimes (Adams 2010). In many parts of the world, crowds of people are forcibly involved in state holidays, public events, state visits, sporting events, and visits from the president or other regional leaders. In many ways, Turkmenistan has continued the Soviet tradition of mass participation in public spectacles (Roche 2001), but such events have been reinvented and adapted to the new national ideology of the independent state. Compared to his predecessor, Berdimukhamedov has made even more use of the tradition of *chare*, or forced passive participation in sport matches, opening ceremonies, presidential visits in the regions, etc. With regularity, spectators and fans are forcibly brought to stadiums to see the matches and form crowds of people. In these cases, "real" fans are not as important as the demonstration of a full stadium with people wearing team clothing. The largest sporting event in the country and a point of personal pride for the president, Aziada-2017, will require officials to ensure that stadiums are full of "fans" for the events. In line with the tradition of *chare*, one can expect an enormous manipulation of the population in order to fill each stadium with sufficient spectators, who will primarily be comprised of people gathered from Ashgabat, as well as regional state employees, students, and other easily collectivized organizations.

In addition to their forced participation in future sports mega-events, substantial segments of the population in Ashgabat and the surrounding areas will contend with social dislocation resulting from special construction projects and its frequent prerequisite: demolition. Even though the venue's location was not densely populated, the Ashgabat Olympic complex's construction has resulted in substantial violations of citizens' property rights, and a wave of forced migration and demolitions in the city center. Despite the area being revamped prior to Ashgabat's bid for the event, housing problems occurred in surrounding neighborhoods not directly connected with the future Olympic City. Ostensibly part of the urban beautification agenda, local officials launched a campaign to eliminate satellite dishes and air-conditioning systems, which previously had been criticized by the president (KT 2015a). In addition, several small villages or cottage communities with private gardens at Ashgabat's fringes (e.g., Choganly), were destroyed by bulldozers in 2014–15. Allegedly visible from planes approaching the Ashgabat airport, the demolitions were officially justified by claiming that the continued presence of rural-looking settlements on the city's outskirts would give a "bad outlook" for Aziada-2017 visitors (ANT 2015b, 2015c). Property owners have received little or no compensation from the government.

Meanwhile, resources available for construction of the Olympic City decreased substantially with falling export incomes due to the collapse of world energy prices in 2015 (Turkmenistan is heavily dependent on exporting natural gas). As a result, the Olympic City budget has met with significant shortfalls, which the government has sought to make up by turning to the population. The leadership has employed various tactics to obtain the desired funds, including delays with contracted payments, cuts from state employee salaries (of 10–30 percent), and racketeering to force entrepreneurs to make contributions for the alleged needs of Aziada-2017 (KT 2015b). The government has also recently shifted to paying state employees's salaries direct to their bank accounts, which require plastic debit cards in order to access their funds (Babaev 2015). This has limited the flow of cash because debit cards have extremely limited utility in Turkmenistan, due to a lack of ATM machines and terminals (even in large centers and cities, especially in bazaars, which are the most popular places for shopping). As a result, access to salaries suddenly became seriously complicated and bought time for state officials to divert these resources to continuing construction for the Olympic complex. In late 2015, the government introduced yet another measure: partial, but compulsory payments of state salaries through state bonds (Durdyjan 2015; KT 2015c).

In assessing the social impact of Aziada-2017, we see that the involvement of Turkmen society has already and will continue to involve the usual mixture of spectacular events, opening ceremonies, and efforts to present the country as an athletic power by gaining as many medals as possible. Workers will be mobilized, forcibly gathered as spectators to fill the stands of Ashgabat's new marble-clad stadiums. However, in looking beyond the immediacy of the event and its sporting significance, it is clear that certain actors within Berdimukhamedov's governmental apparatus have used Aziada-2017 as a tool to settle pet issues unconnected with the Games. Whether advancing their financial interests through controlling the flow of money for substantial parts of society, or seeking to entrench their political control, the event has opened many opportunities for the regime.

The related urban beautification campaign has been particularly useful for officials to further their long-term effort to destroy some parts of Ashgabat by expropriating or destroying citizens' movable and immovable property, as well as cutting off alternative sources of information, which citizens had previously accessed through satellite programs. Salary cuts and limits to accessing salary funds, implemented in the name of Aziada-2017, marks a shift in the Turkmen people's mass participation in sport and, potentially, other events. Up to now, Turkmenistan's leadership has not used such measures systematically and certainly not on at the scale of the entire country. The case of Aziada-2017 is thus a harbinger for the future approach of Berdimukhamedov and his government toward Turkmenistan's citizenship.

Conclusion

The 2017 Asian Indoor and Martial Art Games, or "Aziada-2017," will become the single most important and largest sporting event ever organized in independent Turkmenistan. The level of organization is expected to meet the highest global standards as athletes will discover excellent conditions for their specific sporting events. The games may indeed improve the image of Turkmenistan regionally, and possibly globally, allowing the leadership to demonstrate its increasing openness to the world. In this respect, Aziada-2017 is part of a general shift in the international sporting landscape, which is increasingly involving less-well-known and more authoritarian host countries for mega-events. The easy allocation of financial funds regardless of public opinion, mass mobilizations, and the ability to rebuild urban space for necessary sports facilities without public representation spurs the current trend to organize mega-event such as the Olympic Games and the Asian or European games in authoritarian regimes (on this shift, see Koch and Valiyev 2015). Although strategically justified through nationalist rhetoric, Aziada-2017 is ultimately being organized for the external promotion of the country, or in some cases, for the legitimization of the ruling regime, which is keen to present an image of benevolence, at least during the time of the event.

At the same time, many questions remain unanswered, which can challenge the overall positive image of the country. The measures adopted in connection with, or justified by, Aziada-2017 are hardly acceptable for many citizens. Demolition of several neighborhoods, removal of satellite dishes and air-conditioning systems, and the clearing of streets and quarters of trees further alienates the population and poisons their attitude toward the Games and the regime itself. Nonetheless, such an anti-regime effect may not be a uniform outcome for all citizens. The potential created by Aziada-2017 could in fact strengthen regime ideology and the personality cult surrounding the president. However, up to now the performance of Turkmen leadership and the overall political culture in the country creates skepticism regarding the further development of sport culture – a declared aim of Aziada-2017. The Olympic City complex, in its grandiose mega-event design, does not promise to be used extensively in the future, while the lack of appropriate maintenance and funding for this purpose are likely to cause it to deteriorate rapidly. As preparations for Aziada-2017 have shown thus far, ordinary people will continue to be forced to participate in leaders' sports farces in both active and passive ways. But when used solely as a form of propaganda and a metaphor for an authoritarian regime's ideology, as in Turkmenistan, sport itself will also remain a farce.

Notes

1 It is important to acknowledge that there is no strict division between liberalism and authoritarianism – certain aspects of both are always present in both systems, alongside problematic issues such as corruption, nepotism, and spectacular architecture. However, as Müller and Pickles (2015: 124–5) point out, in the case of sport mega-events, the difference between more liberal and more authoritarian regimes corresponds to a more natural urban regeneration versus a spectacular modernization and construction.

2 In this respect, the Aziada-2017 example most resembles the 2011 Almaty–Astana Winter Asian Games, which were presented as a personal success of the Kazakhstani President Nursultan Nazarbayev (Pugasov 2011).

3 Belorussian ice-hockey players participating in the tournament in Ashgabat as part of the Turkmenistan team have been the most visible example.

4 The monumental architecture in Ashgabat was not designed for everyday use, but, rather, for performative displays aimed at outsiders and/or singular sporting events. Only some sporting facilities have become places popular for the public (e.g., the Old Ice Palace opened in 2006). In some cases, constructing athletic facilities becomes a rare investment in the infrastructure of regional cities in lieu

of more essential infrastructural updates (ANT 2015a). Other athletic fields, however, were used for rare and infrequent events.

5 Though some buildings in the new Olympic city are not directly connected with Aziada-2017, they are generally considered an integral part of the overall project. The Ashgabat Winter Sports complex, including the Ice Palace for ice hockey and figure skating, the student hostel for ice hockey, and a figure skating school became the most important buildings of this kind.

References

Adams, L. (2010). *The Spectacular State: Culture and National Identity in Uzbekistan*. Durham: Duke University Press.

ANT (2015a). Bekdash: Gorod Poluprizrak v Epokhu Mogushchestva i Schast'ia [Bekdash: The Semi-Ghost City in the Period of Might and Happiness]. *Al'ternativnyie novosti Turkmenistana*, January 14. Available at: http://habartm.org/archives/1879 (accessed January 21, 2015).

ANT (2015b). Choganly: Zhitelei Lishili Vody, Gaza i Elektrichestva [Choganly: The Residents were Deprived of Water, Gas and Electricity]. *Al'ternativnyie Novosti Turkmenistana*, May 7. Available at: http://habartm.org/archives/2715 (accessed May 26, 2015).

ANT (2015c). Ashkhabadskii Raion Gaja Snesen, Na Ocheredi Khitrovka [Ashkhabad District Demolished, Khitrovka is in Line]. *Al'ternativnyie novosti Turkmenistana*, September 17. Available at: http://habartm.org/archives/3601 (accessed November 12, 2015).

Arup (2015). Ashgabat Olympic Complex Phase I. *ARUP*. Available at: www.arup.com/Projects/Ashgabat.aspx (accessed May 17, 2015).

Babaev, E. (2015). Beg Na Meste Ochen' Ukrepliaiushchii ... V Turkmenistane Vse Resursy Brosili Na Podgotovku Ob'jektov k Aziade-2017 [Running in Place is Very Strengthening.... All Sources were Put to Preparing an Icon For Aziada-2017]. *Centrasia.ru*, October 17. Available at: www.centrasia.ru/newsA.php?st=1445068500 (accessed December 14, 2015).

Bishop, H., and A. Jaworski (2003). "We Beat 'em": Nationalism and the Hegemony of Homogeneity in the British Press Reportage of Germany Versus England During Euro 2000. *Discourse & Society* 14(3): 243–71.

Broudehoux, A.-M. (2007). Spectacular Beijing: The Conspicuous Construction of an Olympic Metropolis. *Journal of Urban Affairs* 29(4): 383–99.

CSM Strategic (2014). Master Plan for the 5th Asian Indoor and Martial Arts Games. *CSM Strategic*, December 4. Available at: www.csmstrategic.com/master-plan-for-the-5th-asian-indoor-and-martial-arts-games/ (accessed June 25, 2015).

Durdyjan, M. (2015). Obligatsiia ili Abligatsiia? [Obligation or Bond?]. *Gundogar.org*, December 21. Available at: http://gundogar.org/?013051653100000000000011000000 (accessed January 5, 2016).

Garcia, D. (2015). The Desert Kingdom of Bouyguestan. *Le Monde Diplomatique*. 20(2). Available at: http://mondediplo.com/2015/02/11bouyguestan (accessed July 13, 2015).

Gorokhov, V. (2015). Forward Russia! Sports Mega-Events as a Venue for Building National Identifies. *Nationalities Papers* 43(2): 267–82.

Grix, J. (2008). The Decline of Mass Sport Provision in the German Democratic Republic. *International Journal of the History of Sport* 25(4): 406–20.

Hazan, B. (1982). *Olympic Sports as Propaganda Games: Moscow 1980*. London: Transaction Publishers.

Horne, J., and G. Whannel. (2012). *Understanding the Olympics*. London: Routledge.

IWPR (2009). Turkmenistan: Pravitel'stvo Ozabotilos' Razvitiiem Sporta [Turkmenistan's Government Paid Attention to the Development of Sport]. *Central Asia Regional News Digest*, September 25. Available at: https://ca-news.info/2009/09/29/59 (accessed July 17, 2015).

IWPR (2011). Turkmen Sport Teams Yet to Shine, 2011. *IWPR.net*, January 26. Available at: https://iwpr.net/global-voices/turkmen-sports-teams-yet-shine (accessed July 15, 2015).

Koch, N. (2012). Urban "Utopias": The Disney Stigma and Discourses of "False Modernity." *Environment and Planning A* 44(10): 2445–62.

Koch, N. (2013). Sport and Soft Authoritarian Nation-Building. *Political Geography* 32: 42–51.

Koch, N., and A. Valiyev (2015). Urban Boosterism in Closed Contests: Spectacular Urbanization and Second-Tier Mega-Events in Three Caspian Capitals. *Eurasian Geography and Economics* 56(5): 575–98.

KT (2012). Sport v Turkmenistane i Turkmenskiie Sportsmeny Za Granitsei [Sport in Turkmenistan and Turkmen Sportsmen Abroad]. *Khronika Turkmenistana*, September 5. Available at: www.chrono-tm.org/2012/09/sport-v-turkmenistane/ (accessed July 14, 2015).

KT (2013). Turkmensko–Belorusskii Khokkeinyi Record [Turkmen–Belarussian Ice-Hockey Record]. *Khronika Turkmenistana*, February 14. Available at: www.chrono-tm.org/2013/02/turkmeno-belorusskiy-hokkeynyiy-rekord/ (accessed November 11, 2015).

KT (2015a). Ubrat' vse! V Ashkhabade Griadet Aziada [Remove all! Aziada bursts in Ashgabat]. *Khronika Turkmenistana*, February 22. Available at: www.chrono-tm.org/2015/02/ubrat-vsyo-v-ashhabade-gryadet-aziada/ (accessed February 25, 2015).

KT (2015b). Aziada Na Narodnyie Den'gi [The Aziada based on the People's Money]. *Khronika Turkmenistana*, June 17. Available at: www.chrono-tm.org/2015/06/aziada-na-narodnyie-dengi/ (accessed June 29, 2015).

KT (2015c). Salaries of Turkmen Residents to Be Paid Partly in Bonds. *Khronika Turkmenistana*, December 15. Available at: www.chrono-tm.org/2015/12/chast-zarplatyi-obligatsiyami/ (accessed January 5, 2016).

Kunysz, N. (2012). From Sultanism to Neopatrimonialism? Regionalism within Turkmenistan. *Central Asian Survey* 31(1): 1–16.

Lehrer, U., and J. Laidley (2008). Old Mega-Projects Newly Packaged? Waterfront Redevelopment in Toronto. *International Journal of Urban and Regional Research* 32(4): 786–803.

Müller, M. (2011). State Dirigisme in Megaprojects: Governing the 2014 Winter Olympics in Sochi. *Environment and Planning A* 43(9): 2091–108.

Müller, M., and J. Pickles (2015). Global Games, Local Rules: Mega-events in the Post-Socialist World. *European Urban and Regional Studies* 22(2): 121–7.

Nam-Gil, H., and J. A. Mangan (2010). Ideology, Politics, Power: Korean Sport Transformation, 1945–92. *The International Journal of the History of Sport* 19(2–3): 213–42.

NT (2006). V Ashkhabade Sostoialos' Zasedaniie Ispolkoma Olimpiiskogo Soveta Azii [Meeting of the Executive Committee of Asian Olympic Council Took Place in Ashkhabad]. *Neitral'nyi Turkmenistan*, 4 August.

NT (2010a). Teper' Turkmenistan Mozhet Mechtat' Priniiat' u Sebia Olimpiiskiie Igry! [Turkmenistan Can Now Dream of Hosting the Olympic Games!]. *Neitral'nyi Turkmenistan*, November 6.

NT (2010b). Aziada-2017 Budet Provedena v Turkmenistane! [Aziada-2017 Will Take Place in Turkmenistan!]. *Neitral'nyi Turkmenistan*, December 21.

NT (2010c). Turkmenistan – Sportivnaia Derzhava: Prezident Gurbanguly Berdymukhamedov Priniial Uchastiie v Torzhestvakh Posviashchennykh Aziiade-2017 [Turkmenistan – Sport Power: President Gurbanguly Berdymukhamedov Took Part in the Celebrations Dedicated to Aziada-2017]. *Neitral'nyi Turkmenistan*, December 30.

NT (2011a). Aziiatskiie Igry Stanut Simvolom Utverzhdeniia Turkmenistana v Kachestve Sportivnoi Derzhavy [The Asian Games Will Become a Symbol of the Approval of Turkmenistan as the Sport Power]. *Neitral'nyi Turkmenistan*, August 19.

NT (2011b). Navstrechu Slavnomu Iubileiiu Nezavisimosti [Toward the Glorious Anniversary of Independence]. *Neitral'nyi Turkmenistan*, August 22.

NT (2011c). Torzhestvo Epokhi Velikikh Svershenii: Zasedaniie Soveta Stareishin Turkmenistana [The Triumph of the Great Achievements Age: The Meeting of Turkmenistan Council of Elders]. *Neitral'nyi Turkmenistan*, October 26.

NT (2012). Kursom Novatsii i Progressa vo Imia Blagopoluchiia i Schast'ia Naroda [On the Path of Innovation and Progress in the Name of Prosperity and Happiness of the People]. *Neitral'nyi Turkmenistan*, April 10.

NT (2013a). Razshirennoe Zasedaniie Kabineta Ministrov Turkmenistana [Extended Meeting of the Turkmenistan Cabinet of Ministers]. *Neitral'nyi Turkmenistan*, July 13.

NT (2013b). Dzhanni Merlo: "My Gordimsia Partnerstvom s Turkmenistanom" [Jeannni Merlot: "We Are Proud of the Partnership with Turkmenistan"]. *Neitral'nyi Turkmenistan*, November 29.

NT (2014a). Jego Prevoskhoditel'stvu Gospodinu Gurbanguly Berdymukhamedovu [To His Majesty Mr. Gurbanguly Berdymukhamedov]. *Neitral'nyi Turkmenistan*, December 8.

NT (2014b). Vystupleniie Prezidenta Turkmenistana Na Video-Selektornom Rabochem Soveshchanii [Speech of the President of Turkmenistan on the Video-Conference Working Meeting]. *Neitral'nyi Turkmenistan*, December 23.

Polese, A., and S. Horák (2015). A Tale of Two Presidents: Personality Cult and Symbolic Nation-Building in Turkmenistan. *Nationalities Papers* 43(3): 457–78.

Polimeks (2015). *Polimeks Holding*. Available at: www.polimeks.com/eng/UstyapiProjeler.aspx (accessed July 15, 2015).

Pugasov, M. (2011). Belaia Aziada: Triumf Dukha Pobedy [White Aziada: the Triumph of the Victory Spirit]. *Kazpravda*, February 10, 2011.

Ren, X. (2008). Architecture and Nation-Building in the Age of Globalization: Construction of the National Stadium Beijing for the 2008 Olympics. *Journal of Urban Affairs* 30(2): 175–90.

Riordan, J. (1980). *Sport in Soviet Society.* New York: Cambridge University Press.

Roche, M. (2001). Modernity, Cultural Events and the Construction of Charisma: Mass Cultural Events in the USSR in the Interwar Period. *International Journal of Cultural Policy* 7(3): 493–520.

Shimizu, S. (2014). Tokyo: Bidding for the Olympics and the Discrepancies of Nationalism. *The International Journal of the History of Sport* 31(6): 601–17.

Šír, J. (2008). The Cult of Personality in Monumental Art and Architecture: The Case of Post-Soviet Turkmenistan. *Acta Slavica Iaponica* 25: 203–20.

Tétrauld-Farber, G. (2015). Turkmenistan Outs Itself as Unlikely Sporting Mecca. *Moscow Times*, April 6. Available at: www.themoscowtimes.com/news/article/turkmenistan-outs-itself-as-unlikely-sporting-mecca/518707.html (accessed June 29, 2015).

Trubina, E. (2014). Mega-Events in the Context of Capitalist Modernity: The Case of 2014 Sochi Winter Olympics. *Eurasian Geography and Economics* 55(6): 610–27.

Wagg, S., and D. A. Andrews (2007). *East Plays West: Sport and the Cold War.* London: Routledge.

Witcher, T. (2014). Turkmenistan Spends Billions for Sporting Glory. *Dawn*, 4 December. Available at: www.dawn.com/news/1148605 (accessed 30 June 2015).

Witt, G. (1984). Mass Participation and Top Performance in One: Physical Culture and Sport in the German Democratic Republic. *Journal of Popular Culture* 18(3): 159–74.

Xu, X. (2006). Modernizing China in the Olympic Spotlight: China's National Identity and the 2008 Beijing Olympiad. *The Sociological Review* 54(2): 90–107.

Zhang T., and M. Silk (2006). Recentering Beijing: Sport, Space, and Subjectivities. *Sociology of Sport Journal* 23(4): 438–59.

Chapter 5

Sports and politics in Israel

Settler colonialism and the native Palestinians

Magid Shihade

Introduction

In the field of Middle Eastern Studies, popular culture remains a marginalized field of study and research. The main focus is typically instead placed on formal politics, elites, states, economies, conflicts, and wars while a cultural phenomenon such as sport remains of marginal inquiry. In studies of Israel/Palestine, the same pattern is evident. Scholars have studied the history of the state, the history of Palestinians, and Israeli society/Palestinian society with little attention to the many cultural phenomena that can further contribute to understating both the state and society. When studying Palestinian society, little attention has been paid to its secular life or its cultural and political agency. Even more perplexing is the dearth of detailed studies of daily life. The focus on the Israeli state has been dominated by its political process, "peace" talks, policies, and regional security issues. The intimate aspects of state power and how it penetrates even "small" issues like sports within the Palestinian community are often ignored.

This chapter thus aims to fill a gap in this area, illustrating how infrequently studied topics such as sport can help scholars understand the politics of peoples and states in the region. Through the case of soccer in Israel/Palestine, I show how sport is highly connected to politics, power, and state policies. The chapter also highlights how the present and past are connected when it comes to the relationship between the state and its society; this is especially the case for a settler-colonial state and its native citizens/subjects. My research is based on three years of local archival, fieldwork, and interviews with local witnesses in the village Kafr Yassif – in Galilee, Israel. I also analyze the Israeli government's own fact-finding committee's report on the violence that erupted around a soccer game in the village in 1981.

After summarizing the event and its aftermath, I provide a general overview of the history of Palestinians with Israeli citizenship and a history of the Israeli state. I show why categorizing this state and society as a settler-colonial case is more helpful for understanding that relationship. Moreover, this lens assists in understanding state policies, even those not officially declared, as was the case with the violence surrounding the soccer game in Kafr Yassif. I will discuss how state security and police apparatuses operated in the time surrounding that event. I conclude by arguing that popular culture, and sport in particular, is an important area for the study of societies and states, and, in the case of Israel, reveals much about the relationship between each.

The soccer game and its aftermath

On April 11, 1981, a soccer game between teams from two neighboring Palestinian villages in Galilee – Kafr Yassif and Julis – occurred at the stadium in Kafr Yassif. The game would decide which of the two teams would be promoted to the upper division of the Israeli soccer league. Kafr Yassif is a mixed village with a Christian majority while Julis is a Druze village. Druzes serve in the Israeli military and can bear arms. A few days before the game, team managers received threatening phone calls from Julis stating that Julis must win the game or the Kafr Yassif team and village residents would pay the price. The team manager consulted with the local council and the Kafr Yassif mayor decided to inform his counterpart in Julis of the threatening phone calls. He also called the regional police station to inform them and request a stronger police presence during the game to prevent possible violence between the fans. Police presence is common during soccer games in Israel; during especially tense or decisive games, the Ministry of Interior deploys larger numbers of police. However, in the Kafr Yassif case, the police department sent only three policemen to the game – despite the phone calls from the mayor and the manager of the local soccer team.

During the game, on Saturday afternoon, a fight between the fans of the two teams broke out, and one person from each village was killed. Fans from Julis used firearms and hand grenades. The three policemen who were present did nothing; they did not even fire warning shots to stop the fighting but simply stood watching the fighting unfold in front of their eyes. The story did not end there.

On Saturday night, the mayor of Kafr Yassif received a phone call from Julis demanding that the person who killed the Julis fan be identified or the whole village of Kafr Yassif would be attacked. The mayor responded in multiple ways. First, he convened a meeting of the local council and, after consultations, the members decided to notify the regional police station of the development and request more police presence in the village. He also contacted members of parliament, who helped in contacting the Minister of Interior to ask for swift intervention. Finally, he contacted community leaders from the village and the region for help with initiating a traditional conflict resolution/management method common to the Palestinian Arab community, the "*Sulha.*"

A *Sulha* committee is comprised of community members of different social, economic, political, and educational backgrounds who are respected in the community and thus have an influence in shaping public opinion. The committee's work starts by contacting the two parties in dispute to initiate an end to the hostilities (a "*Hudna*"). They then investigate the point of dispute in consultation with representatives of both parties and in conversation with eyewitnesses of the event or incident in question. The principles of this method are not based on "an eye for an eye" absolute justice, nor do they work to cover up the wrongdoing. The party found guilty must publicly assume the blame and ask for forgiveness. It is also asked to pay a monetary compensation to the injured party. The details of the resolution to the conflict are put in writing and all parties sign. This sometimes occurs during a public ceremony to share the details, and the wrongdoer publicly acknowledges their mistake and asks for forgiveness from the rest of the community. The method has been used in Palestine and the region for centuries (for more on *Sulha*, see Jabbour 1996). Among the Palestinian community in Israel, it is used with extra vigilance because of the lack of trust that the community has vis-à-vis the state – a topic that will become clearer later in the chapter.

In Kafr Yassif, the *Sulha* committee was able to achieve a truce (*Hudna*) on Saturday night, after making contacts with the mayor and community leaders in Julis. Their message to community leaders and the mayor in Kafr was assuring and stated that a resolution was highly likely (as is normally the case with other disputes within the community). However, by Sunday afternoon, the *Sulha* committee contacted community leaders and the mayor in Kafr Yassif to inform them of a shift of position in Julis. Citing heavy interference from individuals connected to the Israeli government, they argued that a resolution was in jeopardy. Still, the committee promised that it would continue to put more effort toward avoiding an attack on Kafr Yassif. Worried at the possibility of a failing resolution by the *Sulha* committee, the mayor and leaders from Kafr Yassif community again contacted the regional police station asking more police officers be sent to Kafr Yassif to prevent a possible attack. The head of the regional police department continued to downplay the incident, assuring callers that nothing would happen under his watch. Furthermore, the mayor contacted members of parliament to update them on the saga. They reached out to the Minister of Interior, who is responsible for the police department, and personally asked him to send police reinforcements to prevent an attack against Kafr Yassif.

Despite all these efforts and media exposure about the unfolding event, at around noon on Monday, April 13, 1981, Kafr Yassif was attacked by hundreds of men from Julis. They were equipped with Israeli military vehicles, arms, and communication equipment. For almost two hours, they shot at village residents, attacked and bombed homes, and burned vehicles and property. The violence culminated in two more deaths in Kafr Yassif, with dozens injured and extensive damage to private property, a local church, a bank, and the village council buildings. For many of Kafr Yassif's older generation, the scene looked like another round of what occurred in 1948 to many Palestinian villages at the hands of Zionist troops. For the younger generation born after 1948, it seemed as surreal as a Hollywood movie – though it aligned with the oral histories they had heard about the devastation in Palestine in 1948.

Despite the anger at the attackers from Julis, the residents in Kafr Yassif held the Israeli authorities responsible. Their claims were corroborated by eyewitnesses in the village, who saw police officers who were present during the Monday events communicating with the attackers while the atrocities were underway. Wireless communications between the attackers and the police also showed that the police force was not concerned with stopping the attack. Instead, they withdrew from village neighborhoods as the attackers entered each street and they worked to clear the roads to ensure that the attackers finish their mission. The apparent coordination between the attackers and the police force in the village was corroborated by individuals from neighboring villages who came to help Kafr Yassif but were blocked by police from entering the village. With over 40 policemen, the police force was present in larger numbers and managed to block two of the three main entrances to Kafr Yassif. Blocking these two main entrances blocked hundreds from neighboring villages who had friends and relatives in Kafr Yassif from coming to help. The only entrance the police did not block was the narrowest; it was through this entrance that the attackers entered the village. The Interior Ministry/Israeli government's fact-finding committee that looked into the events in Kafr Yassif acknowledged this incriminatingly suspicious ability to block the two major entrances and also the inability to block one narrower entrance. The excuse, according to the report, was to prevent the escalation of violence (more details of the incident are found in Shihade 2005, 2011).

The leadership in Kafr Yassif continued to blame the Israeli government and asked for an independent investigation committee to look into the police force's behavior during the events. The Israeli government refused and was content with its self-appointed fact-finding commission. This committee's report concluded that regional police stations should take future incidents in Arab villages more seriously, given the prevalence of violence within Arab society. If the Israeli officials' narrative about the endemic violence within the Palestinian society was true, why did these same officials not expect violence to occur during the soccer game and three days later, despite the calls for intervention? Such contradictory statements also reflect the pattern of Israeli Orientalism (Said 1978) that naturalizes the prevalence of violence within Arab society, which pervaded the rhetoric of Israeli officials and media commentators during that time.

How are we to make sense of this double-speak? That is, why did the Ministry of Interior and the police department under its authority fail to prevent the violence during the soccer game and during the attack on Kafr Yassif three days later, if they truly believed that violence is "endemic" to Arab society? How do we explain the government's refusal of an independent investigation of the police force's behavior? And how do we make sense of the apparent duality of weakness/strength of the Israeli state and its security organs? Eyewitness accounts provide some insight, but to answer these questions, it is useful to review a brief history of the Israeli state, its relationship to the Palestinian community as a whole, the history of Kafr Yassif, and to consider whether other incidents can explain or indicate a policy pattern around the issue of violence within the Palestinian community.

Israel/Palestine: the community and the state

There is hardly any serious dispute in the academic literature on the origin and history of the state of Israel and its relationship to the native Palestinians there (Khalidi 1987; Lloyd 2012; Masalha 2013; Pappe 2010; Said 1979; Sayegh 1965; Wolfe 2006). If there is a dispute or disagreement, it is around the reasons why the state was established (Morris 2001), though this question is not crucial for this chapter. What is crucial to understanding the relationship between the Israeli state and its Arab-Palestinian citizens is what structured that relationship, such that the Israeli security behaved in the manner it did in Kafr Yassif in 1981, and more generally in response to violence within the Palestinian community.

The Zionist Movement's plan to create a state for Jewish people worldwide targeted Palestine, ultimately selected after entertaining and exploring other sites in Africa, Latin America, and elsewhere. This plan received the support of the British government, as stated in the Balfour Declaration issued in 1917. Soon after World War I, through a resolution at the League of Nations (a precursor to the United Nations), Britain was entrusted with a Mandate rule over Palestine. The Mandate was supposed to allow Britain to prepare the local population for self-governance and independence after a certain period of time. However, what the British Mandate government accomplished during its control of Palestine from 1922 to 1948 was, on one hand, a systematic repression of political and economic development of the native Palestinians, and on the other hand, institutionalized support of the Zionist settler enterprise in Palestine. Comprised mainly of European Jewish settlers, they managed to build a semi state-like economic, political, and military structure during the time of British rule.

Using the opposition of native Palestinians to Zionist colonization of their lands and the violence between Zionist military and paramilitary groups and between local native Palestinians, the British government eventually declared its intention to end its Mandate over Palestine and turn the question of Palestine to the United Nations. In 1947, the United Nations General Assembly issued a resolution to partition Palestine into two states: one Arab and one Jewish. Palestinian natives rejected the partition plan, but the Zionist Movement went on to implement the plan through its military and paramilitary groups. The process culminated in the War of 1948, which resulted in over 400 villages and towns being destroyed and about 85 percent of the local native Palestinian population being turned into refugees (mainly fleeing or deported to neighboring Arab states). In May 1948, the leadership of the Zionist Movement declared the creation and independence of a new state – Israel – in the Palestinian territories that it managed to control by the end of the war.

The remaining 15 percent of the native Palestinian population in these lands became subjects/citizens of the newly created state of Israel – a state that was built on the destruction of their own society. From the start, the Israeli state viewed these remaining Palestinians with contempt and suspicion. Not only did officials continue to confiscate Palestinian lands, they implemented various policies aimed at undermining their economic and political development, controlling them, and suppressing any possible collective resistance. The government also designed policies to divide the native Arab community, turning them into a collection of sects/religious groups rather than treating them as a collective. Officials then worked to coopt these sects and recruited (primarily through economic incentives) two local native groups, the Druze and Bedouin, into its military – effectively cutting them off from the larger unified Palestinian Arab community (Cohen 2010; Firro 1999; Jiryis 1968; Khalidi 1987; Lloyd 2012; Lustick 1980; Masalha 2013; Pappe 2010; Robinson 2013; Sa'di 2013; Said 1979; Sayegh 1965; Shihade 2014, 2015).

Israeli policies of sectarianism are crucial for understanding the Kafr Yassif case because the two villages in question, Julis and Kafr Yassif, are divided around these lines. Julis is a Druze village, whose residents regularly serve in the Israeli military. In addition to the training that Druzes receive in the Israeli military, they are also indoctrinated into a culture that casts Arabs as a hostile target and enemy. The Israeli state also turned the Druzes from their historic category as a Muslim religious sect into an ethnic group different from the rest of the local Arab community. The Druzes have been defined in this way not only through Israeli laws, regulations, and state documents including national identification cards, but also through a policy of separate educational systems designed specifically for the Druze community that highlighted links between Druzes and Jews, which has had the effect of downplaying and even erasing the shared history of Druzes and the larger Arab community (Firro 1999; Parsons 2000; Shihade 2011, 2012).

Kafr Yassif, on the other hand, is a mixed village, and its history is crucial to understanding how state security organs behaved during the events in 1981. While predominantly Christian, it includes a large Muslim population and a very small number of Druzes. Soon after the creation of the Israeli state in 1948, village residents and leadership participated in resisting Israeli policies of repression, discrimination, and marginalization. Its leadership, under the mayor Yanni Yanni, created a local alliance of different political groups. He worked toward creating a countrywide political coalition to unify the native Arab population in opposition to discriminatory Israeli policies, such as land confiscation. Kafr Yassif also hosted a large number of refugees who fled their destroyed villages in 1948, and both the village leadership and the larger community resisted the Israeli military's attempts to deport these refugees. As a result, the village became a target for state repression, underfunding, and the provocation of sectarian politics.

The Israeli state's policy toward Kafr Yassif is documented by many studies. Despite its mixed demographics, some policies resemble how the Israeli state treated its native Palestinians subjects; this fits into a wider pattern whereby the Israeli security apparatus actively encouraged violence within the Palestinian community (Shihade 2011, 2012). Some of these policies were openly declared, while others were secretly planned (only becoming available with the opening of archives). Yet others came about by default, due to the nature of the state treating its local native Palestinian population as an obstacle to the Israeli state's *raison d'être* – that is, for the purpose of settler colonialism of gathering Jews from around the world and building a state for their sole benefit. When seen as a "fifth column" and an obstacle to the Zionist settler-colonial project, policies to undermine the collective organizing of native Palestinians were easily justified (Cohen 2010; Jiryis 1968; Masalha 2013; Pappe 2010; Robinson 2013; Sa'di 2001, 2013; Sayegh 1965; Shihade 2015, 2011).

As Lustick (1980) shows, Israeli government and security personnel did not need an official order for how to treat native Palestinians; the issue became tacitly understood through the overarching structure of the state's suspicious relationship with this community. However, Lustick's (1980) study sums up the relationship between the Israeli state and its Arab citizens by stating that Israel cannot be categorized as a police state, but a democracy – despite its use of methods to co-opt, repress, control, and pacify its local Arab citizens. Rouhana (1997) challenges this framing and other studies that present the local Arab community as docile, "loyal," or pacified by demonstrating how the majority of local Palestinians are clearly alienated from the state as a norm. A recent example of this alienation is the vote for the Joined Arab List, a political organization in clear opposition to the main ideas and goals of Zionism, for which the majority of Palestinians with Israeli citizenship voted. Lustick's dismissal of the Israeli state as a repressive police state is challenged by many works, including studies of resistance using the case of Kafr Yassif, among others, as an example of collective local resistance to state policies (e.g., Cohen 2010; Jiryis 1968; Masalha 2013; Pappe 2010; Robinson 2013; Sa'di 2001, 2013; Shihade 2011, 2012, 2015; Sultany 2003).

This recent scholarship has made it clear that the Israeli state has, since before its establishment and to this day, designed and worked to implement policies of repression, discrimination, and marginalization toward the local native Palestinian community. These policies, I argue (as do many others), are a natural outcome of a settler-colonial state and its structured policy of excluding native populations – as defined by the Zionist leadership itself since before 1948 and as seen by the native Palestinian population (Sayegh 1965; Shihade 2012, 2015; Wolfe 2006). Categorizing the state as democratic or as an ethnic democracy is not helpful in that regard (see e.g., Smooha 1997; Yiftachel 2006). It can also be a form of mystification (Fanon 2005) and part of a public relations campaign that tries to normalize the Israeli state and mystify its settler-colonial nature which structures its relationship to the native Palestinian community (like any other settler-colonial state).

The foundation of the state as a settler-colonial one is crucial in understanding the relationship between the state and its different agencies (including the security branch) and the native Palestinian community. Simply categorizing the Palestinian community as pacified, coopted, or docile (Lustick 1980) can lead to a misunderstanding of the relationship between resistance and violence in the study of politics in colonial settings. That is, if attention is only paid to physical violence, this can obscure seeing the violence of colonialism in many other forms that also encompass cultural, social, political, and economic violence that targets the colonized group – as well as the resistance to it that is just as diverse. Categorizing the state as a settler-colonial state thus is not simply a matter of polemics, but is informative because it helps to explain the relationship between the state and its native Palestinian community (Khalidi 1987; Lloyd 2012; Masalha 2013; Pappe 2010; Sayegh 1965; Shihade 2015; Wolfe 2006). It also helps to explain the behavior of the security apparatus in the Kafr Yassif case, operating as the determining context for the events that transpired around the soccer game in 1981, to which I return by way of conclusion.

Not just a soccer game: understanding Kafr Yassif and its aftermath

Set against the context of the preceding discussion about the nature of the state and its relationship to the native Palestinian community, let us return to the behavior of the various parties involved in the soccer game violence and its aftermath. When the Kafr Yassif team manager received the threating call from Julis, and then contacted the authorities for reinforcements, he and the mayor were aware of the presence of arms within that community. Druze soldiers in Julis were seen on a daily basis carrying their arms in public, and these weapons had even been used in previous fights within the Druze community itself. To outside observers, it might seem contradictory for Kafr Yassif to call on the police, given the village's problematic relationship with state security forces in the past. However, as many interviewees involved in that decision argued, they felt the only option was to continue to hold the state responsible for the safety of its citizens. They also claimed to have contacted other parties, including members of parliament and other community leaders in the region, to alert them to the situation. After the soccer game, they asked community leaders to initiate a *Sulha* with Julis, hoping to prevent further escalation of violence against the village. These decision-makers and members of the *Sulha* committee argued that the *Sulha* would have worked, as it often does when such conflicts arise, if it was not for the intervention of the Israeli government through its local strongmen.

After the attacks against the village, residents in Kafr Yassif considered the behavior of the police force and concluded that the events had transpired in coordination with Israeli officials. The police department did not send reinforcements to the game, as requested by the mayor and soccer team of Kafr Yassif, and the three officers present at the game stood idly by, making no efforts to calm the fighting. During the larger attack three days later, the police behavior was similarly revealing. Not only did they facilitate the Julis assailants' access to Kafr Yassif, they simultaneously barred entry to hundreds of people from neighboring villages that came to help stop the attack and defend the unarmed residents of the village.

When Israeli journalists and officials such as the Minister of Interior tried to whitewash the role of the state and the police department by arguing that the police did not expect such violence, and claiming that violence is endemic to the Arab society, they ultimately reproduced the contradictory logic and discriminatory structures of Orientalism (Said 1978), which pervade Israeli Jewish society. While the official narrative presented the police force as a passive and a weak party in the events, it ignored the ability of the same police force to block a larger number of people who came to help the village residents against the attack. It also ignored other aspects: the history, ability, and willingness of the police force to pull the trigger when it comes to dealing with Palestinian Arabs; Israeli security forces that are quick and efficient in shooting at, injuring, and killing members of the Palestinian community (especially when it is about that community's collective activism and resistance to state policies). Lastly, in refusing an independent investigation of the events, the Israeli state's behavior in the Kafr Yassif case is indicative of the wider history of state violence against the local Arab community – before and after 1948 – in which certain forms of violence can unfold with impunity. In stark contrast to any attempt at violence against any member of the Jewish community, the Israeli state has never held anyone in the Arab community responsible when violence is directed inwardly (i.e., against the community itself).

The behavior of Israeli officials and the local police force present during the events surrounding the Kafr Yassif soccer match is not unusual. They have acted similarly before and after that event in other Arab villages. The history and ideology of the state and its various branches is informed by a settler-colonial logic that looks at these remaining Palestinians as an obstacle to achieving the plan of Zionism based on the doctrine of "a land without a people for a people without a land." But since people have been on the land for a long time, and since they cannot be completely eliminated physically, the Palestinian community has been targeted by a multiplicity of alternative modes of repression, always shifting and updated according to sensibilities of time and space. This includes, as we have seen here, a simple activity that they might enjoy, such as soccer. Since that game in 1981, the village has lost its central role in the region's soccer scene, and has been going through different social, political, and cultural changes, many of which are a product of a structure of settler colonialism since 1948.

As this case study of the Kafr Yassif game illustrates, popular culture, and sport in particular, is an important site for the study of societies and state, and, in the case of Israel, reveals a great deal about the relationship between the two. Further, small events, intimate relations, and the daily life of local Palestinians are crucial areas of analysis because they illuminate the nature of the Israeli state and how it intervenes to unsettle even the simplest pleasures of native Palestinians. Not only does this reflect the pathology of such a state, but it also reveals the intent of state-based actors to target local natives – even if the issue is unrelated to armed resistance to the state. The violence of the state is clearly exposed in these small local incidents. Even if people wanted to forget about politics, forget or ignore the state's capacity to control them, and enjoy a simple thing such as soccer, they cannot escape the violent nature of a settler-colonial state.

References

Cohen, H. (2010). *Good Arabs: The Israeli Security Agencies and the Israeli Arabs, 1948–1967.* Berkeley: University of California Press.

Fanon, F. (2005). *The Wretched of the Earth.* Trans. R. Philoux. New York: Grove/Atlantic, Inc.

Firro, K. (1999). *The Druzes in the Jewish State: A Brief History.* Leiden: Brill.

Jabbour, E. (1996). *Sulha: Palestinian Traditional Peacemaking Process.* Montreal: House of Hope Publications.

Jiryis, S. (1968). *The Arabs in Israel*. Beirut: Institute of Palestine Studies.

Khalidi, W. (1987). *From Heaven to Conquest: Readings in Zionism and the Palestine Problem until 1948*. Beirut: Institute of Palestine Studies.

Lloyd, D. (2012). Settler Colonialism and the State of Exception: The Example of Palestine/Israel. *Settler Colonial Studies* 2(1): 59–80.

Lustick, I. (1980). *Arabs in the Jewish State: Israel's Control of a National Minority*. Austin: University of Texas Press.

Masalha, N. (2013). *The Zionist Bible: Biblical Precedent, Colonialism and the Erasure of Memory*. London: Acumen.

Morris, B. (2001). *Righteous Victims: A History of the Zionist-Arab Conflict, 1882–1999*. New York: Alfred A. Knopf.

Pappe, I. (2010). *The Forgotten Palestinians: A History of the Palestinians in Israel*. New Haven: Yale University Press.

Parsons, L. (2000). *The Druze between Palestine and Israel, 1947–1949*. New York: Palgrave Macmillan.

Robinson, S. (2013). *Citizen Strangers: Palestinians and the Birth of Israel's Liberal Settler State*. Palo Alto: Stanford University Press.

Rouhana, N. (1997). *Palestinian Citizens in an Ethnic Jewish State: Identities in Conflict*. New Haven: Yale University Press.

Sa'di, A. (2001). Control and Resistance at Local-Level Institutions: A Study of Kafr-Yassif Local Council under the Military Government. *Arab Studies Quarterly* 23(3): 31–47.

Sa'di, A. (2013). *Thorough Surveillance: The Genesis of Israeli Policies of Population Management, Surveillance, and Political Control towards the Palestinian Minority*. Manchester: Manchester University Press.

Said, E. (1978). *Orientalism*. New York: Pantheon Books.

Said, E. (1979). *The Question of Palestine*. New York: Vintage Books.

Sayegh, F. (1965). *Zionist Colonialism in Palestine*. Beirut: Palestine Liberation Organization Research Center.

Shihade, M. (2005). Internal Violence: The State's Role and Society's Responses. *Arab Studies Quarterly* 27(4): 31–43.

Shihade, M. (2011). *Not Just a Soccer Game: Colonialism and Conflict among Palestinians in Israel*. Syracuse: Syracuse University Press.

Shihade, M. (2012). Settler Colonialism and Conflict: The Israeli State and Its Palestinian Subjects. *Settler Colonial Studies* 2(1): 108–23.

Shihade, M. (2014). Not just a Picnic: Settler Colonialism and Mobility among Palestinians in Israel. *Biography* 37(2): 77–99.

Shihade, M. (2015). The Place of Israel in Asia: Settler Colonialism, Mobility, Memory, and Identity among Palestinians in Israel. *Settler Colonial Studies* doi:10.1080/2201473X.2015.1024379.

Smooha, S. (1997). Ethnic Democracy: Israel as an Archetype. *Israel Studies* 2(2):198–241.

Sultany, N. (2003). *Citizens without Citizenship: Israel and the Palestinian Minority*. Haifa: Mada Al-Carmel, Arab Center for Social Science Research.

Wolfe, P. (2006). Settler Colonialism and the Elimination of the Native. *Journal of Genocide Research* 8(4): 387–409.

Yiftachel, O. (2006). *Ethnocracy: Land and Identity Politics in Israel/Palestine*. Philadelphia: University of Pennsylvania Press.

Chapter 6

Sports fields and corporate governmentality

Gazprom's all-Russian gas program as energopower

Veli-Pekka Tynkkynen

Introduction

Russia's biggest enterprise, a parastatal energy company Gazprom, has adopted many societal tasks, which are typically considered as the responsibility of states or regional self-governing authorities, in the communities where it operates. This practice is not unique globally and has firm historical roots in post-socialist space. Developing sports facilities is a prime example and one way that Gazprom has sought to craft a positive image for itself throughout Russia. However, the way these amenities are chosen and produced as part of Russian national gas program, *Gazifikatsiya*, raises questions about the positive connotations accorded to the chosen amenities and how they are utilized to control and govern the Russian populace from afar. Accordingly, this chapter will scrutinize the state-enterprise–population relationship by looking at the construction of sports facilities tied to the all-Russian gas program via a case study from one Russian region, Karelia.

By studying the words and deeds of Gazprom's governmentality through its *Gazifikatsiia* program, it is possible to unravel how power, truths, and identities are being constructed in and through energy networks. Pivotal to this study is the understanding that the materialities, spatialities, and infrastructures related to energy constitute a form of agency. This understanding views the social as ultimately an assemblage of the human and the non-human, as elaborated by scholars working with the ideas of Bruno Latour's actor–network theory (e.g., Alcadipani and Hassard 2010; Collier 2011; Dolwick 2009; Murdoch 1998). Actor–network theory posits that materialities, such as infrastructure or the natural environment, produce both inertia and action due to the social norms and practices that are tied to them. This chapter, therefore, examines the material roots of the governmentality practiced by Gazprom. The *Gazifikatsiia* program is analyzed using a methodological power-analytics approach informed by the research traditions of both Foucault (1991) and Latour (2005).

The *Gazifikatsiia Rossii* gas-distribution program (Gazprom 2012a) sends a clear message to the Russian people: regions without gas are left outside development and economic modernization. Prosperous regions and communities are thus said to choose gas, while backward regions choose other sources of energy and they are consequently doomed to battle scarcity. Moreover, a settlement that chooses to join Gazprom's network becomes part of President Vladimir Putin's state-building enterprise of gas-pipelines extending from Arctic production sites to Russian and foreign consumers. This expansive network is viewed by the company and its statist stakeholders as the material manifestation of Russia's new global role as an energy superpower (e.g., Bouzarovski and Bassin 2011; Gazprom 2012a). This chapter aims to explore how the gas-distribution program constructs new kinds of power, truth, and identity, and how the promotion of sports and constructing sport infrastructure are utilized in this task. This construction can be understood by considering it alongside geographically and anthropologically inclined governmentality analytics.

From biopolitical to energopolitical governmentality

Governmentality, as initially articulated by Michel Foucault in the 1970s, is a collective way of thinking about different modes of governing, and especially a government's relation to the governed (Dean 1999; Foucault 1991). Scholars have used the concept of governmentality to study far more than state-defined systems of government, applying it also to non-governmental actors, such as companies and civil society organizations (e.g., Lehtinen 2003; Rivera Vicencio 2014; Rooker 2014). Governmentalities can be understood by simultaneously studying the practices that amalgamate actions and collective modes of thinking about government that prevail in a particular location, institution, or state. Governmental practices, thus, consist of both words and deeds, regardless of whether or not they are conscious or intentional. In any given context, certain actors are better positioned than others to promote their rhetorical and material visions of government, which give rise to "dominant discourses" that come to represent certain truths, or, as Foucault (2008: 35) terms them, "regimes of veridiction." A question posed by the governmentality literature, therefore, is how both the conscious and unconscious "truth" construed by dominant discourses is produced as part of governmental practice (Mills 1997: 2–8). An analytics of government is defined by three central dimensions: power, truth, and identity (Dean 1999: 18), and producing these requires expertise, imagination, and tactical skills (Foucault 1991: 87).

In this chapter, I consider the gas program as an manifestation of the two interrelated aspects of discourse: (a) the action, as exemplified in the social responsibility programs "Gazprom – for children" and "Sponsoring

Sports" that are designed to tell the story of Gazprom's supposed popular approval, and (b) the collective "mentality" of a company that is closely tied to the actions and thinking of president Putin's regime. In liberal societies, governing operates primarily through biopolitical tactics because disciplinary power contradicts its core principles of individual liberty. In a system defined by biopower, the population living in the territory of the state is subjugated to techniques that have the goal of optimizing its health, welfare, and life (Dean 1999: 20). Therefore, biopolitical governmentality has to be seen as an inseparable part of the logic of the actions of neoliberal states, including Russia. A significant literature now exists on Soviet and post-Soviet governmentalities (e.g., Kharkhordin 1999; Kotkin 1995; Matza 2009; Prozorov 2014). However, these studies are confined in one pivotal manner: they do not look explicitly at the material and spatial in their analysis.

Stephen Collier's (2011) *Post-Soviet Social*, by contrast, takes an explicitly material approach. He argues that post-Soviet Russia is a prime example of a country where, stemming from the Soviet-era objectives and norms, the objectives of both the social welfare state and classical liberalism have come together to form modern biopolitical practices. He concurs with most analysts of post-Soviet power that governmentalities in today's Russia are neoliberal, but with a de-politicizing twist: responsibilities saddled to individuals are thought to benefit the state economy, but not to liberalize and democratize state governance. Accordingly, as Coleman and Agnew (2007: 332) suggest, in today's Russia we are not witnessing a leap from the goals of the modern into the aims, logic, and action of the postmodern; rather, we are seeing the mutual inclusion and adaptation of these two goals. But this raises the question of precisely *how* these transformations are taking place. Through what networks and agencies are governmentalities being reworked in post-Soviet Russia? Given the prominence of Russia's energy economy, scholars have considered energy companies as one of the most important sites of analysis in answering this question.

Energy studies scholars have introduced the concept of "energopower" to unite their traditional inquiries into material cultures with recent critical social science scholarship on power. Boyer (2014) defines energopower as "a genealogy of modern power that rethinks political power through the twin analytics of electricity and fuel." Thus, governmental concern over energy supplies has to do with both the biopolitical aims of guaranteeing the (bio)security of the population, as well as the exertion of control over populations and the production of economic accumulation by keeping energy flowing in grids and pipelines. In developing an "energopolitical" approach, scholars underline that they do not wish to replace the traditional concept of biopower with energopower; rather, it would complement Foucault's original conceptual toolkit. Rogers (2012, 2014), for example, examines how Russian energy companies utilize the materiality of oil and gas to build local and national allegiances, deploying their power to produce truth and identity. In the end, all modern biopolitical technologies are in one way or another "wired" into energy systems. Scholars have emphasized that energopower is an analytical tool that can help people understand how power and the materialities of energy are intertwined. Likewise, Collier (2011) has urged us not to consider society as a pre-given category, but as an assemblage of things, rationalities, discourses, and actions that constitute biopolitics.

The concept of energopower is particularly useful in this study of Gazprom's *Gazifikatsiia* programs, as it explicitly reminds us of the binary nature of contemporary energy systems: they both enable and constrain. Modern energy systems and their extensions (such as communal infrastructure) are a means of delivering amenities, as well as of controlling the population. Taking a specifically geographic approach, I am interested in what kind of truth and identities Gazprom is constructing with its *Gazifikatsiia* program as it expands to peripheral Russia. I focus on the spatiality of gas infrastructure and ask how its "epiphytes" – those ancillary apparatuses and infrastructures, such as sports halls – potentially serve as conduits of disciplinary power.

State priorities in Gazprom's corporate governmentality strategies

Gazprom is the successor of the Soviet Ministry of Gas Industry and has been an open joint-stock company since 2005, with the Russian state owning the majority of the shares (50 percent plus one stock). Modern-day Gazprom has more than 450,000 employees and, in addition to the energy sector, it is active in finance and media (Gazprom 2015a). Although it is technically a commercial enterprise, given its strong relationship with the Russian government Gazprom can be defined as a "parastatal company" (versus a completely state-controlled corporation, such as the nuclear giant Rosatom). As a parastatal company, Gazprom is subject to the authority and decisions of the Russian state and President Putin's entourage – far more than its corporate legal status would suggest. All major strategic choices, operations abroad, large infrastructure decisions, and national programs, such as the *Gazifikatsiia* program and other corporate social responsibility operations, are made with the blessing of Putin and his peers. This is not to suggest that decision-making in the company is entirely politically motivated; its executives clearly exhibit that a business rationale is the main motivation for operational decisions taken by the company (Kivinen 2012). Moreover, Gazprom is a vast company with dozens of regional daughter companies, each with differing objectives and political voices, operating in the Russian provinces and internationally (Gazprom 2015b). Overall, however, when analyzing the corporate governmentality practices of Gazprom, we are dealing with a parastatal company that is steered by the country's elite and therefore enjoys privileges in the Russian economic and political context unlike any other company.

Gazprom's position in the Russian domestic energy sector is therefore exceptional. However, in the 2010s Gazprom lost its monopoly, legally speaking, over gas exports and control of the domestic gas-pipeline system. Now, other gas producers, such as private gas firm Novatek as well as oil companies, have the right to feed gas into the national system and export it. Despite the fact that more competition is now tolerated, Gazprom's monopolistic practices prevail, which enables it to diminish competitors' chances to increase their share in regional energy markets (Tynkkynen 2013). Since the Russian energy scene cannot be further dominated by Gazprom, the company's decision-makers perceive a need to engage in branding or "imago-promotion" activities, such as social responsibility programs and infrastructure construction, in order to safeguard its position in the market and minds of Russian citizens. Perceiving the latter to be of increasing importance, Gazprom engages in a wide range of corporate social responsibility activities. Sponsoring sports has been one of the central means of enacting this agenda (Gazprom 2015c). In welfare societies, which the Soviet Union and its successor Russia purport to be (at least on paper), local and regional governments have traditionally been delegated the responsibility of developing communal amenities and infrastructures, including public sport and health facilities. Thus, in assuming responsibility for developing such facilities, Gazprom has been granted – and itself taken on – responsibilities that are traditionally considered government tasks.

Sport, "Greatpowerness," and Gazprom

In approaching sport, the critical social sciences take as a starting point that it is as political as any other realm in international relations and cooperation (e.g., Sugden and Tomlinson 2002). Sport is political in at least three senses. First, doing sports and exercising is tied to the health of an individual as well as the population. Constructing sports facilities to promote sports and the health-oriented lifestyle it entails, therefore, is an essential social policy question in modern societies. Second, a healthy population links sport to soft-power issues, such as the national economy (*individual as worker*), but also to security and hard-power topics, such as military potential (*individual as soldier*). This promotion of the ideal citizen as an able-bodied worker-soldier is related to the third way sport is political: it is about competition and the international pursuit of victory over other nations. Success in sport is not only seen as important for the self-esteem of an individual, but it can also function as one of the building blocks of national or ethnic identity. Faring well in global competition has, thus, long been understood as crucial to promoting a positive national image in the eyes of the international community (e.g., Grix and Lee 2013; Houlihan 1997; Koch 2013; Smith and Porter 2004; Wong and Trumper 2002).

Sport was an essential part of the Cold War rivalry between the capitalist and socialist worlds, led by the United States and the Soviet Union. In the Soviet Union, it was utilized to persuade global audiences that the socialist economic and societal model was better than capitalism. Significant investments were therefore made in sports training and coaching, but also in sport infrastructures and facilities of all kinds (e.g., Edelman 1993; Peppard and Riordan 1993; Riordan 1977, 1999). Indeed, many Russians today are nostalgic for the perceived success of the Soviet state in socio-political and cultural realms, including sports (Emaliantseva 2011; Larson and Shevchenko 2014; Lee 2011; Mankoff 2009; Mckee *et al.* 2013). In the context of the recent surge in Russia's great-power ambitions, Russians continue to emphasize success in sports on global arenas as one supposedly objective indicator of "*derzhava*" or "greatpowerness" (Jokisipilä 2011). For example, organizing and doing well at the 2014 Sochi Olympic Games was widely framed by the media and the state as important for the self-esteem of ordinary Russians, which Putin's regime strategically leveraged as a tool to promote national pride (Persson and Petersson 2014). In Sochi, as well as in nearly all Russian regions, major state-owned or dominated corporations have been obliged and ready to sponsor sport infrastructure construction and the communal infrastructures needed to operate these premises (e.g., Müller 2011; Trubina 2014). Gazprom and the state-dominated oil company Rosneft were accorded the widest responsibilities in this field. The Sochi games thus illustrated a wider triangle uniting Russian sports, energy, and Great Power status – with accumulated energy wealth not only being invested in the military apparatus to expand Russia's "greatpowerness" (Baev 2008), but also poured into sports and sporting infrastructure.

Gazprom's extensive social responsibility programs, namely "Gazprom – for children" (Gazprom 2015d) and "Sponsoring Sports" (Gazprom 2015e), are part of the company's general strategy and operations. The largest share of Gazprom's sport sponsorship goes directly to ice hockey and soccer clubs and associations. For example, from 2008 to 2014 the Director-General of Gazprom Export, Alexander Medvedev, was the President of Russia's Continental Hockey League (KHL), which is only economically viable due to generous funding from the national energy giants Gazprom and Rosneft. Seen by some observers as a "soft" geopolitical tool of President Putin's Great Power agenda, the KHL has expanded beyond the borders of Russia to purchase and include teams from regional neighbors, including Serbia, Slovakia, Latvia, Finland, and Kazakhstan (Jokisipilä 2011). In ice hockey, the link between the state and the energy sector is the strongest, yet Gazprom is also a major sponsor of European soccer. Internationally, Gazprom's sport sponsorship is primarily justified on the economic grounds of promoting visibility in its main market area, but soft power aims of the Russian state also play a role.

Domestically, sponsorship of and investments in sports are overrepresented in both the gas commodity chain's upstream (energy producing) and downstream regions (those with little or no gas coverage). The highly visible and spatially extensive social responsibility projects in the sphere of sports are thus treated as one of Gazprom's tools for promoting the national gas program in these key areas. Sport is an ideal means to do so, as it has so many positive connotations for Russians, both individually and on a broader sociocultural level. By amalgamating the gas program with sports-related social responsibility, Gazprom can cultivate an image of "doing good" for society, while simultaneously promoting the less benign objectives of the Russian state and the present regime in biopolitical and energopower terms (namely, emphasizing the importance of a physically and mentally healthy population that suits the needs of the Russian economy and military). The pact of energy and sports advances a conservatively defined communality (communitarianism) via sport halls and clubs, and fosters a national identity based on an idea of Russia as a great power. For example, as part of Gazprom's "Sponsoring Sports" program, in addition to more than 1,000 sports infrastructure projects carried out since the mid-2000s in the form of ice hockey halls, tennis courts, sports halls, and various athletics fields, the company promotes a Russia-wide program of physical training and sports called "Ready for Work and Military Defense" (*Gotov k trudu i oborone*) led by the Ministry of Sports (Gazprom 2015f; Ministerstvo Sporta RF 2015). Gazprom sponsors this national sport and military preparedness program and has also started to require its employees to take the battery of physical tests, including short- and long-distance running, swimming, skiing, pull-ups, long jump, as well as (artificial) grenade throwing and shooting with a rifle.

Another example emphasizing the biopolitical objectives (i.e., that physically and mentally fit bodies serve economic but also military and other patriotic ends) is visible in the social responsibility program, "Gazprom – for Children." This program is dominated by local-level sports sponsorship and infrastructure construction projects carried out by Gazprom and its regional daughters; but it also includes a patriotic song contest called "Flare of Hope" ("*Fakel Nadezhdy*") (Gazprom 2015h). If the sports projects aim at physically fit patriotic citizens, this project aims specifically at producing mentally strong and unified youth that share the government's patriotic goals that benefit the country economically and militarily. A quote from the head of Culture and Arts Department of the City of Orenburg on Gazprom's website advertising the song contest makes the connection clear: "I am sure these children will grow up as good, wise people who will make this country more powerful and richer. Thank you, Gazprom, for loyalty towards traditions!" (Gazprom 2015g). Traditions, here, can be understood as a reference to traditions of the Russian state – with its emphasis on Great Power status, loyalty to authoritarian rule and its leader, and the compliant citizen as a patriotic ideal.

Case study: Russian gas and sports fields displacing local renewables in Karelia

Gazprom's numerous projects and programs are firmly tied to the country-wide gas program *Gazifikatsiia Rossii*. On the grounds of enhancing energy security, promoting economic growth, regional investment, and environmental protection, Gazprom and the Russian government assert the importance of extending the country's gas distribution network to its peripheries. The Republic of Karelia, which borders Finland, is one such peripheral region. Exemplifying the themes discussed so far, a case study of Gazprom's projects in Karelia is the subject of the remainder of this chapter.

The *Gazifikatsiia* program has been running since the mid-2000s, but the most intensive phase started only in 2010–11 (Gazprom 2012a). The international demand for Russian-piped gas had decreased significantly at that time, as Europe, Russia's main gas market, experienced an economic downturn and the company encountered more competition in the growing liquefied natural gas markets (Rodova 2012). Meanwhile, the eastward export of gas to Asia has been moderate, with major pipeline projects only in the planning stages (Bradshaw 2013). Policymakers, thus, looked to domestic market expansion as a partial answer to the slowdown in foreign demand. Accordingly, Gazprom introduced its extensive domestic gas infrastructure investment program in 2011, which enabled it to further consolidate its role in the domestic market at a time when independent gas producers were beginning to challenge the company's dominance (Paszyc 2012).

A specific feature of *Gazifikatsiia* is that a social infrastructure component is tied to all gas-pipeline projects and gas-powered plants built by Gazprom. In the case of Karelia, this has been significant: in its Ladoga district, a deal was struck in 2012 to invest six billion rubles in gas infrastructure, while at the same time earmarking two billion rubles for social infrastructure (Nika-Media 2012; Peterburgregiongaz 2012). These figures may be staggering, but Gazprom, along with other major Russian enterprises, is in fact legally obliged by the government to carry out certain philanthropic activities. As Gazprom cannot evade these obligations, its executives prioritize acts of charity that can maximize gains for both the company and its backers in the state. As discussed below, Gazprom-branded sports halls and athletics fields have been at the top of the list of preferred projects.

In Karelia, settlements predominantly import their electricity from outside the region and heat supplies have traditionally come from oil or coal, though the region is rich in wood resources and has a long history of local forestry. As a whole, the Republic of Karelia imports 70 percent of its energy, indicating that the forest industry, in supplying the remaining 30 percent, is responsible for a significant share of the region's local energy. In fact, Karelia has made several plans and agreements since 2001–3 to decrease energy import dependency by constructing new power plants running on woodchips and peat (Pravitelstvo RK 2001; Solovej 2003). But, by 2004–5, Gazprom started negotiations to expand its gas-distribution pipelines in Karelia and to construct gas-burning heat plants. This resulted in an agreement between Gazprom and the government of the Republic of Karelia in 2006 on "Gasification of the Republic," with Gazprom launching pipeline and heat plant construction in 2007 that amounted to 490 million rubles through 2010.

In 2011, Gazprom invested an additional 180 million rubles in the Karelian heat and power sector (Peterburgregiongaz 2012). All these investments served as a prerequisite for the 2012 Ladoga deal mentioned above, in which Gazprom was to undertake the gasification of the Northern Ladoga territories of Karelia at the cost of six billion rubles for gas infrastructure (pipelines and power and heat plants), plus two billion rubles for social infrastructure – predominantly indexed for constructing sport facilities (Stolitsa na Onego 2012). However, the gas investment program was not simply sold to Karelian politicians and authorities on the basis of economic and energy security arguments, but with promises of social infrastructure construction in the form of several sport halls and fields. Such projects offered links to "positive" national objectives, making gas look more appealing than local energy sources and energy self-sufficiency. In the Ladoga region, these social sports projects consumed one quarter of all money invested in all of Karelia. By prioritizing these sport facilities over other potential social infrastructure projects, Gazprom's initiatives have helped to further entrench the nationalist valorization of sports as united with Great Power aspirations, while also advancing the state's biopolitical and energopolitical objectives.

While these national biopolitical objectives are certainly pivotal for Gazprom's programs to gain acceptance and support inside Putin's regime, the local practices evolving in and around such programs are implicated in a more nuanced and multifaceted set of power relations. During the 1990's, before the era of state corporations' social responsibility programs and sport facility sponsorship in the Russian regions, Karelian municipal and regional leaders preferred visible infrastructure construction and renewal projects. These included favoring paving streets, building pedestrian streets and shorelines, and statues and fountains over invisible, yet more vital, renewal projects – such as enhancing drinking water safety by investing in obsolete water treatment plants and deteriorating drinking water and sewage-pipeline systems (Tynkkynen 2001). Sports facilities have increasingly become one such visible project preferred by regional leadership.

As highly visible sites in urban centers impacting and "traversing" the everyday life of many, Gazprom-sponsored sport facilities play a multidimensional role in allowing locales to reassert power and control within national hierarchies. For example, one strategy for local and regional politicians in Karelia to remain in positions of power is to promote the objectives set by the nation's corporate champions, such as Gazprom, so that central officials in the Kremlin see them as reliable and submissive technocrats. However, sport halls and athletics fields that structure urban space are also a way to legitimize chosen policies in the eyes of the local inhabitants and to show the people that the local elite is aligned with national power and its supra-local objectives. Furthermore, sport infrastructure construction is a highly profitable business, offering regional leadership the opportunity to divert money to their entourage, and is thus a means to build and fortify allegiances and local centers of power. Indeed, across Russia and the post-Soviet space, the state-sponsored sport facility construction business is not only lucrative, but also enables corruption better than other businesses (Koch and Valiyev 2015; Müller 2011; Trubina 2014). Therefore, this "promise" of lubricating local power machines is possibly one central motivation for local and regional politicians and authorities to promote social responsibility programs set by the central government, which include building sport infrastructure.

As seen in the Karelia case, Gazprom's decision to emphasize sports facilities that are highly visible "commercial" objects raises a question as to whether these projects are appropriately categorized as social charity. This in turn raises a related question: do such projects have more to do with the company's marketing campaign – aimed at casting itself as a socially responsible actor and "white-washing" its image – than engaging in philanthropic activities that would promote the well-being of the populace in a more substantive fashion (e.g., developing social housing, hospitals, schools, etc.)? By claiming to be socially responsible via providing sport facilities, the state giant signals in a markedly neoliberal–biopolitical way that "social responsibility" entails promoting fit citizens who might benefit society, its economy, and military might (i.e., its Great Power ambitions) through self-help and exercise. The state and the company cooperate to provide a setting that enhances communitarianism via local sport institutions. The individual and communities, however, are ultimately held responsible for accomplishing biopolitical objectives set by the state.

Undoubtedly, Gazprom's *Gazifikatsiia* campaign produces positive impacts as it expands to new areas, increasing the reliability of energy deliveries compared to peripheral settlements being dependent on imported oil and coal. At the same time, connecting new areas to centrally governed pipelines makes these territories and regional actors much more dependent on Gazprom and the state. As scholars have pointed out, pipes matter (Bridge 2009, 2011; Collier 2011) – especially in the post-Soviet context. Not only do gas pipelines construct dependencies and interdependencies between Russia and its consumers (mainly in Europe), but they are also key to forming and sustaining structures of power inside Russia. Gazprom-funded sports infrastructure, thus, acts like an extension of gas infrastructure, an "epiphyte" both luring and compelling towns and settlements to join the nation-building project, *Gazifikatsiia Rossii*. It is here that the national energy, cultural, and military "Great Power" narratives converge.

Conclusions: sport, energopower, and corporate governmentality

Discursive (biopolitical) and coercive (anatomopolitical) governmentality come together in the energopower practiced by Gazprom and the Russian state. The amalgamation of energy and sports enables the state to practice discursive and coercive power cunningly, as the "presence" of the state is made concrete through both gas pipelines and visible and spatially extensive sport facilities. Gazprom's all-Russian gas program and its practices on the local level, as exemplified via the Karelia case study, may be a form of corporate white-washing, but they also advance the Great Power ambitions of Putin's regime in the name of social "responsibility." Parastatal Gazprom has managed to construct a truth: that sports-related investments are a form of "responsible" social provisioning and infrastructure development. Yet genuine philanthropy, with investments in basic social infrastructure and communal amenities, such as schools and hospitals, pure drinking water and non-toxic sewage, or assisting the disabled and alleviating poverty, does not take place.

   Thus, the position of major energy corporations in post-socialist Russia to formulate what is worth knowing, what is the truth, is exceptionally strong. This is partly due to the fact that Russian people demand and expect patronage from the state and its corporations, as they did during the Soviet era.

   For the most part, the population and local and regional stakeholders find themselves agreeing with the hegemonic discourse where the state defines what is good for the people and the regions. However, as a Foucauldian theoretical approach suggests, power produces counter-power that both opposes more hegemonic claims to truth, but also adapts to their objectives by changing slightly and adding contextual nuances and peculiarities (e.g., Tynkkynen 2009). In the Russian regions, therefore, we find that the national patriotic agenda is utilized locally not just to maintain power, but also to challenge it – and Russians actively demand concessions from the state. For example, in the Perm region bordering the Urals, where

Gazifikatsiia has been carried out far longer than in Karelia, the municipalities, the local power and heat providers, as well as private households have come to expect inexpensive delivery of gas as a civil right. And, as Gazprom has steadily raised gas prices, the communal companies and households have refused to pay. In 2013 in the Perm region alone, municipalities had accrued a debt to Gazprom worth approximately 2 billion rubles. Gazprom may thus "deliver" state power along with gas pipelines and its sporty "epiphytes" as it enters new regions such as Karelia, but at the same time it is aware of the oppositional potential of communities to both counter and redeploy the hegemonic discourse of state patronage.

Ultimately, however, Gazprom's sports-oriented social program aims to achieve the responsibilization of individuals to take care of both the well-being of the self and the nation along with its economy and military might. Its unique form of corporate governmentality can thus be defined as a marriage between the energy superpower ideal and military Great Power identity that are constructed with the help of sports metaphors, values, and infrastructures. Thus, sport is utilized to steer energy policies on the local and regional level, as is clearly shown in the Karelian case when the gas program pushed local bioenergy and energy self-sufficiency goals out of the regional agenda. The compelling nationalist narratives manifested in the triangle uniting Russian sports, energy, and Great Power status are thus just as important as the mundane energy security objectives, which persuaded Karelian leadership and communities to join *Gazifikatsiia Rossii*.

References

Alcadipani, R., and J. Hassard (2010). Actor–Network Theory, Organizations and Critique: Towards a Politics of Organizing. *Organization* 17(4): 419–35.

Baev, P. (2008). *Russian Energy Policy and Military Power: Putin's Quest for Greatness*. Abingdon: Routledge.

Bouzarovski, S., and M. Bassin (2011). Energy and Identity: Imagining Russia as a Hydrocarbon Superpower. *Annals of the Association of American Geographers* 101(4): 783–94.

Boyer, D. (2014). Energopower: An Introduction. *Anthropological Quarterly* 86(1): 309–33.

Bradshaw, M. (2013). Progress and Potential of Oil and Gas Exports from Pacific Russia. In *Russian Energy and Security up to 2030* eds. S. Oxenstierna and V.-P. Tynkkynen. London: Routledge, 192–212.

Bridge, G. (2009). Material Worlds: Natural Resources, Resource Geography and the Material Economy. *Geography Compass* 3(3): 1217–44.

Bridge, G. (2011). Past Peak-Oil: Political Economy of Energy Crises. In *Global Political Ecology* eds. R. Peet, P. Robbins, and M. Watts. Abingdon: Routledge, 307–24.

Coleman, M., and J. Agnew (2007). The Problem with Empire. In *Space, Knowledge and Power: Foucault and Geography* eds. J. Crampton and S. Elden. Aldershot: Ashgate, 317–39.

Collier, S. (2011). *Post-Soviet Social: Neoliberalism, Social Modernity, Biopolitics*. Princeton: Princeton University Press.

Dean, M. (1999). *Governmentality: Power and Rule in Modern Society*. London: Sage.

Dolwick, J. (2009). 'The Social' and Beyond: Introducing Actor-Network Theory. *Journal of Maritime Archaeology* 4(1): 21–49.

Edelman, R. (1993). *Serious Fun: A History of Spectator Sports in the USSR*. New York: Oxford University Press.

Emaliantseva, E. (2011). Russian Sport and the Challenges of its Recent Historiography. *Journal of Sports History* 38(3): 361–72.

Foucault, M. (1991). Governmentality. In *The Foucault Effect: Studies in Governmentality* eds. G. Burchell, C. Gordon, and P. Miller. Chicago: University of Chicago Press, 87–104.

Foucault, M. (2008). *The Birth of Biopolitics: Lectures at the Collège de France 1978–1979*. New York: Picador.

Gazprom (2012a). Gazifikatsiia [Gasification Developments]. Available at: www.gazprom.ru/about/production/gasification/ (accessed November 25, 2012).

Gazprom (2015a). Gazprom in Questions and Answers. Available at: www.gazpromquestions.ru/fileadmin/f/2014/download/view_version_eng_9.07.2014.pdf (accessed January 23, 2015).

Gazprom (2015b). Companies with Gazprom's Participation and Other Affiliated Entities. Available at: www.gazprom.com/about/subsidiaries/list-items/ (accessed January 23, 2015).

Gazprom (2015c). Charitable Actions. Available at: www.gazprom.com/social/ (accessed January 23, 2015).

Gazprom (2015d). "Gazprom – Detiam" ["Gazprom – for Children"]. Available at: www.gazprom.ru/social/children/ (accessed June 25, 2015).

Gazprom (2015e). Podderzhka Sporta [Promoting Sports]. Available at: www.gazprom.ru/social/supporting-sports/ (accessed June 25, 2015).

Gazprom (2015f). "Gazprom Transgas Mahachkala" Proveli Sdachu Norm Kompleksa GTO ["Ready for Work and Military Defense" Ltd. Took Part in the GTO]. Available at: www.gazprom.ru/about/subsidiaries/news/2015/may/article225993/ (accessed June 25, 2015).

Gazprom (2015g). "Fakel Nadezhdy" Junyh Patriotov ["Flare of Hope" of Young Patriots]. Available at: www.gazprom.ru/about/subsidiaries/news/2011/october/article121965/ (accessed September 20, 2015).

Gazprom (2015h). Gimn Festivalia 'Fakel' – Pesnia 'Fakel Nadezhdy' [The Hymn of Flare Festival – Song "a Flare of Hope"]. Available at: www.youtube.com/watch?v=gg9Sqqo6L3g (accessed September 20, 2015).

Grix, J., and D. Lee (2013). Soft Power, Sports Mega-Events and Emerging States: The Lure of the Politics of Attraction. *Global Society* 27(4): 521–36.

Houlihan, B. (1997). Sport, National Identity and Public Policy. *Nations and Nationalism* 3(1): 113–37.

Jokisipilä, M. (2011). World Champions Bred by National Champions: The Role of State-Owned Corporate Giants in Russian Sports. *Russian Analytical Digest* 95(April 6, 2011): 8–11.

Kharkhordin, O. (1999). *The Collective and the Individual in Russia: A Study of Practices*. Berkeley: University of California Press.

Kivinen, M. (2012). Public and Business Actors in Russia's Energy Policy. In *Russia's Energy Policies: National, Interregional and Global Levels* ed. P. Aalto. Cheltenham: Edward Elgar, 45–62.

Koch, N. (2013). Sport and Soft Authoritarian Nation-Building. *Political Geography* 32: 42–51.

Koch, N., and A. Valiyev (2015). Urban Boosterism in Closed Contexts: Spectacular Urbanization and Second-Tier Mega-Events in Three Caspian Capitals. *Eurasian Geography and Economics* 56(5): 575–98.

Kotkin, S. (1995). *Magnetic Mountain: Stalinism as a Civilization.* Berkeley: University of California Press.

Larson, D. W., and A. Shevchenko (2014). Russia Says No: Power, Status, and Emotions in Foreign Policy. *Communist and Post-Communist Studies* 47(3–4): 269–79.

Latour, B. (2005). *Reassembling the Social: An Introduction to Actor-Network-Theory.* Oxford: Oxford University Press.

Lee, M. (2011). Nostalgia as a Feature of "Glocalization": Use of the Past in Post-Soviet Russia. *Post-Soviet Affairs* 27(2): 158–77.

Lehtinen, A. (2003). Samhällsgeografi and the Politics of Nature. In *Voices from the North: New Trends in Nordic Human Geography* eds. J. Öhman and K. Simonsen. Aldershot: Ashgate, 233–58.

Mckee, R., E. Richardson, B. Roberts, C. Haerpfer, and M. Mckee (2013). Things Can Only Get Better? Changing Views of the Past, Present and Future in the Former Soviet Union. *Europe-Asia Studies* 65(7): 1466–78.

Mankoff, J. (2009). *Russian Foreign Policy: The Return of Great Power Politics.* Lanham: Rowman and Littlefield Publishers.

Matza, T. (2009). Moscow's Echo: Technologies of the Self, Publics, and Politics on the Russian Talk Show. *Cultural Anthropology* 24(3): 489–522.

Mills, S. (1997). *Discourse: The New Critical Idiom.* London: Routledge.

Ministerstvo Sporta Rossiiskoi Federatsii (2015). Vserossiiskii Fizkulturno-Sportivnyi Kompleks "Gotov k Trudu i Oborone" [All-Russian Physical Exercise and Sports Complex "Ready for Work and Military Defense"]. *GTO.* Available at: www.gto.ru/ (accessed June 25, 2015).

Müller, M. (2011). State Dirigisme in Megaprojects: Governing the 2014 Winter Olympics in Sochi. *Environment and Planning A* 43(9): 2091–108.

Murdoch, J. (1998). The Spaces of Actor–Network Theory. *Geoforum* 29(4): 357–74.

Nika-Media (2012). Sortavala, Pitkiaranta i Olonets Poluchat FOKi ot Gazproma [Sortavala, Pitkäranta and Olonets receive FOKs from Gazprom]. Available at: http://nika-media.ru/blog/vse-novosti/economy/sortavala-pitkyaranta-i-olonec-poluchat-foki-ot-gazproma/ (accessed November 25, 2012).

Paszyc, E. (2012). Gazprom's Position on the Russian Gas Market Weakening. *OSW Commentary*, February 23. Available at: www.osw.waw.pl/en/publikacje/osw-commentary/2012-02-23/gazprom-s-position-russian-gas-market-weakening (accessed November 12, 2012).

Peppard, V., and J. Riordan. (1993). *Playing Politics: Soviet Sport Diplomacy to 1992.* Stamford: JAI Press (Elsevier).

Persson, E., and B. Petersson (2014). Political Mythmaking and the 2014 Winter Olympics in Sochi: Olympism and the Russian Great Power Myth. *East European Politics* 30(2): 192–209.

Peterburgregiongaz (2012). Gazprom Possmotrit Vozmozhnost Stroitelstva Dvuh Gazoprovodov-Otvodov v Respublike Kareliia [Gazprom is Looking for Possibilities to Construct Two Gas Pipelines in the Karelian Republic]. Available at: www.peterburgregiongaz.ru/639 (accessed November 25, 2012).

Pravitelstvo RK (2001). Pazporiazhenie ot 22 Oktiabria 2001 Goda N 241r-P [Decree From the 22nd of October 2001 No. N241r-P]. Available at: http://kodeks.karelia.ru/api/show/919308348 (accessed June 25, 2015).

Prozorov, S. (2014). Foucault and Soviet Biopolitics. *History of the Human Sciences* 27(5): 6–25.

Riordan, J. (1977). *Sport in Soviet Society: Development of Sport and Physical Education in Russia and the USSR*. Cambridge: Cambridge University Press.

Riordan, J. (1999). The Impact of Communism on Sport. In *The International Politics of Sport in the 20th Century* eds. J. Riordan and A. Krüger. New York: Routledge, 48–86.

Rivera Vicencio, E. (2014). The Firm and Corporative Governmentality. From the Perspective of Foucault. *International Journal of Economics and Accounting* 5(4): 281–305.

Rodova, N. (2012). Exports of Russian Natural Gas to Europe to Drop 4–5% on Year in 2012. *Platts*, November 20. Available at: www.platts.com/RSSFeedDetailedNews/RSSFeed/NaturalGas/8928237 (accessed November 25, 2012).

Rogers, D. (2012). The Materiality of the Corporation: Oil, Gas, and Corporate Social Technologies in the Remaking of a Russian Region. *American Ethnologist* 39(2): 284–96.

Rogers, D. (2014). Energopolitical Russia: Corporation, State, and the Rise of Social and Cultural Projects. *Anthropological Quarterly* 87(2): 431–51.

Rooker, T. (2014). Corporate Governance or Governance by Corporates? Testing Governmentality in the Context of China's National Oil and Petrochemical Business Groups. *Asia Pacific Business Review* 21(1): 60–76.

Smith, A., and D. Porter (2004). *Sport and National Identity in the Post-War World*. New York: Routledge.

Solovej, J. (2003). Problemy Podgotovki Biotopliva, Ili Kogda Loshad Budet Idti Vperedi Telegi? [Problems Related to Production of Biofuels, or When the Horse is Going to Run Before the Cart?]. *Promyshlennyi Vestnik Karelii*, Vol. 52. Available at: www.karelexpo.ru/news/sovremennoe-energo05fektivnoe/internet-konferenciya/problemy-podgotovki-biotopliva (accessed November 25, 2012).

Stolitsa na Onego (2012). Gazprom Nameren Vlozhit' V Gazifikatsiiu Karelii 8 Mlrd Rublei [Gazprom Aims to Invest 8 Billion Rubles to Gasify Karelia]. Available at: www.stolica.onego.ru/news/225944.html (accessed November 25, 2012).

Sugden, J., and A. Tomlinson (2002). Theory and Method for a Critical Sociology of Sports. In *Power Games: A Critical Sociology of Sports* eds. J. Sugden and A. Tomlinson. Abingdon: Routledge, 3–21.

Trubina, E. (2014). Mega-Events in the Context of Capitalist Modernity: The Case of 2014 Sochi Winter Olympics. *Eurasian Geography and Economics* 55(6): 610–27.

Tynkkynen, V.-P. (2001). Water Related Health Risks and Preventative Policies in the Karelian Republic. In *The Struggle for Russian Environmental Policy* eds. I. Massa and V.-P. Tynkkynen. Helsinki: Kikimora Publications, 123–58.

Tynkkynen, V.-P. (2009). Maantieteellisesti Spesifi Hallintatapa ja Aluesuunnitte-
lun Valtatutkimus [Geo-Governmentality and Studying Power in Urban and
Regional Planning]. *The Finnish Journal of Urban Studies* 47(3): 24–37.

Tynkkynen, V.-P. (2013). Russian Bioenergy and the EU's Renewable Energy
Goals: Perspectives of Security. In *Russian Energy and Security up to 2030* eds.
S. Oxenstierna and V.-P. Tynkkynen. Abingdon: Routledge, 95–113.

Wong, L., and R. Trumper. (2002). Global Celebrity Athletes and Nationalism:
Fútbol, Hockey, and the Representation of Nation. *Journal of Sport and Social
Issues* 26(2): 168–94.

Chapter 7

Athletic autocrats

Understanding images of authoritarian leaders as sportsmen

Natalie Koch

Introduction

Politicians from many different political systems are frequently portrayed as being sports aficionados or engaged in playing sport. Indeed, some autocrats seem to have a unique penchant for donning a sporting persona. One of the most circulated images of Russian president Vladimir Putin, for example, shows him bare-chested, riding a horse, while on holiday in the countryside. But he has also been portrayed doing many other sports, such as judo, ice hockey, and cycling. The Italian fascist president Benito Mussolini (d. 1945) was also frequently photographed bare-chested while engaged in sport, and he was a vocal supporter of soccer and automobile racing. Sheikh Zayed (d. 2004) of the United Arab Emirates (UAE) was a major proponent and practitioner of the sport of falconry. Kim Jong Il (d. 2011) in North Korea was touted for his supposed golfing prowess, while the brutal Ugandan dictator Idi Amin (d. 1979) was a famed boxer and rugby player. Chinese Communist Party Chairman Mao Zedong (d. 1976) was an advocate of swimming and his celebrated 15-kilometer swim across the Yangtze River in 1966 later became a yearly spectacle, with thousands of participants. Stretching even to ancient history, Roman Emperors Nero and Commodus showed a special interest in publicly displaying their skills as charioteer and gladiator, respectively.

Why is it that certain autocrats are frequently portrayed as athletes? In many cases, as with the examples just noted, it is clear that the individuals have a personal passion for sport and, in some cases, have real talent. The discussion here, while not discounting the importance of a leader's character, focuses on a wider set of political and contextual factors to explain why autocrats are routinely portrayed as sportsmen. Adopting a cross-regional approach, I take a closer look at three cases of "athletic autocrats": Russian President Vladimir Putin, Sheikh Zayed bin Sultan Al Nahyan of the UAE, and Chinese Communist Party Chairman Mao Zedong. I explore how this phenomenon factors into local regimes of legitimating authority in authoritarian states, including personalistic rule, nationalism, and paternalism.

Sport, nationalism, and masculinity in authoritarian states

In considering the connections between sport and nationalism in authoritarian states, many scholars have shown how nondemocratic regimes frequently use their athletes' success and sporting spectacles as a way to promote domestic pride and garner international legitimacy (e.g., Dennis and Grix 2012; Houlihan 1997; Koch 2013; Lee and Bairner 2009; Merkel 2010; Riordan 1991; Riordan and Arnaud 1998). Others have demonstrated how authoritarian regimes can use mass sport and spectator sports as a vehicle for promoting nationalist sentiments – this being a staple of authoritarian systems in the twentieth century, including fascist Italy and Germany, and later, the Soviet Union and East Germany (Falasca-Zamponi 1997; McDonald 2006; Riordan 1991; Teja 1998).

While a number of these studies touch on the issue of sport being used as a form of propaganda in authoritarian states, in this chapter I propose an alternative approach to the relationship between sport and authoritarianism. Guided by the discursive analysis methods of critical geopolitics (Dittmer 2010), I scrutinize the use of sporting "personas" as a way to legitimate the authority of autocratic heads of state. A discursive approach means focusing on text- or media-based materials, though my aim is not to replace more embodied or performative analyses of sports. Rather, a specifically semiotic tack is complementary to these studies insofar as it suggests that sport is implicated in – and constitutive of – a much larger set of identity discourses that extend far beyond the baseball stadium, football pitch, or swimming pool (as suggested by nearly every other chapter in this volume). Or, as Michael Billig (1995: 120) has argued, "sport is never merely sport," but "has a social and political significance, extending through the media beyond the player and the spectator."

In this chapter, I consider one such extension of sporting discourse: the portrayal of autocrats engaged in sporting activities. These men – for I know of no female cases (and women dictators are historically rare) – exemplify the most personalistic variants of authoritarian rule. In such systems, the government's legitimacy is staked to the merits of the leader himself – typically his wisdom, acumen, vitality, and strength (actual and metaphorical) – as well as his ability to manifest nationalist ideals and values. Sport, as a historically favored social and political metaphor, represents an ideal way for a leader and his public relations (PR) apparatus to illustrate to citizens that he possesses all these desirable attributes and, in turn, legitimate his authority. While the motivating fiction of personalistic regimes is that the leader is all-powerful, I argue that analyzing an autocrat's persona alone is insufficient. This is because broader narratives, such as nationalism and paternalism, are also essential to sustaining political legitimacy under personalistic authoritarian regimes.

Nationalism and paternalism have important gender dimensions, which become readily apparent in the images of "athletic autocrats" I explore here. As feminist geographers and other gender studies scholars have long argued, "masculinity" and "femininity" are socially constructed through a wide range of performances – and many of these are tied to particular understandings of the "nation" (Connell 1995; Mayer 2000; van Hoven and Hörschelman 2005; Yuval-Davis 1997). The scholarship on gender and sport has shed light on the social construction of male/female roles in a wide range of contexts, and this work has tended to fit into one of two approaches. First, the majority of studies on gender and sport have focused on what I see as the "embodied" side of sporting practice, through a close analysis of the body, as well as people's lived experiences as athletes or fans (e.g., Hargreaves and Vertinsky 2006; Jensen 2010; Messner 1992, 2005; Messner and Sabo 1990; Woodward 2009). Second, a smaller subset of the literature has emphasized the media's gendered presentation of sport, through what Messner (2005: 320) calls the "cultural turn" in sports studies (e.g., Andrewes 1998; Burstyn 1999; Fuller 2006; Kibby 1998; Senyard 1998).

While I see the two approaches as complementary, I adopt the latter in this chapter to understand the political relations that give rise to, and are sustained by, the portrayal of autocrats as athletes – following Jackson and Balaji's (2011) focus on the media to analyze how cultures of masculinity are constructed and perpetuated locally and globally. Laden with wide-ranging cultural significance, discourses around sport have historically worked as an important conduit for constructing hegemonic masculinity. But this is certainly not limited to the realm of professional or even everyday sport: the mere symbolism of sport is significant in many social realms. When united with politics, sports metaphors are commonplace. Indeed, the trope of portraying politicians as athletes is found in varied international settings.

Karin Wahl-Jorgensen (2000), for example, has analyzed the heavy use of sporting imagery by candidates in the 1992 United States presidential campaign. Often treated as a whimsical metaphor in the media, as with the widely circulated image of Clinton and Gore jogging together captioned as "running mates," she argues that such portrayals are far from neutral. Rather, the images of presidential candidates engaged in sports generally worked to trivialize the complexity of politics, while rhetorically constructing the presidency as a hyper-masculine position and transforming the leader "into a personalized emblem of the gendered nation-state" (Wahl-Jorgensen 2000: 57). When political or media-based actors use it to downplay the gravity of certain political questions, sporting imagery can thus have a *de-politicizing* effect. Yet, as the cases analyzed below suggest, when deployed in formal politics sporting rhetoric generally, and the regime-promoted images of "athletic autocrats" specifically, are deeply political.

Putin, Zayed, and Mao: the leaders and their sporting personas

The remainder of this chapter considers how and why three particular leaders have been cast as sportsmen. Russian President Putin, the late Sheikh Zayed of the UAE and Chairman Mao of China are illustrative of three common themes in the semiotic portrayal of athletic autocrats, but some brief context is first needed to situate each in their political milieu. First, President Vladimir Putin is among the best-known contemporary examples, given how much international attention has been given to his media-based sporting persona. Putin has been at the helm of Russia's government since 1999, with a short interregnum as Prime Minister from 2008 to 2012. When he first came to power, he was best known for his love of judo and images of him engaged in the sport circulated widely. In 2007, the Kremlin disseminated pictures of him fishing and horseback riding – bare-chested – during his summer holiday in Tuva. Causing a sensation domestically and internationally, he has since been portrayed in highly stylized photo-ops doing almost every sport imaginable, from ice hockey, to car racing, rafting, swimming, cycling, skiing, weight-lifting and more (Figure 7.1).

The second leader considered here, Sheikh Zayed bin Sultan Al Nahyan, oversaw the founding of the United Arab Emirates (UAE) as a federation of seven hereditary monarchies in 1971, at the end of the British colonial

Figure 7.1 President Putin fishing in Tuva in August 2007 (source: kremlin.ru)

protectorate in the Trucial States. As the Emir of Abu Dhabi until his death in 2004, he was the leading political force of the UAE and is widely described as the "father of the nation." While many sporting facilities and tournaments around the UAE are today named for him, Sheikh Zayed's own sporting interest lay almost exclusively with falconry. Well-known for his love of the sport, images glorifying him and his accomplishments frequently portray him with his falcons or on hunts. His image as an expert falconer has been harnessed to promote a wide range of falconry-related initiatives – including the UAE-based International Falconry Festival and the Abu Dhabi Falcon Hospital – but also more generally, as an icon of Emirati nationalist pride and heritage (Figure 7.2).

Also deemed a "founding father," Mao Zedong ruled the communist People's Republic of China as the Chairman of the Communist Party from 1949 until his death in 1976. In one of Mao's (1917) earliest articles, "A Study of Physical Culture," he touted the benefits of regular exercise for strengthening both the bodies and minds of the Chinese population. Mao was himself especially fond of swimming and he is now remembered for his love of the sport – but it was only after 1966 that images of him engaged in the sport began to proliferate. In that year, he participated in a spectacle of swimming 15 kilometers across the Yangtze River and, at the age of 72, his success became a focus of nationalist propaganda and glorification of the leader for many years to come (Figure 7.3).

From this brief sketch, it is clear that the differences between Putin, Zayed, and Mao are many. However, they also have much in common and local media portrayals of the three reflect broader trends in how authoritarian leaders are portrayed as sportsmen. The three themes outlined in the next section are certainly not exhaustive of the way that sporting discourse is harnessed in such portrayals, but they are among the most important aspects of how these images are used to support the efforts of personalistic authoritarian regimes to achieve popular legitimacy. Thus, in considering the commonalities across the sporting images of Putin, Zayed, and Mao, this analysis offers an insight into the nature of such political systems, as well as the local cultures of paternalist masculinity and nationalism upon which they are built.

Personalistic rule: enacting the leader's superhuman prowess

Portraying an autocratic head of state as a sportsman is typically one element of a broader "imaging" project, in which the leader is held up as no ordinary man, but possesses a range of superhuman or extraordinary talents or attributes. As with kings, emperors or sultans of times past and present, the royal aura of a ruler's inherent superiority must be actively constructed through a range of symbols, rituals, spectacles, and

Figure 7.2 Typical display of images of Sheikh Zayed and falconry at the Sheikh Zayed Heritage Festival in December 2014 (source: Natalie Koch).

Figure 7.3 1967 poster reading: "Commemorate the first anniversary of Chairman Mao's swim over the Yangzi – Follow Chairman Mao in moving forward in wind and waves!" (source: IISH/Stefan R. Landsberger Collections, chineseposters.net).

performances. This superiority is, after all, the claim to the leader's legitimacy and right to rule. Paul Veyne (1990: 382) elaborates:

> The personal superiority expressed by display extends to everything, since the master commands by the right to command which belongs to a higher species. Those who belong to that higher species eat better and live more luxuriously. Luxury and pleasures form part of the display.

While Veyne considers this display of luxury and pleasure in terms of ancient Roman Emperors portraying themselves as charioteers or gladiators, Simonetta Falasca-Zamponi (1997: 68) has noted the same dynamic much later in fascist Italy under Benito Mussolini, whose regime constantly portrayed him as superhuman and a master of a range of sporting feats, including skiing, fencing, swimming, and horseback riding. She also notes that, under Italy's fascist regime, it was the very saturation of these images of Mussolini that created the impression of his superhuman state, investing him "with a magical, mystical aura that placed him above common people—or better, above mortals" (Falasca-Zamponi 1997: 86).

This image of being more than a "mere mortal" is clearly at work in portrayals of Putin, Zayed, and Mao. The broad and constant coverage of President Putin's heroic deeds suggests that he can do everything (Foxall 2013; Goscilo 2013; Sperling 2015). Consistent with representations of

Chairman Mao as a godlike figure and "nothing less than the physical representation of Revolution, History, the Fate of China, and the People's Aspirations" (Barmé 1996: 24), representations of his swimming prowess also worked to deify him. Running counter to the actual manner in which Mao swam – which consisted of floating downstream with the current, as vividly described in the widely cited memoirs of his private physician Zhisui Li (1994) – he was described after his celebrated Yangtze crossing as having swum faster than an Olympic athlete. At the age of 72, this was clearly a superhuman feat (if exaggerated).

Sheikh Zayed, for his part, is commonly described by local sources as "unrivalled" for his falconry skills (Al-Saggar 2004), but it is actually more frequently his commitment to environmental conservation and to falconry as a form of intangible heritage that has been used to highlight his super-human traits. He is consistently referred to as being a rare visionary and the pioneer of ecological sustainability in the Arabian Peninsula, and indeed the entire world (Koch 2015; Krawietz 2014; Ouis 2002). This is vividly exemplified in the *Al-Saggar* (2004) magazine article on Sheikh Zayed as "the first falconer":

> Dubbed as the fore-runner of contemporary falconers and conserva-tionists across the world, the late Sheikh Zayed Bin Sultan Al Nahyan (may God bless his soul) was born a conservationist. Although he was born into a harshly inhospitable environment of the Arabian Desert where the Bedouins eked out a living through hunting, young Zayed foresaw the need to strike a balance between preservation of the ances-tral heritage of falconry and hunting on the one hand, and ensuring the long-term survival of falcons and their prey on the other. This view, by any stretch of imagination, was a transcendental and far-sighted vision that modern conservationists today know as "sustain-able hunting." Clearly, Sheikh Zayed was not only ahead of his own generation but also far ahead of the entire worldwide conservationist movement.

When considering these narratives, it is natural to ask whether people in the respective polities actually "believe" them. In many ways this question is irrelevant because, regardless of what people believe, these narratives offer a formula for speaking of the leader as omnipotent (for more on this point, see Veyne 1988). This very image of omnipotence is the crux of per-sonalistic authoritarian regimes' claim to power.

The idea of a singular leader in control of all political decisions in a given country is necessarily fictitious, but it is the motivating fiction of a personalistic regime. Rather than legitimacy being staked in democratic institutions, for example, legitimacy in such systems hinges on an indi-vidual citizen or subject's commitment to a leader. For example, in Rome's

Imperial era, Veyne (1990: 293) explains, "the kingly style replaced the appeal to each man's civic sense by an exaltation of their personal virtues of the Emperor. Instead of obeying out of devotion to the state, people were to trust the sovereign's providence." Geremie Barmé (1996: 24) has noted this same dynamic under Mao, whereby individual citizens' devotion to the leader – or rather his public persona – "created a relationship that bypassed government and Party structures created to regulate the nation." For the general population to understand the figure of the leader as possessing unparalleled skill, insight, or visionary acumen, this must be communicated through ritual – which in more contemporary authoritarian settings has taken shape in state-controlled media outlets.

While sporting images are a useful way to illustrate the leader's superordinary set of skills, they can also illustrate his physical vigor. As I discuss further below, physical vigor exhibited through sport is a common metaphor for the vigor of the nation. Yet in the case of personalistic authoritarian regimes, the individual leader's health takes on an added significance because the state's legitimacy is tied to his continued survival and his physical fitness to rule. In the cases at hand, this is especially evident in the rhetoric and imagery used to portray Putin as athletic. Since his first days as president, Putin has defined his persona around leading a healthy and substance-free lifestyle. In explicit contrast to his predecessor Boris Yeltsin, who was a notoriously sloppy drunk, he positioned himself as an "eternally young, sport man" (Sperling 2015: 61). His many escapades over 15 years at the helm routinely underscore his physical fitness to govern, with top-down and bottom-up media campaigns fetishizing his body as an ideal that men aspire to and women desire (Goscilo 2013; Sperling 2015).

Under Chairman Mao's political apparatus, his famous 15-kilometer swim of the Yangtze was also used to advertise his supposed vitality at the age of 72. Post facto portrayals claimed that he "swam faster and more vigorously than any Olympic swimming champion" (Karl 2010: 126), and articles in the press boldly proclaimed: "The news of Chairman Mao's swim in the Yangtse stirred all hearts and brought immense inspiration and strength to everybody" (quoted in Barmé 1996: 61). Yet Mao was in fact suffering from poor health, and had been seen relatively little in public; the images of him swimming were strategically designed to illustrate his continued – if grossly exaggerated – vitality. Like so many other autocrats, sporting images of Mao and Putin display an uncommon concern with the leader being seen as eternally youthful. Whether a fixation of the leader or his apparatus, the image of immortality is especially important in personalistic authoritarian regimes – systems that tie legitimacy so closely to one human being's continued survival. Eternal youth may be mythical, but it is a powerful myth that regimes strategically promote through sporting rhetoric, which is designed to show the leader's age-defying, superhuman character.

Nationalism: manifesting the leader's nationalist spirit

Sport can also be an important way for an authoritarian leader to prove that he shares what Veyne (1990: 398) terms "popular feelings." In non-democratic polities, displays of leaders engaged in popular pastimes are not solely about effecting legitimacy through cultivating a positive image of the leader; they also show that he is "one of them," "multiplying proofs that at least he reigns for them" (Veyne 1990: 402). While the governmental portrayals of Putin, Zayed, and Mao's sporting prowess tend toward a superhuman idealization of the leader, elevating him above the general population, sporting narratives also show that he is nonetheless in touch with the people and shares their values, both with respect to nationalist sports and the nationalistically imagined landscapes with which they are associated.

Portrayals of Sheikh Zayed during his falconry excursions, for example, explicitly rely on nationalist landscapes to buttress the idea that his sport is a national pastime, rather than a simple case of the leader engaging in globalized sport. Although many photographs of him hunting are from his expeditions in Pakistan or Morocco, these images do not stress the local landscapes, but rather portray scenes from the group's camp (as in the top image of Figure 7.2). As I have argued elsewhere, the image of the desert camp is an important trope in Gulf nationalism and, even when detached from the Arabian Peninsula, the camp indexes a Gulf national identity and, as such, is a national landscape in itself (Koch 2015). As it is practiced today, however, Gulf falconry is a decidedly elitist sport, "often associated with royalty, as it is only the very wealthy who can afford to travel abroad to hawk with their birds" (Wakefield 2012: 283). Yet, in the images surrounding Sheikh Zayed and falconry, this elitist aspect is stripped away. He is often shown "roughing it," with minimalist supplies at desert camps, rather than the luxurious arrangements of contemporary Gulf elites' hunting expeditions. This is important in part because of the way that falconry is locally narrated as a "heritage sport" that hearkens back to an imagined primordial Arab way of life. More importantly, this image of minimalism is also required to portray Sheikh Zayed as an ordinary man, who was not inherently privileged, but rose out of this time of widespread poverty to unite his people around a unified Emirati identity and lead them on a path to great wealth and prosperity. Falconry-related rhetoric around Sheikh Zayed thus underscores the claim that, "even when he became President ... he was neither swayed by the affluence of modern life nor by many responsibilities which he had to shoulder" (Al-Saggar 2004).

In the case of Putin, his sporting photographs clearly evoke nationalist landscapes of the Russian countryside. The widely circulated images of his bare-chested fishing and horseback riding, for example, were taken during his summer holidays in Tuva, with the carefully orchestrated images being set in the midst of dramatic river and mountain landscapes (Foxall 2013: 144). But the rugged Siberian countryside is not just a passive backdrop: it is iconic of the Russian *rodina*, or motherland, and is essential to constructing Putin's sporting body as a decidedly nationalist body. Similarly, in his sporting endeavors, Mao embraced China's rivers as the ideal site for swimming. So fused was Mao's persona with the idea of a quintessential Chinese landscape, that he was often symbolized with images of the sun, dawn, mountains, and the sea in film and theater (Barmé 1996: 24). While he would occasionally swim in pools, he preferred to swim in rivers, where the current would allow him to drift for hours. Despite the anxiety of his circle of attendants about the polluted state of the rivers, he always insisted that it was no matter and that others simply lacked the courage to face the unique sporting challenge presented by the wild waters (Li 1994). He frequently lectured his entourage about this and, in the 1950s, declared to the Chinese public: "Swimming is a sport in which the swimmers battle against Nature; you should go into the big rivers and seas to temper yourselves" (quoted in Barmé 1996: 25). Official portrayals of Mao's love for swimming were thus typically set on the banks of a vast river.

In addition to fixing the leader in a nationalist landscape, sporting images allow authoritarian regimes to strategically paint a leader as an exemplar of the physically fit national body, metaphorically symbolizing the vigor of the nation as a whole. Sport-related metaphors have a long history in nation-building discourse, and are especially common in "transformational" nationalisms, i.e., those aimed at redefining the nation in contrast to some previous national era. For example, leadership in the three great authoritarian systems of the twentieth century, fascism in Italy, Nazism in Germany, and Stalinism in the Soviet Union, were all especially fond of using sport to define these regimes as representing a marked difference from the previous regimes. Often having a military dimension, mass sporting displays, such as the Soviet "physical culture" parades, were also about advertising national fitness and discipline – of both body and mind. In these parades, as with similar displays in Nazi Germany, the leaders (Stalin and Hitler) were metaphorically framed as the "expert sculptor," creating "bodily symbolism, where naked tanned flesh and well-developed muscles stood for the might of the ... nation" (Petrone 2000: 32–3).

Similarly, the sporting body and sporting success have long been treated as indicators of national status and international prestige in China (Xu 2008). Drawing on many principles of fascist physical cultures, Mao was an early advocate and practitioner of physical education for revolutionary ends. For him, physical discipline and sport were "constantly linked to the issue of China's rejuvenation and progress" (Barmé 1996: 24), and he imagined a fit body to reflect inner discipline and other nationalist values:

Those whose bodies are small and frail are flippant in their behaviour. Those whose skin is flabby are soft and dull in will. Thus does the body influence the mind. The purpose of physical education is to strengthen: the muscles and the bones; as a result, knowledge is enhanced, the sentiments are harmonized, and the will is strengthened.

(Mao 1917)

Though his sporting persona was certainly embellished by his PR apparatus, Mao felt that it was important to personally model this vision. Treated as exemplars of regime and national ideals, autocratic leaders such as Mao are frequently cast as manifesting these virtues themselves. Of course, there are differences in the balance between this being mere propaganda and the leader's actual behavior, but suffice it to say that no true talent is necessary for a leader to be transformed into an "athletic autocrat." Mao was, after all, mostly a floater.

Paternalism: performing the leader's masculinity

Paternalism is a way of legitimating authority by behaving as a protective or benevolent father, removing both responsibility and choice from those being controlled or governed, who are treated as children. Personalistic authoritarian regimes are often also paternalistic and, for this reason, how regimes construct the leader's masculinity are especially important. As gender studies scholars have shown, "control over access to the benefits of belonging to the nation is virtually always gendered" (Mayer 2000: 2). So when a leader asserts his masculinity, he is also asserting his legitimacy as a leader and his right to speak for the "nation."

Ideals about masculinity are of course not static, nor are they the same everywhere, but in paternalistic systems local norms and ideals surrounding masculinity are a primary conduit for power relations. This is especially clear in the way that men in such systems are imagined as a "personalized image of the nation," expected to defend its "moral consciousness" (Mayer 2000: 6). In various international contexts, men are imagined (passively and actively) as "defenders" of the nation, whereas women and children are seen as those in need of protection (Young 2003). In the three cases at hand, this masculinist "protector" ideal comes out vividly in the glorification of their "strong handed" rule: the leaders' PR apparatuses draw heavily on tropes of paternalism to validate the prevailing autocratic power structures.

Local cultures of masculinity are commonly narrated through sport and sporting rhetoric. Just as Kibby (1998: 20) demonstrates in her study of nostalgia in 1980s sports films, we find in the images of athletic autocrats a certain "mis-remembering" of "hegemonic masculinity in providing an arena where individual success, male-male bonds, the reaffirmation of the father, and the rejection of the feminine, [can] be comfortably accommodated." In this context, the language of sport becomes an easy means to define the authoritarian leader's stylized masculinity. In Russia, this "mis-remembered" or imagined "traditional" masculinity is frequently tied to "the idea that the 'man of the house' (or political leader) is responsible for protecting 'his' family (or 'his' nation)" (Sperling 2015: 34). Accordingly, Vladimir Putin's public persona has consistently drawn on paternalist tropes.

Scholars have amply explored what has been termed his "hypermasculinity" – the product of a designed PR campaign. Although his image has more recently been sexualized by his many supporters treating him as object of women's sexual desire, he is more generally framed as an exemplar of the strong Russian man: a rock in the face of perceived challenges to Russian supremacy and territorial integrity on many fronts (see also Foxall 2013; Goscilo 2013; Sperling 2015; Tynkkynen, Chapter 6 this volume). In this respect, Putin represents a typical father figure, the strongest and bravest man in Russia prepared to defend the nation and its people. In a truly paternal fashion, he is imagined as their protector. Putin's masculinity and paternal authority is narrated through images of him engaged in sport endeavors, as well as the related discussions of his muscular body, work ethic, and clean lifestyle – all of which are essential to promoting him in this protector role.

The sporting images of Putin have additionally stressed the theme of male bonding with his right-hand man, Prime Minister Dmitry Medvedev. Images of Putin and Medvedev together are just like those in the 1992 US presidential election discussed by Wahl-Jorgensen's (2000: 60–1): designed to "illustrate the level of trust and collaboration between presidential and vice presidential candidates." But in these moments of bonding, the power hierarchy is always clear: whether in their series of photos cycling or weightlifting together, Putin is always depicted in the dominant position, often instructing Medvedev in a fatherly fashion as to proper form in their sporting activities (see especially BBC 2015; Longbottom 2011). Although it is common for politicians to emasculate their direct opponents, Putin's sporting displays set him apart from Medvedev's ostensible weakness or femininity and thus strengthen his machismo and paternalist credentials.

Male bonding in politics thus remains a distinctly uneven terrain, rather reinforcing vertical hierarchies than breaking them down – a dynamic that is also at play in the Chinese context. For example, in Li's (1994) and other accounts of Mao's swimming escapes, we routinely see him reproving his (all-male) entourage for their unwillingness to join him in the rivers – and for making a laughing stock of those who had difficulty when they did enter the water. He was also particularly fond of giving others instructions about how to "improve" their swimming form (this being a dubious designation given that he was typically teaching them to float rather than

swim). Whether emasculating others in his jest, or in his paternalist instructions, Mao's masculinity was clearly a relative matter – and something that
sport allowed him to strategically narrate.

The theme of male bonding is especially pertinent in the case of Sheikh
Zayed, whose masculinity is also on clear display in his sporting images.
The desert camp is a particular space of male bonding and communion – a
point that is emphasized in the *Al-Saggar* (2004) article on Zayed and falconry, quoted above. The authors went on to note that Zayed's attraction
to falconry rested not just with the sport, but in the "companionship of the
hunt," bringing him "closer to the hearts and minds of his compatriots"
and winning him "love and prominence that none of the other leaders in
the whole region had enjoyed at that time." The images of Zayed engaged
in falconry also stress his delicate and caring interactions with the birds
themselves. As Birgit Krawietz (2014: 138) notes, Zayed, like "most of the
other Arab Gulf rulers can be seen with either falcons, horses and/or
camels to naturalize their qualities as considerate leaders." The staged
images of Arab rulers with animals, she suggests, allows them to display
their "softer," loving side in public. Equally, the diffusion of images of
Zayed with his falcons broadcast a tender and affectionate image –
attributes that build his image as a caring father and solidify his paternalist
authority. This paternalist care for the animals and his people are also par-
alleled in the narratives about Sheikh Zayed's concern for the Arabian
Peninsula's ecology, discussed above. In his media-promoted sporting
persona, the Emirati leader is thus not only a "man of the people," but the
"father of the nation." And the nondemocratic system of governance he
institutionalized is imagined as uncontested and unproblematic, for it is
imagined to originate in his deep paternalist care and affection.

Conclusion

In considering the semiotic confluence of identity narratives surrounding
sport, nationalism, and masculinity – through the peculiar trope of portraying an autocratic leader as a sportsman – this chapter raises the question of whether there is something unique about autocratic contexts. I
suggest here that there is. Although Michael Billig (1995: 96) notes the
trend toward the "politician-as-celebrity" in liberal settings, thanks to
digital media, autocracies have arguably always been characterized by such
a dynamic. In personalistic regimes, the political figurehead is imagined
and treated as a celebrity whose words and everyday activities their followers and media apparatuses quickly transform into aphorisms and the
deeds of a superhuman. This process of exalting a single individual is
fundamental to authoritarian regimes' narrative fiction that the leader
(whether he is called president, emir, or chairman) is all-powerful. As I
have shown in this chapter, we often see leaders of such regimes construed

as an athlete or engaged in vigorous sporting activity because of the wide-ranging tropes that it affords to narrate their singular authority – based on the grounds of his exemplary or superhuman nature, his nationalist spirit, and his masculinity and paternalist care for the nation and its well-being.

But the idea of an autocrat being the ultimate source of power in a personalistic regime is and always will be a fiction. This is because, as French theorist Michel Foucault's transformative discussions of power emphasize, its exercise can never emanate from one person alone, but is constituted through a vast range of agencies, materialities, and contingencies. Power, he argues, must be analyzed:

> as something which circulates, or rather as something which only functions in the form of a chain. It is never localised here or there, never in anybody's hands, never appropriated as a commodity or piece of wealth. Power is employed and exercised through a net-like organization.
>
> (Foucault 1980: 98)

Even in highly centralized political systems, many actors are working together, with differing resources at their disposal, to produce the desired effect of retaining positions of power, influence, and, often, wealth. This notwithstanding, authoritarian regimes have a vested interest in making it look like power is indeed localized in the hands of the central leader. This is because, by creating the image of an infallible individual, or a man with unparalleled vision to govern, these regimes seek to erase the need for political contest. If endowed with such a remarkable man to steer the nation's course, democracy is narrated as obsolete. Fictitious though it may be, this authoritarian vision is the broader phenomenon that explains the strangely common images of authoritarian leaders as sportsmen – the "athletic autocrats" such as President Putin, Sheikh Zayed, and Chairman Mao.

References

Al-Saggar (2004). Sheikh Zayed Bin Sultan Al Nahyan: The First Falconer. *Al-Saggar Magazine*. Available at: www.falconryfestival.ae/about-the-festival/zayed-falconer/ (accessed November 17, 2015).

Andrewes, F. (1998). Demonstrable Virility: Images of Masculinity in the 1956 Springbok Rugby Tour of New Zealand. *The International Journal of the History of Sport* 15(2): 119–36.

Barmé, G. (1996). *Shades of Mao: The Posthumous Cult of the Great Leader*. Armonk: M. E. Sharpe.

BBC (2015). Russia's Putin and Medvedev Work Out Together. *BBC News Services*, August 30. Available at: www.bbc.com/news/world-middle-east-34102651 (accessed December 20, 2015).

Billig, M. (1995). *Banal Nationalism*. Thousand Oaks: Sage.

Burstyn, V. (1999). *The Rites of Men: Manhood, Politics, and the Culture of Sport.* Toronto: University of Toronto Press.

Connell, R. W. (1995). *Masculinities.* Berkeley: University of California Press.

Dennis, M., and J. Grix (2012). *Sport under Communism: Behind the East German "Miracle."* New York: Palgrave Macmillan.

Dittmer, J. (2010). *Popular Culture, Geopolitics, and Identity.* Lanham: Rowman & Littlefield.

Falasca-Zamponi, S. (1997). *Fascist Spectacle: The Aesthetics of Power in Mussolini's Italy.* Berkeley: University of California Press.

Foucault, M. (1980). *Power/Knowledge: Selected Interviews and Other Writings, 1972–1977.* New York: Pantheon Books.

Foxall, A. (2013). Photographing Vladimir Putin: Masculinity, Nationalism and Visuality in Russian Political Culture. *Geopolitics* 18(1): 132–56.

Fuller, L. (2006). *Sport, Rhetoric, and Gender: Historical Perspectives and Media Representations.* New York: Palgrave Macmillan.

Goscilo, H. (2013). *Putin as Celebrity and Cultural Icon.* New York: Routledge.

Hargreaves, J., and P. Vertinsky (2006). *Physical Culture, Power, and the Body.* New York: Routledge.

Houlihan, B. (1997). Sport, National Identity and Public Policy. *Nations and Nationalism* 3(1): 113–37.

Jackson, R., and M. Balaji (2011). *Global Masculinities and Manhood.* Urbana: University of Illinois Press.

Jensen, E. (2010). *Body by Weimar: Athletes, Gender, and German Modernity.* Oxford: Oxford University Press.

Karl, R. (2010). *Mao Zedong and China in the Twentieth-Century World: A Concise History.* Durham: Duke University Press.

Kibby, M. (1998). Nostalgia for the Masculine: Onward to the Past in Sports Films of the Eighties. *Canadian Journal of Film Studies* VII(1): 16–28.

Koch, N. (2013). Sport and Soft Authoritarian Nation-Building. *Political Geography* 32: 42–51.

Koch, N. (2015). Gulf Nationalism and the Geopolitics of Constructing Falconry as a "Heritage Sport." *Studies in Ethnicity and Nationalism* 15(3): 522–39.

Krawietz, B. (2014). Falconry as a Cultural Icon of the Arab Gulf Region. In *Under Construction: Logics of Urbanism in the Gulf Region* eds. S. Wippel, K. Bromber, C. Steiner, and B. Krawietz. Farnham: Ashgate, 131–46.

Lee, J., and A. Bairner (2009). The Difficult Dialogue: Communism, Nationalism, and Political Propaganda in North Korean Sport. *Journal of Sport & Social Issues* 33(4): 390–410.

Li, Z. (1994). *The Private Life of Chairman Mao: The Memoirs of Mao's Personal Physician.* New York: Random House.

Longbottom, W. (2011). Fancy a Bike Ride in the Park? How an "Informal" Meeting in Moscow Could Decide Who Runs Russia Next Year. *Daily Mail*, June 11. Available at: www.dailymail.co.uk/news/article-2002504/Fancy-bike-ride-park-How-informal-meeting-Moscow-decide-runs-Russia-year.html (accessed December 20, 2015).

McDonald, I. (2006). Political Somatics: Fascism, Physical Culture and the Sporting Body. In *Physical Culture, Power, and the Body* eds. J. Hargreaves and P. Vertinsky. New York: Routledge, 52–73.

Mao, Z. (1917). A Study of Physical Culture. *New Youth* 3(4).

Mayer, T. (2000). *Gender Ironies of Nationalism: Sexing the Nation*. New York: Routledge.

Merkel, U. (2010). Bigger Than Beijing 2008: Politics, Propaganda and Physical Culture in Pyongyang. *The International Journal of the History of Sport* 27 (14–15): 2467–92.

Messner, M. (1992). *Power at Play: Sports and the Problem of Masculinity*. Boston: Beacon Press.

Messner, M. (2005). Still a Man's World? Studying Masculinities in Sport. In *Handbook of Studies on Men & Masculinities* eds. M. Kimmel, J. Hearn, and R. Connell. Thousand Oaks: Sage, 313–25.

Messner, M., and D. Sabo (1990). *Sport, Men, and the Gender Order: Critical Feminist Perspectives*. Champaign: Human Kinetics Books.

Ouis, P. (2002). "Greening the Emirates": The Modern Construction of Nature in the United Arab Emirates. *Cultural Geographies* 9(3): 334–47.

Petrone, K. (2000). *Life Has Become More Joyous, Comrades: Celebrations in the Time of Stalin*. Bloomington: Indiana University Press.

Riordan, J. (1991). *Sport, Politics, and Communism*. New York: St. Martin's Press.

Riordan, J., and P. Arnaud (1998). *Sport and International Politics*. New York: E. & F.N. Spon.

Senyard, J. (1998). The Imagined Golf Course: Gender Representations and Australian Golf. *The International Journal of the History of Sport* 15(2): 164–75.

Sperling, V. (2015). *Sex, Politics, and Putin: Political Legitimacy in Russia*. Oxford: Oxford University Press.

Teja, A. (1998). Italian Sport and International Relations under Fascism. In *Sport and International Politics* eds. J. Riordan and P. Arnaud. New York: E. & F.N. Spon, 147–70.

van Hoven, B., and K. Hörschelmann (2005). *Spaces of Masculinities*. New York: Routledge.

Veyne, P. (1988). *Did the Greeks Believe in Their Myths? An Essay on the Constitutive Imagination*. Chicago: University of Chicago Press.

Veyne, P. (1990). *Bread and Circuses: Historical Sociology and Political Pluralism*. London: Penguin Press.

Wahl-Jorgensen, K. (2000). Constructing Masculinities in U.S. Presidential Campaigns: The Case of 1992. In *Gender, Politics and Communication* eds. A. Sreberny and L. van Zoonen. Cresskill: Hampton Press, 53–77.

Wakefield, S. (2012). Falconry as Heritage in the United Arab Emirates. *World Archaeology* 44(2): 280–90.

Woodward, K. (2009). *Embodied Sporting Practices: Regulating and Regulatory Bodies*. New York: Palgrave Macmillan.

Xu, G. (2008). *Olympic Dreams: China and Sports, 1895–2008*. Cambridge: Harvard University Press.

Young, I. (2003). The Logic of Masculinist Protection: Reflections on the Current Security State. *Signs* 29(1): 1–25.

Yuval-Davis, N. (1997). *Gender & Nation*. London: Sage.

Chapter 8

Playing identity politics

The Gaelic Athletic Association in modern Ireland

Arlene Crampsie

Introduction

In an increasingly globalized sporting world, indigenous sports have become ever more marginalized as they fail to compete successfully with international codes for both players and spectators. The Gaelic Athletic Association (GAA) stands apart as one of a small number of exceptions, which has maintained and even increased in popularity and reach. The oft-cited explanation for this success is that the GAA is, and always has been, more than simply a sporting organization. Established in 1884, both as part of the nineteenth century cultural nationalism movement and the Victorian sporting revolution, the GAA was initially founded to preserve and cultivate Irish national pastimes. The Association spread rapidly across Ireland and today is widely reckoned as the largest amateur sporting organization in the world with 1,616 clubs in Ireland and another 398 across the globe (Duffy 2015: 78–9). From these local clubs the GAA expands upwards and outwards to a sporting body with an increasingly international profile, and yet, it remains a grassroots-driven, volunteer-led sporting organization.

The association's two main sports are the men's sports of hurling and Gaelic football. Ladies Gaelic football and camogie (an adapted form of hurling for women) have their own separate organizations, but fall under the broad umbrella of Gaelic games, as do handball and rounders. The GAA has carved the island of Ireland into a network of club territories, based largely around the Roman Catholic parish network, ensuring the presence of the GAA in every community. The resultant clubs form the grassroots base unit of the GAA, grounded in specific geographic territories. Each club is affiliated with a county board, which is answerable to a provincial council, and the overall structure is managed at an all-Ireland level by a central council and a management committee. The administrative and sporting home of the GAA is Croke Park in Dublin, the largest sports stadium in Ireland and the third largest in Europe. The association's competitions pit territories against territories at club, county, and provincial levels. Spectator interest in the games is high with over 1.5 million supporters attending inter-county games in 2014. In addition to capacity attendance in Croke Park (82,300), the 2015 All-Ireland football and hurling finals recorded peak viewership figures on Irish television channel RTÉ with 1.08 million and 919,000 respectively (Duffy 2015: 3; RTÉ Press Centre 2015).

In his seminal work, John Bale (2003: 14) discusses the ability of sport to "bind people to place through ascription," noting that it can become a medium for collective identification. Throughout its history, the GAA's commitment to preserving and promoting Irish culture and strengthening national identity has remained a strong facet of the association, as indicated by its explicitly nationalist purpose statement: "The Association is a National Organisation which has as its basic aim the strengthening of the National Identity in a 32 County Ireland through the preservation and promotion of Gaelic Games and pastimes" (GAA 2015: 5). However, unlike many other sporting organizations that promote national ideals through international competition, the GAA's commitment to identity construction has been internally focused. From its inception the GAA promoted participation in the organization as an expression of nationalism, a way for members to participate in a tangible national community. Furthermore, as both a sporting and nationalist organization, the GAA has been closely entwined with Irish politics since the association's inception as an anti-colonial force.

Despite the relatively recent emergence of academic research on sports organizations in Ireland, a number of studies from a range of disciplinary perspectives from history to political science, sociology to sports science, have examined the political elements of the GAA. These can be loosely categorized as having a focus variously on the role of the GAA in the late nineteenth century cultural nationalism movement (e.g., Garnham 2004; Rouse 1993), the fight for Irish freedom (e.g., Mandle 1987; Murphy 2009), in the contested spaces of Northern Ireland (e.g., Bairner 2003; Hassan 2003, 2005a, 2005b; Sugden and Bairner 1993), and as a nationalist identity marker in the aftermath of independence (e.g., Cronin 1998; Moore 2012).

While much of this work covers core geographic themes, geographers have been almost entirely absent from these studies (for exceptions, see Nolan 2005; Storey 2012; Whelan 1993). Another significant absence from the extant work has been any sustained critical engagement with the non-political, cultural, and social aspects of the GAA in modern Ireland (but see Conner, Chapter 13 this volume; Cronin et al. 2009, 2011; Ó Tuathaigh 2009). This chapter addresses some of these gaps by critically interrogating the role of the GAA in identity creation and evolution in modern Ireland from a geographical perspective. In doing so, I intend to expand debates over the GAA's role in identity formation beyond straightforward historical narratives of national identity to how the modern GAA has actively sought to foster a variety of socially and culturally based Irish identities. An expanded approach, I argue, requires us to examine the contested and conflicted geographies of power that emerge as attempts are made to maintain a nationalist identity in the context of a post-conflict, modern, politically divided Ireland. This chapter offers just one of a myriad ways that the GAA might be critically engaged by sport geographers, but hopefully lays the groundwork for others to follow different trajectories – both in Ireland and globally – to provide a fuller picture of the geographies that emerge when sporting associations combine the organization of their games with explicitly stated cultural and political aspirations.

The promotion of Irish national identity through the early GAA

Before embarking on an analysis of the modern GAA, it is important to understand the evolution of identity politics and geographies of power within the association. Although most GAA writers discuss the early years of the GAA in a colonial context, debates on where Ireland stood in the spectrum of colonial–imperial relations in this period abound. As Anderson and O'Dowd (2007) have noted, Ireland was at once colony and imperial center, having been incorporated as a constituent part of the United Kingdom of Great Britain and Ireland under the 1801 Act of Union. At the time of the GAA's formation in 1884, Irish nationalists were campaigning not for freedom from colonial oppression, but for independence from the imperial core (Crampsie 2014: 209–13). Regardless, Ireland was one of many nations across Europe engaged in promoting its perceived unique national identity and clamoring for official state recognition. The GAA was created, at least in part, to further this agenda.

An exemplary case of what scholars have termed "sporting nationalism," the codification of Gaelic games was an effort to promote "sporting national self-determination" (Sugden and Bairner 1993). The inscription of nationalist ideals was clear from the first meeting of the association, held on 1 November 1884. The mission statement of the meeting was to form an organization for "the preservation and cultivation of our National Pastimes and for providing rational amusement for the Irish people during their leisure hours" (*United Ireland* 1884, cited in Cronin *et al.* 2009: 4). This latter comment reflecting the Sabbatarian influence in British sports and athletics codes, which ensured that games were not played on a Sunday, the only day of rest for the average Irish person (Garnham 2004: 71–3). The selection of hurling, with its long history in Irish folklore and mythology, and the choice of three patrons representing the main pillars of Irish nationalism – the Roman Catholic church, political nationalism, and militant nationalism – ensured that, from its inception, the GAA became embroiled in the cultural nationalism movement, utilizing cultural activities to advance the cause of an Irish-Ireland. However, as the GAA spread across Ireland "like a prairie fire" (*United Irishman* 1898, cited in Garnham 2004: 65), it was the newly codified games of Gaelic football and hurling – and not necessarily the nationalist zeal of the leaders of the association – that attracted a wide-ranging membership. This amateur, community-based sporting organization quickly became an integral part of life in the communities in which it was established and has remained so up to the present day.

The overarching cause of strengthening Irish national identity was however a unifying mission of the association, particularly in its early years. In addition to actively promoting the Irish language, music, song, and dance, this was borne out in a range of rules and regulations, which limited the use of GAA spaces to loyal GAA supporters, which in turn curtailed their use of other sporting spaces. Specific legislation was enacted and enforced to ensure the primacy of Gaelic games among the nationalist community, which had the simultaneous impact of reducing competition from other sports. Of particular importance were a series of bans which blocked members of the British security forces participating in the association (Rule 21), prevented members of the GAA attending or participating in "foreign games" including soccer, rugby, cricket or hockey (Rule 27), and prohibited the playing of "foreign games" on GAA grounds (Rule 42). The GAA also placed limitations on the cultural activities of its members, similarly expelling members who were reported for attending "foreign dances," also under Rule 27.

These rules were enforced through complex webs of power, including a network of local vigilance committees, composed of a secret membership that operated as the association's secret police. They were responsible for attending foreign games and reporting individuals found in breach of the regulations to the county committee, which would then hold an inquiry and decide on the punishment. Penalties usually took the form of suspensions from the association, though repeat offenders could be expelled entirely. Nationalism thoroughly imbued the GAA's governance – so much so that all official motions, nominations, and appeals of match reports, suspensions, and bans were to be published on Irish watermarked paper and written in Irish. Failure to comply with this particular rule resulted in many motions being deemed illegal, which ensured that key decisions were often made on the basis of nationalist fidelity rather than an accurate application of the rules of the games (Cronin *et al.* 2009: 278). Thus, in order for a player or club to be successful in the GAA they were compelled to engage fully with both the sporting and nationalistic aspirations of the association, even when the rules superseded the sporting activities. For many members, those nationalistic ideals placed significant limits on their use of alternative sporting and entertainment spaces, while simultaneously socially and spatially excluding those deemed unworthy of the GAA.

While only members and those actively excluded knew the intricacies of the GAA's rules, its nationalist ethos was evident for all to witness in the spectacles of nationalist allegiance surrounding GAA games and events. As Till (2004: 355) notes "landscapes are constitutive settings made and used by individuals performing a 'recognizable' identity." For the GAA, it was through the spectacular landscapes conjured during major inter-county matches that its most explicit markers of nationalist identity were laid bare. Early GAA matches abounded in nationalist pageantry with marching bands playing nationalist anthems as teams were paraded to locations selected for the contest. Flags and banners were bedecked with nationalist symbols, as were club and county jerseys. GAA clubs and fields were given names commemorating key local and national political figures or events (Cronin 1998). Just as Johnson (1999: 53) has noted that formal iconography and symbolism associated with events such as this assist in cultivating public memory, the GAA's pre-match parades and the games themselves were central to the association's effort to cultivate a collective public memory around Irish nationalist ideals.

In 1913, the GAA acquired a new headquarters and permanent home for its games with the purchase of Jones' Road in Dublin, later renamed Croke Park. The fate of this site and Irish nationalism were to become inextricably linked on Sunday, November 21, 1920. In retaliation for the murder of British intelligence officers that morning, the British army entered Croke Park during a match between Dublin and Tipperary and opened fire, killing 14 people. This was one of the most vicious days of the War of Independence, entitled for that reason "Bloody Sunday." Croke Park was thereafter indelibly associated with both the Irish independence movement and bloodshed at the hands of British forces. In the aftermath of independence in 1921, Croke Park continued as a beacon for nationalist Ireland, hosting one of the most significant displays of nationalist spectacle: the Tailteann Games. Held in 1924, 1928, and 1932, these games were to be a modern version of the mythical annual sporting occasion begun in ancient Ireland, and were accompanied by extensive nationalist pageantry. The Games were envisioned as an opportunity to show that Ireland was taking its place once more among the free nations of the world. The staging of this state-building exercise in Croke Park further reinforced the links between the national sporting body and the emergence of the now post-colonial Irish state.

However, the post-colonial Irish state consisted of only 26 of the 32 Irish counties. The creation of Northern Ireland divided the island into two political territories, allowing northern unionists to remain part of the imperial core, while the minority northern nationalist population, many of whom were GAA members, remained colonial subjects. For the GAA, with its full 32-county organizational remit and commitment to the ideal of a united Ireland, there could be no immediate throwing off of anti-colonial rhetoric. Yet for the majority of GAA members, while they were sympathetic to the plight of those in Northern Ireland, theirs was a post-colonial reality. Although it worked as a key link between nationalists in both territories, the GAA took on a split role: a marker of post-colonial Irish identity, but also a marker of subaltern identity for those who remained in a colonial state. As the divergent realities of the two new Irelands began to evolve in the Free State and Northern Ireland, administering a political–sporting organization that provided a welcoming space for all shades of nationalism would require some very complex negotiations of power dynamics and symbolic acts on the part of the GAA.

Contesting identity politics in modern Ireland

Discussing contemporary Ireland, Alan Bairner (2003: 159–60) has succinctly observed: "there is no such thing as a single Irish national identity. Nor can one even talk legitimately of two national identities on the island of Ireland." Geographers have long called for studies of how post-colonial experiences vary across territories and through time and Craggs (2014: 39–41) has recently stressed the need to engage with "the precise periods, places and processes of decolonization" as "people, institutions and states negotiated, performed and experienced becoming postcolonial" (see also Blunt and McEwan 2002; Gilmartin and Berg 2007; Loomba 1998; Sidaway 2000). Treating the GAA as such an institutional case study, the remainder of this chapter examines how a non-state institution mediates the contrasting views of members who share a coherent national identity, but politically inhabit two different colonial spaces.

The GAA is infamous for its sluggish pace of change. This is, in part at least, a result of the complex power structures which have developed. The GAA is a committed grassroots organization with a bottom up governance structure, which enhances the democracy of the association and prevents the implementation of reactionary legislation. Conversely, this also results in frustrating delays between the conception of ideas and their execution at a national level (for more, see Hassan 2010). On several occasions in its history, the association has been seen to lag behind the will and demand of the majority of its membership. Some of the most controversial delays have occurred when issues pertaining to the association's explicitly nationalist ideals have been tabled for discussion – especially those related to removing or altering the various ban rules.

The first major nationalist rule considered for removal was Rule 27, the ban on foreign games and dances. While the association had voted to retain the legislation in the aftermath of independence, by the 1950s it had become clear to even the most casual GAA supporter that it was more often ignored than enforced. In fact, many club committees and county board officials actively assisted the breach of bans by variously ignoring violations or by placing prominent players who refused to obey the legislation on the secret vigilance committees – or "vigilante" committees as they were colloquially known (Crampsie and Fitzpatrick 2014). Throughout the 1960s, Rule 27 was the subject of heated debates. Some challenged it on the grounds that the advent of television meant that members could watch foreign games in the privacy of their own homes, while only those who went to live matches risked suspension. Others questioned the need for a ban in an independent Ireland, where the anti-colonial ideals of the early GAA were no longer relevant. To more republican-minded members and those in the north of Ireland, such partition-blindness was anathema. Those in favor of maintaining the ban argued that its removal would water down the association's nationalist ideals and its explicit commitment to achieving a 32-county Ireland. As debates wore on, the media increasingly portrayed the ban as an outdated, sectarian piece of legislation, which was exclusionary rather than protective. Eventually, the GAA voted to remove the most iconic of its anti-colonial ideals in 1971. While the GAA mantra regularly posits this decision as an indication of how the GAA moved forward and changed with public opinion, for some this loss of nationalist idealism was unforgiveable and they simply left the association. For others, they were forced to accept the decision of the majority and move forward.

Naturally, the removal of Rule 27 meant that other ban regulations were now more susceptible to repeal. However, any serious consideration of the removal of the ban on the British security forces was lost with the development of the Troubles in Northern Ireland (1968–98). Throughout this time, the GAA in the North was increasingly sought out as a key marker of a nationalist identity and, as a result, both GAA personnel and property were frequently targets of attack and suspicion. Players and supporters travelling to matches were regularly stopped, questioned, and searched by security personnel, often having their equipment impounded. Lily Spence, an Antrim camogie official, for example, recalled being stopped outside Newry en route to a game and having the team's hurls confiscated. When she opened the newspaper the following day, a headline caught her eye: "amongst the lethal weapons taken were hurling sticks" (Spence 2010). Outside of these more mundane experiences with policing, the association was also subject to attack from Loyalist paramilitaries. Despite the GAA's effort to position itself as an apolitical organization, Loyalists viewed the GAA as "the IRA at play." While it is undoubted that individual members of the association were involved in the IRA, this was never condoned nor supported by the official association. Indeed, as it attempted to maintain its apolitical stance, the GAA faced internal rancor from members who felt it should be doing more to support the nationalist cause in Northern Ireland (see Short 1984).

With the signing of the Good Friday Agreement in 1998, this internal dissent refocused around the role the GAA should play in promoting peace and reconciliation in post-conflict Ireland. A turning point in Anglo-Irish relations, the accord also marked a shift in colonial positioning across the island. The agreement required the Irish Constitution to be significantly altered so that the state no longer claimed a right to the whole territory of the island, while also introducing a condition that unification could only occur subject to majority consent in both jurisdictions. This was a historic moment, recognition of the need for grand gestures and compromise on all sides to facilitate a lasting peace. In this context pressure was brought to bear on the avowedly nationalist GAA to make a similar gesture of conciliation. This gesture was not an alteration of the GAA's commitment to achieve a 32-county Ireland, but rather the removal of Rule 21, which banned members of the British security forces from playing Gaelic games. Many GAA members felt that this symbolic gesture would show the willingness and commitment of the organization to the peace process. For these, Rule 21's elimination was a natural next step and one which had been periodically debated since 1995 (Hassan 2005b). But for those whose reality had been persecution at the hands of those same forces, this was viewed as a step too far, too soon, and one which they had always strenuously resisted. After much debate, the rule was rescinded by a majority vote in 2001. The vote drew a stark line between the GAA in the North, and the rest. Down, which had proposed the resolution, was the only northern county to support the rule's removal, while the other five northern counties stood alone in opposition.

While each of the above decisions were generally viewed as timely, the membership seemed to have little appetite to remove the last remaining anti-colonial ban, Rule 42, which prohibited the playing of foreign games on GAA grounds. These physical spaces were purchased, developed, and maintained by the work of GAA volunteers across the country, albeit with the support of various government subsidies. The idea of allowing other competing sports bodies to share in the fruits of the GAA's labor was totally unthinkable. At least, that was, until Lansdowne Road, the home of Irish soccer and rugby, was closed for redevelopment in 2007, temporarily leaving the national teams with no home venue for their international games. With Rule 42 still in effect, soccer and rugby had no option but to look across the Irish Sea for the nearest suitable stadium. Faced with the prospect of thousands of Irish sports fans leaving Ireland to support Irish teams at "home" fixtures in Cardiff or England while the recently refurbished Croke Park, a beacon of modern Ireland, lay empty, the GAA was forced to consider lifting the ban.

Once more, the association was asked to remove one of the key elements of its nationalist constitution in order to facilitate the needs of others and once more the membership was torn. This time, however, the debates were not confined to the membership; this was a national issue and all shades of sporting and political opinion weighed into the debate. The media, politicians, the general public, and a large proportion of its own membership were all cognizant of the substantial government funds that assisted in building Croke Park, and they brought this pressure to bear on the GAA. Emotional politics were also played as the GAA was variously charged with forcing Irish teams to play on foreign soil and abandoning its nationalist ideals. Those in favor of the ban stressed that opening Croke Park to soccer and rugby would necessitate welcoming foreign sports teams, including English teams and allowing the British national anthem to be played on a ground where British forces had killed innocent Irish people. For them, Croke Park was too shrouded with the weight of collective memory about the atrocities of the colonial regime during Bloody Sunday.

In the end, however, the GAA congress of 2005 voted by 227 to 97 to suspend Rule 42, paving the way for the opening of Croke Park to soccer and rugby. Despite protests outside the grounds at the first matches, the public reaction was overwhelmingly positive. When "God Save the Queen" was played for the first time in Croke Park, it was observed with full respect. The rendition of the Irish national anthem that followed, however, was the most memorable part of the occasion, ringing out across the home of Irish nationalism from voices full of emotion. The GAA and the Irish nation had taken its place as an equal beside its former colonial oppressor; there had been no catcalling and no protest within the stadium itself. For the Republic of Ireland, nationalists in Northern Ireland, and the GAA, the post-colonial era had finally begun.

A post-colonial GAA?

The status quo in Ireland's major sporting venues returned with the opening of the Aviva stadium, which replaced the old Lansdowne Road – but the GAA had changed forever. As the GAA's most trenchantly nationalist legislation was removed, the association slowly transitioned from an anti-colonial body to a body approaching a post-colonial state. Yet the erosion of the GAA's ultra-nationalist positioning was part of an ongoing repositioning that helps to explain the shifts detailed above. One of the earliest symbolic nationalistic links to fade was that between the GAA and the Roman Catholic Church. By the end of the 1970s, the playing of "Faith of Our Fathers" had ended and church dignitaries were no longer invited to throw in the ball to start matches. The exact end date of these practices is generally disputed, indicating the unremarked nature of their passing and reflecting the wider and yet very gradual diminution of the status of the Roman Catholic Church in all aspects of Irish life across the spaces and spectacles of the GAA. That is not, however, to suggest the complete decoupling of the church and sport in Ireland. On the contrary, in many areas local Catholic clergy still act as patrons of local clubs and county boards, while the recently appointed Archbishop of Cashel and Emly accepted the invitation to retain the link between his position and the patronage of the association (albeit with minimal publicity outside of his own diocese). It is clear that these are now figurehead positions that reflect the GAA membership's majority Catholic demographic but such exchanges are no longer associated with any power dynamic or national symbolism.

With the removal of both the overtly anti-colonial and religious aspects, the GAA has repositioned its nationalist rhetoric more in terms of culture and less in politics. In terms of cultural rhetoric, the place of the Irish language in the association remains strong and forms a key part of every match and related event. Announcements about substitutes, additional time to be played, safety announcements, and official attendances are all made bilingually, in Irish first. Players and their clubs are similarly introduced initially in Irish, while victory speeches from officials and winning team captains on final days also contain at least a smattering of Irish. It is this latter element that is critiqued as mere lip-service attachment to the Irish language, but GAA grounds nonetheless remain one of the few public spaces where Irish is regularly used as the primary operational language. The gap, however, between official practice and the use of Irish by players and supporters has also recently been addressed by engaging a number of high profile inter-county players in Irish language promotion campaigns and appointing dedicated Irish Language and Cultural Officers within each club. These officers are also responsible for running the Scór cultural competition, which was introduced just before the removal of Rule 27 in 1969, and fulfils the GAA's wider remit in terms of promoting Irish cultural activities such as music, song, and dance.

The GAA's culture-focused positioning was also evident at its 125th Anniversary Celebrations in 2009, where the more recent nationalistic past of the association was quietly bypassed in favor of events reinforcing the association's ancient origins in a mythical Irish past, and the role of the GAA in modern Irish society. Among a wide calendar of events were two major spectacles, both widely publicized and held in Croke Park. The first of these was the sell-out opening match of the National Football League between Dublin and Tyrone, which took place under the recently installed floodlights and was accompanied by a "spectacle of light" and entertainment from leading Irish musicians and singers. This event was designed to showcase the modern GAA's technological innovations and facilities, and its strong popular support: that an opening round league game could attract a stadium-capacity crowd was framed as a statement of the association's strength. The second event was a more traditional affair, showcasing the history and culture of the GAA and timed to coincide with the highlight of the club calendar, the club All-Ireland finals held on St. Patrick's Day. The GAA's importance in modern Ireland was once more highlighted, as key GAA figures were invited to lead the St. Patrick's Day

Parade in Dublin, before moving to Croke Park, where the parade expanded into a full-scale performance on the pitch in the interval between the hurling and football club finals. The pageantry included representations of the games of the association, the mythical Cúchulainn, and a procession of flags and traditional Irish music.

During the 125th Anniversary Celebrations, there was no mention of the early anti-colonial ethos of the GAA nor was there any reference to the deeply divisive political issues of previous years. This event could therefore be read as an attempt to rework the association's origin myth, using the long history of hurling to firmly ground the GAA in a depoliticized Irish past, which might appeal to all inhabitants of the island of Ireland, regardless of creed or politics. The event's timing to coincide with the local club finals was indicative of the direction the continuing identity repositioning of the GAA would take – as a national cultural organization operated by and for local communities. Refocusing the GAA as a champion of local community was initially made explicit by the inclusion of a Lá na gClub (Club Day) in the official calendar of 125 events and its continuation in 2010. The importance of the local club to the national organization has also become the GAA's mantra in its marketing and branding campaigns. Under sponsorship from Allied Irish Banks, high profile advertising campaigns for the club championships have stressed the importance of the club to local communities. Similarly, Supervalu's "believe in local" ad campaign asserts the significance of the local club alongside the supermarket chain's own ethos of supporting local produce.

That the GAA needed to re-emphasize the importance of the local club is uncontested and reflects on a central challenge of its increasing corporatization. Branding and marketing campaigns, a corporate tier in the redeveloped Croke Park, international sponsorship, increasing commercialization of the games, and the increasing professionalization of management levels have all created a significant gap between the grassroots membership and the national organization. In tandem with the perceived overemphasis on the inter-county championships to the detriment of club fixtures and competition, many members bemoan this altered outlook. It has even led some to suggest that the GAA was neglecting its roots and the importance of the volunteers to the entire association, "forgetting about the grassroots structures [and] forgetting about the people who gave us this wonderful heritage" (Walsh 2010). Interestingly, it has been this disconnect from the grassroots, rather than the GAA's altered political agenda, which has drawn most ire in contemporary Ireland. Viewed in this light, the recent advertisement campaigns take on an additional dimension beyond fostering a post-colonial identity – they are a very functional and practical response to members' concerns about the association's future.

The strengthening of the GAA's corporate arm has also been accompanied by a push for the association to become more inclusive, based on recent Irish demographic changes and the post-conflict context of Northern Ireland. The GAA's Inclusion and Integration Strategy 2009–15 sought to address both these issues, setting a goal that, by 2016, people of "all nationalities, ethnicities, religions, ages and abilities" would feel welcome and able to participate (GAA 2009: 11). While it is too early to judge the success of this strategy, the GAA has seen increased participation by the non-Irish national community, as well as more efforts to promote cross community awareness of Gaelic games in Northern Ireland. Overall, the changed focus of the GAA in the post-conflict era is perhaps best illustrated by the visit of Queen Elizabeth and the Duke of Edinburgh to Croke Park in May 2011, as part of their state visit to Ireland. As with every other event during their stay, they were received in the spirit of goodwill and reconciliation at the hallowed Croke Park stadium. With the backing of a united membership, the GAA as an all-island national association was finally coming to stand as a symbol of a post-colonial Irish society.

Conclusion

Catherine Nash (2002: 221) suggests that one of the most useful aspects of a post-colonial framework is that it "denotes a range of critical perspectives on the diverse histories and geographies of colonial practices, discourses, impacts and, importantly, their legacies in the present – critical engagements that often preceded and must continue long after formal political independence." This chapter has examined one uniquely Irish sporting organization through that framework, highlighting the complicated web of events and geographies through which a post-colonial identity has come to prevail in Ireland. Neither the 26 counties of the Free State of Ireland, nor the GAA can be viewed as uncontested post-colonial entities in the immediate aftermath of the creation of the Free State in 1922. It is clear, however, that the Republic of Ireland achieved a "decolonized" status well before the GAA could claim to have followed. The complicated and competing identity politics across differing segments of the membership challenged the GAA's ability to maintain the unity of an association that was all-island based. The result was the evolution of complex geographies of power within the association that saw variously an organization led from below, from above, and forced into action from outside. The GAA's complex governance structures are often blamed for its belated reaction to important issues, but, in many ways, the slow turning of the wheels of power is precisely what allowed the GAA to bring its members to consensus. In doing so, and in spite of occasional internal rancor, the GAA has overwhelmingly remained united, evolving into the largest amateur sporting organization in the world today.

In becoming post-colonial, the GAA has not entirely divested itself of its nationalistic symbolism. The tricolor is still flown and the national anthem is still played at the start of every major match. And within the GAA Official Guide, two explicitly anti-colonial statements remain:

> Since she has not control over all the national territory, Ireland's claim to nationhood is impaired. It would be still more impaired ... if she were to forsake her own games and customs in favour of the games and customs of another nation. If pride in the attributes of nationhood dies, something good and distinctive in our race dies with it. Each national quality that is lost makes us so much poorer as a Nation. Today, the native games take on a new significance when it is realised that they have been a part, and still are a part, of the Nation's desire to live her own life, to govern her own affairs.
>
> (GAA 2015: 4)

> *1.2 Basic Aim.* The Association is a National Organisation which has as its basic aim the strengthening of the National Identity in a 32 County Ireland through the preservation and promotion of Gaelic Games and pastimes.
>
> (GAA 2015: 5)

Rarely mentioned and little known, readers in Ireland today are likely to view these statements not as an active commitment by the GAA to engage in anti-colonial activity, but as relics of the rule book and a nod to a greater, more politically active past.

While it is doubtful that current GAA members would readily ascribe to this politicized rhetoric, it does beg the question of why these statements remain. The GAA and Irish nationalists have, in practice, entered a post-colonial era, but the nationalist affinities of the GAA remain firm. The change to the Irish constitution in 1998 removed the legal ideal of ownership and all-island unity, but, for the GAA, this unity is a reality. While the Irish state has only ever operated across 26 counties, the GAA has operated over 32 for its entire history. Even in the context of a post-conflict Northern Ireland, removing the organization's explicit commitment to this territorial reach would undoubtedly engender anger and discontent. It is perhaps easier to maintain the status quo of the rulebook, while simultaneously engaging in a modernizing, depoliticizing repositioning around a more local, community-focused ideology than to remove the last vestiges of the actively nationalistic, anti-colonial sporting association founded in 1884.

References

Anderson, J., and L. O'Dowd (2007). Imperialism and Nationalism: The Home Rule Struggle and Border Creation in Ireland, 1885–1925. *Political Geography* 26(8): 934–50.

Bairner, A. (2003). Sport, Nationality and Postcolonialism in Ireland. In *Sport and Postcolonialism* eds. J. Bale and M. Cronin. Oxford: Berg, 159–74.

Bale, J. (2003). *Sports Geography*. London: Routledge.

Blunt, A., and C. McEwan (2002). *Postcolonial Geographies*. New York: Continuum.

Craggs, R. (2014). Postcolonial Geographies, Decolonization, and the Performance of Geopolitics at Commonwealth Conferences. *Singapore Journal of Tropical Geography* 35(1): 39–55.

Crampsie, A. (2014). Creating Citizens from Colonial Subjects: Reforming Local Government in Early Twentieth Century Ireland. *Historical Geography* 42: 208–28.

Crampsie, A., and F. Fitzpatrick (2014). Vigilance and Vigilantes: An Oral History of the Gaelic Athletic Association's Ban on Foreign Games. Paper presented at the International Oral History Association Conference, IOHA. Barcelona, Spain.

Cronin, M. (1998). Enshrined in Blood the Naming of Gaelic Athletic Association Grounds and Clubs. *The Sports Historian* 18(1): 90–104.

Cronin, M., M. Duncan, and P. Rouse (2009). *The GAA: A People's History*. Cork: The Collins Press.

Cronin, M., M. Duncan, and P. Rouse (2011). *The GAA: County By County*. Cork: The Collins Press.

Duffy, P. (2015). *Director General's Annual Report for 2014*. Available at: www.gaa.ie/content/documents/2015AnnualReport.pdf (accessed October 22, 2015).

GAA (2009). *Inclusion and Integration Strategy, 2009–2015*. Available at: www.gaa.ie/content/documents/publications/inclusion_and_integration/GAA_Inclusion_Integration_Strategy_100110225137.pdf (accessed October 27, 2015).

GAA (2015). *Official guide – Part 1: Containing the Constitution and Rules of the G.A.A., Revised and Corrected up to date, and Published by Authority of the Central Council*. Available at: www.gaa.ie/content/documents/publications/official_guides/2015%20Official%20Guide%20-%20Part%201.pdf (accessed June 12, 2015).

Garnham, N. (2004). Accounting for the Early Success of the Gaelic Athletic Association. *Irish Historical Studies* 34(133): 65–78.

Gilmartin, M., and L. Berg (2007). Locating Postcolonialism. *Area* 39(1): 120–4.

Hassan, D. (2003). Still Hibernia Irredenta? The Gaelic Athletic Association, Northern Nationalists and Modern Ireland. *Culture, Sport, Society: Cultures, Commerce, Media, Politics* 6(1): 92–110.

Hassan, D. (2005a). Sport, Identity and Irish Nationalism in Northern Ireland. In *Sport and the Irish: Histories, Identities, Issues* ed. A. Bairner. Dublin: University College Dublin Press, 123–39.

Hassan, D. (2005b). The Gaelic Athletic Association, Rule 21, and Police Reform in Northern Ireland. *Journal of Sport and Social Issues* 29(1): 60–78.

Hassan, D. (2010). Governance and the Gaelic Athletic Association: Time to Move Beyond the Amateur Ideal? *Soccer and Society* 11(4): 414–27.

Johnson, N. (1999). The Spectacle of Memory: Ireland's Remembrance of the Great War, 1919. *Journal of History Geography* 25(1): 36–56.

Loomba, A. (1998). *Colonialism/Postcolonialism*. London: Routledge.

Mandle, W. F. (1987). *The Gaelic Athletic Association and Irish Nationalist Politics: 1884–1924*. London: Christopher Helm.

Moore, C. (2012). *The GAA v Douglas Hyde: The Removal of Ireland's First President as GAA Patron*. Cork: The Collins Press.

Murphy, W. (2009). The GAA during the Irish Revolution, 1913–23. In *The Gaelic Athletic Association, 1884–2009* eds. M. Cronin, W. Murphy, and P. Rouse. Dublin: Irish Academic Press, 61–76.

Nash, C. (2002). Cultural Geography: Postcolonial Cultural Geographies. *Progress in Human Geography* 26(2): 219–30.

Nolan, W. (2005). *The Gaelic Athletic Association in Dublin, 1884–2000*. Dublin: Geography Publications.

Ó Tuathaigh, G. (2009). The GAA as a Force in Irish Society: An Overview. In *The Gaelic Athletic Association, 1884–2009* eds. M. Cronin, W. Murphy, and P. Rouse. Dublin: Irish Academic Press, 237–56.

Rouse, P. (1993). The Politics of Culture and Sport in Ireland: A History of the GAA Ban on Foreign Games, 1884–1971. Part One: 1884–1921. *International Journal of the History of Sport* 10(3): 333–60.

RTÉ Press Centre (2015). GAA All-Ireland Football Final is Most-Watched Show on Irish Television So Far This Year as Over One Million Viewers Tune in to Live Match on RTÉ2. *RTÉ Press Centre*, September 21. Available at: http://presspack.rte.ie/2015/09/21/gaa-all-ireland-football-final-is-most-watched-show-on-irish-television-so-far-this-year-as-over-one-million-viewers-tune-in-to-live-match-on-rte2/ (accessed November 9, 2015).

Short, C. (1984). *The Ulster GAA Story, 1884–1984*. Monaghan: Comhairle Uladh CLG.

Sidaway, J. (2000). Postcolonial Geographies: An Exploratory Essay. *Progress in Human Geography* 24(4): 591–612.

Spence, L. (2010). Audio Recording Oral History Interview, OHP/AN/1/3, December 1, by A. Crampsie. *GAA Oral History Project Collection, 2008–2012*, GAA Museum, Croke Park, Dublin, Ireland.

Storey, D. (2012). Heritage, Culture and Identity: The Case of Gaelic Games. In *Sport, History and Heritage: Studies in Public Representation* eds. J. Hill, K. Moore, and J. Wood. Woodbridge: The Boydell Press, 223–34.

Sugden, D., and A. Bairner (1993). *Sport, Sectarianism and Society in a Divided Ireland*. Leicester: Leicester University Press.

Till, K. (2004). Political Landscapes. In *A Companion to Cultural Geography* eds. J. Duncan, N. Johnson, and R. Schein. Malden: Blackwell Publishing, 347–64.

Walsh, W. (2010). Questionnaire Response, OHP/CK/2/21, 18 February, *GAA Oral History Project Collection, 2008–2012*, GAA Museum, Croke Park, Dublin, Ireland.

Whelan, K. (1993). The Geography of Hurling. *History Ireland* 1(1): 27–31.

Part II

Sports, community, and urban space

Chapter 9

Soccer and the mundane politics of belonging

Latino immigrants, recreation, and spaces of exclusion in the rural US South

Lise Nelson[1]

Introduction

"Oh, they don't let Mexicans play on those fields."

This matter-of-fact comment was made to me during a 2010 interview with Alejandro, a 33-year-old undocumented immigrant who had lived and worked in Rabun County, Georgia, for the previous 12 years.[2] His comment emerged in the context of describing how, despite long hours on two different jobs to help support a wife and three children, he loves to play soccer at least once a week. Yet he had never played on the plentiful and often-empty sports fields that happened to be right next to where we were sitting during the interview (see Figure 9.1). His comment led me to

Figure 9.1 Maintained and lighted soccer and baseball fields run by the Rabun County Recreation Department, 2012 (source: Lise Nelson).

ask about soccer as I continued to interview adult male Latinos for a larger study in Rabun County. These subsequent interviews, conducted between 2010 and 2012, repeatedly affirmed that Latino immigrants – documented or otherwise – were not allowed to play soccer on sports fields in the community. This is not a formal rule to be found in any recreation department handbook, but a de facto practice. The only space Latino immigrants could access for soccer was an abandoned parking lot, a space prone to serious injury and bloodletting (see Figure 9.2). Despite the dangers of playing on it, a group of 10–15 Latino men played on this concrete "field" almost nightly during the summer months during our visits to northern Georgia.

This chapter examines daily struggles over belonging and the right to recreation for Latino immigrants living in the rural South, drawing on research in Rabun County, Georgia – a "new destination" community that in 1990 was categorized by the US Census as 99.6 percent white. A small group of researchers, including myself, arrived in Rabun County in 2010 to conduct qualitative research exploring the emergence of immigrant-based labor regimes in the context of rural gentrification. We hypothesized that gentrification processes drove the astonishing 1,760 percent increase in Latino residents in the county between 1990 and 2010, as immigrants were actively recruited to work in construction, landscaping, and a range

Figure 9.2 The concrete parking lot used as a "field" by adult Latino soccer players in Rabun County, GA, 2000s–2014 (source: Lise Nelson).

of service industries tied to the arrival of wealthy, white "amenity" migrants to the area (Nelson *et al.* 2015). Perhaps this growth was not a surprising development given the extent to which immigrant-based labor regimes were expanding numerically and geographically during the 1990s across the United States (Kandel and Cromartie 2004; Zuñiga and Hernández-León 2005). Nevertheless, it was certainly completely new to Rabun County and to scholars of rural gentrification in the U.S., who until recently tended to ignore the arrival of immigrant workers in high-amenity, gentrifying rural locales in the 1990s and beyond (Nelson and Nelson 2011).

To understand shifting labor markets and geographies of social reproduction, as well as explore how employers recruited immigrant workers to relatively isolated locales, we conducted fieldwork in Rabun County between 2010 and 2012. During three visits our research team conducted 128 interviews with employers, workers (immigrant and non-immigrant), gentrifiers (wealthy, white amenity migrants), and city and county officials, as well as other "locals" (the folks who usually trace their heritage back eight to nine generations). We undertook participant observation of public spaces throughout the county, in addition to collecting local textual sources from real estate ads to local planning documents. The focus of our efforts was to gather data on immigrant migration, work, and housing histories; on employer recruitment and labor practices; and on the ways various groups were negotiating belonging in everyday life. In all these areas and topics, we were attentive to the intersections of race, class, gender, and legal status in producing landscapes of production and social reproduction.

Soccer and the politics of public space were not initially on our agenda, yet we were forced to grapple with the significance of the history, contemporary practice, and contested meanings of soccer for Latino male residents in the community (Latina women generally did not play soccer). It became clear that soccer games represent a set of spatial practices that spoke directly to the profound tensions between economic recruitment and social–civic exclusion faced by low-wage, racialized, and "illegal" workers. After our conversation with Alejandro, interviewees again and again confirmed that "Mexicans" (as all Latino residents were often labeled) were not allowed to play soccer on the county's many well-groomed, public fields. It did not matter if one was documented or undocumented, no adult Latino soccer player we met felt entitled to venture onto a formal, public field to play soccer for either a pick-up game or formal one.

Through players' stories and a critical reading of landscape, this chapter explores the history of a short-lived, public Latino soccer league that played for three years between 2001 and 2003 and the subsequent emergence of the "parking lot" status quo for Latino soccer players in Rabun County. The analysis contributes to this volume's effort to apply critical social theory to sports geographies, by considering how the spaces of soccer – including exclusion from such spaces – reflect and enact immigrant residents' social-political exclusion in a new destination community. Spaces of soccer shed insight into how race, class, and narratives of illegality become imbricated into daily life and shape the mundane social relations of belonging, findings that build on the burgeoning literature that uses fine-grained ethnographic approaches to exploring belonging and identity in new destination communities.[3] Before turning to a discussion of soccer, the following section considers the political economic forces that recruited immigrants to Rabun County, as well as overviewing the spatial architecture of life in a place that demands immigrants' productive labor, but excludes their social, including recreating, bodies.

Contexts

Rabun County sits at the southern edge of the Appalachia mountain range in the northeastern corner of Georgia. A triangular jurisdiction sandwiched between North and South Carolina, it can be reached in about 90 minutes from Atlanta. With 377 square miles of area and a total population of less than 16,235 (2013), Rabun County is a decidedly rural place. Beyond its low population density, the county is unique in that nearly 75 percent of its land area is held up by the U.S. Forest Service or Georgia Power Company. Its bucolic agricultural valleys are thus surrounded by largely intact forests, creating pristine views and a deep sense of rurality from a bygone era (on how nostalgia for rurality and nature are important drivers of rural gentrification, see McCarthy 2007; Smith 1998). In addition to "pristine" rural landscapes, the county contains three large reservoirs, created when power generation dams were built in the 1930s: Lake Rabun, Lake Burton, and Seed Lake. Wealthy families from Atlanta began to build cottages along their shores starting in the 1930s; however, the scale and nature of this amenity-driven transformation remained relatively contained until the 1990s. It was in that decade that highway improvements shortened travel time from Atlanta, but, most importantly, the urban "growth machine" linked to globalization allowed Atlanta's elites to accumulate the wealth essential to Rabun's rural gentrification boom (on Atlanta's growth, see Rutheiser 1996). The rustic summer cottages of the 1930s were systematically torn down and replaced with much larger homes designed for long-term (part-year and year-round) residence. These landscape transformations in rural Georgia are representative of national and global phenomena: from Jackson Hole, Wyoming, and Catalunya, Spain, to Uruguay, rural gentrification has become a global phenomenon (Álvarez-Rivadulla 2007; Paniagua 2002).

By the early 2000s, Rabun County was experiencing a construction boom. Rapid expansion of second-home and permanent "amenity migrant" home development occurred not only on the Lakes – now the domain of millionaires and celebrities in homes such as that shown in Figure 9.3 – but also in the valleys throughout the county. A 2005 local newspaper editorial urged readers to see the benefits of this growth:

> At no time in Rabun's history has the growth of the business sector been more pronounced. And the list of business additions doesn't even touch the growth being seen in the construction industry because of the purchase of second and vacation homes here, or the new families that move to Rabun seemingly every week. Change is in the air. Let's not lose sight that change is inevitable and can be an incredibly good thing.
>
> (Clayton Tribune 2005)

While local newspaper coverage of the gentrification boom was robust throughout the late 1990s and 2000s, there was relatively little mention of its relationship to the arrival of Latino immigrant workers during the same period, workers brought in for construction, roofing, landscaping, and other service businesses. Local media coverage of the growing Latino immigrant population instead focused on Latinos who were accused of committing crimes, overcrowded housing conditions in select apartment buildings in town where immigrants were often congregated, or new demands for ELL courses in the local public schools.

Figure 9.3 Home on Lake Burton, GA, emblematic of the kinds of homes being built since the 1990s, and the class of gentrifiers this area has attracted (source: Lise Nelson).

Despite skewed media representations of immigrant residents during the gentrification boom, interviews with *employers* suggest that hiring Latino immigrant workers was key to their ability to meet growing demand for construction, maintenance, landscaping, and other services linked to the arrival of wealthy amenity migrants. In addition to simply meeting a new level of demand, many businesses sought to speed up their operations: if they had typically built a house in nine months, the expectations of wealthy, urban clients pushed that to five months. Through a range of circumstances, employers began to tap into Atlanta-based Latino immigrant labor pools. What may have started out as a stopgap measure led to profound transformation: by the 2000s employers in a number of gentrification-linked sectors viewed Latino immigrants as critical to the productivity and profitability of their businesses. Structural positioning shaped by poverty, race, and "illegality" led many low-wage immigrants to become "compliant workaholics" (Harrison and Lloyd 2012), and less likely to protest uneven work schedules (for details on recruitment strategies and labor regimes, see Nelson *et al.* 2015). Although this proved to be a boon to employers, it relied on inherently exploitative conditions for most immigrants, who were at the same time eyed suspiciously by those white residents not profiting from these new labor regimes.

Spaces of social reproduction for immigrant families and workers mirrored and structured this flexibility of the workforce. During the peak of labor demand (2004–08) one large, overcrowded apartment complex in Clayton (the county seat of Rabun) became coded as "Mexican," as nonimmigrant white residents had largely moved out by the early 2000s. Located in walking distance from downtown, but relatively hidden from the highway, the complex is conveniently located next to a laundromat. This laundromat eventually became the "day laborer" site for the county – a place where white residents would go to find short-term workers for small house projects. A *tienda mexicana* also opened nearby, offering money transfers and fresh tortillas to immigrant residents.

This concentrated space of Latino social reproduction, visible yet invisible because every local knows it is there but it remains largely invisible to the area's aesthetic and commodified landscapes, is complemented in Rabun County by dispersed immigrant housing usually afforded by a trailer, sometimes located deep in the woods but not uncommonly in an employer's backyard. For low-wage immigrant residents in such dispersed settlements, daily highway commutes can be especially challenging: Georgia does not grant driver's licenses to undocumented immigrants and it has expanded the ability of local police to send fingerprints and photos to Homeland Security, and hold suspects while their immigration status is checked (on immigration enforcement and local policing, see Coleman 2012). For many Latino immigrants, work is plentiful but life and spatial mobility is a struggle no matter how hard they work.

Finding a space to play

In 2012, the only space for adult men to play soccer in Rabun County was the parking lot shown in Figure 9.2, though we learned over time that there had been two or three years in the early 2000s when a Latino soccer league formed and played in Rabun County. Lacking any archival sources confirming its existence (the local paper did not cover its games, for example), we reconstructed the history of this short-lived Latino soccer league that stretched from Cornelia, Georgia (45 minutes south of Clayton), to Franklin, North Carolina (25 minutes to the north), through analyzing immigrant residents' narratives. We can speculate *why* local newspapers did not deem this league worth covering despite ample attention to youth and adult sports leagues in the county, but suffice it to say it is a history made visible by the stories of immigrants themselves and not formal textual sources.

José and Pedro, interviewed jointly in July 2011, were among the founders of this soccer league. We approached them for interviews because they worked in gentrification-linked sectors, in their case, restaurants. The two were among the "old-timers" of immigrant residents – they had lived and worked in Rabun County for 16 and 18 years respectively. In talking about their move to Rabun County, and work and life after they arrived, José described the origins of the soccer league:

> In that time [in the early 2000s] I met Pedro. We were younger then, and we both played soccer. We decided to begin a league here in Rabun County.... We were three to four teams. Oh, at first it was just two.... [Pedro] is from Michoacán and I am from Guanajuato. The teams were always divided by place of origin. So we used to say "we are going to play a game on Sunday." There really wasn't anything else to do.

As they planned to organize soccer among their friends, their main difficulty was finding a field. As Pedro described it, "Oh, yes, we went there [to the recreation department] but they said no. [They said] that there *were* leagues and that all the fields were occupied [by other sports], and besides only a minority play soccer." They described finally approaching the Sheriff's office with their request, and he granted them permission to play for two or three seasons on a field behind the library and the civic center (the Sheriff later confirmed this to me in an interview; see Figure 9.4).

It is important to note that the field in question was and is not a sports field. Instead, it is and was an empty, weed-filled space that the players themselves mowed and maintained when they were using it. José described getting access to this field:

Figure 9.4 Field behind the civic center auditorium (three blocks from the center of downtown Clayton), 2012, long after the Latino soccer league had stopped playing there (source: Lise Nelson).

I went to ask for permission to use that field behind the Civic Center. They told me that yes, they would let us use it. I spoke with the Sheriff. I asked him permission to see whether they would let us play, because there were people who wanted to play and instead of them doing something else [i.e., getting into trouble], it would be better if they came to play soccer. They said "yes, as long as there are no problems," but, they said "this field we are going to eventually destroy to make a parking lot. Until this happens, you can play." ... Then a few years later we went again to renew our permission, and they said no. The explanation was that they were going to build the parking lot. But they have not done anything to that field.

It was after they were denied access to the field behind the civic center that the parking lot they currently use (Figure 9.2) became the de facto space for adult male Latino soccer players in the county. Without access to a field, most withdrew from participating in the larger, formal league although handful continued to make the drive to Franklin, North Carolina, to play real games there.

As we began to raise the soccer question with respondents for our gentrification project, conflicting stories arose about *why* they were kicked off the empty, unused space in 2003–04 (timelines are fuzzy in these reconstructed narratives). The most common explanation we heard from immigrant soccer players was that "we brought it on ourselves" because spectators (not players, was the general consensus) would drink beer as they watched. Many respondents acknowledged that it sometimes got out of hand, and there were often garbage issues that were not always success-fully managed, despite the players putting out trashcans. This, some argued, precipitated the waning of the police department's original support for their use of the field, but it also created other problems. One player, Ramón (age 42 in 2011), reported that, after a few years of the league,

> the police would put up *retenes* [checkpoints] right here on this street leaving the field. And because many people watching were drinking they knew that it was a secure way of getting money – when you are driving drunk and have no license, that costs you $1,200 in fines.

He thought these checkpoints made more people nervous about playing and watching. The Sheriff, when interviewed, was vague about the reasons for withdrawing support for the league's field access, but he also men-tioned drinking at the game and a sense that it was becoming unruly.

While they lasted, the soccer games represented an important site for immigrant residents in Rabun County to gather socially – for kids and families to watch the game, and enjoy food and beer together. This is not surprising given the social norms and sense of community that emerges from local soccer matches throughout Latin America (Nadel 2014). There, local soccer teams are often a regular gathering place, not just for players but for whole communities. It is a time for eating, drinking, and socializ-ing. Yet as this normal cultural practice from the perspective of immigrants became more regular, and the crowds became larger during a period of increased immigrant settlement in Rabun County (it increased steadily until the 2008 housing bust), one can imagine that white residents came to view them explicitly, or responded to them subconsciously, as a racialized threat. In listening to the history of the league, one wonders whether, as the crowds grew over time in the "hidden" field behind the civic center, the broader, overwhelmingly white community began to get explicitly nervous (e.g., sending in complaints), or whether the police shut down the space after a few years in *anticipation* of complaints. This is speculation, since no white respondents during our interviews, except for the Sheriff himself, acknowledged or claimed awareness that the league existed. Although seeing immigrants in spaces of labor had become normalized by the early 2000s, their gathering and socializing in *public space* was rare outside the coded "Hispanic" space of the laundromat and *tienda mexicana* men-tioned earlier.

The different explanations for why the league was kicked off the civic center field beg the question of why they were denied access to regular facilities run through the recreation department in the first place. If the players had access to the recreation department facilities, it might have been easier to regulate drinking, trash collection, etc., such that it would not put the onus on the players themselves to "police" the crowds and their use of the space. The fact that the Latino adult soccer league was only allowed to play in marginalized, unimproved, and semi-hidden space not only embodies their socio-political and racialized subordination, but it could easily have contributed to the local communities' perception of the newcomers as a threat to prevailing social and spatial orders. They were playing in marginal, unsanctioned space – or at least unsanctioned in the public eye, as it was the result of a private and verbal agreement with the Sheriff and not covered in the local paper. As the crowds grew, this anxiety may have deepened in ways less imaginable if (instead) Latino bodies had been gathering at a lighted and designated sports field next to the county recreation center.

Thus the most interesting, and troublesome, continuity in hearing the players' stories was not the lack of unanimity about why they were kicked off the unmaintained civic center field, but the universal normalization of their exclusion from *formal* sports fields. No immigrant or white resident we spoke to explicitly contested this exclusion. While a number of immigrant participants did acknowledge "racism" as a cause for getting kicked off the civic center field, it was not framed as something they considered questioning. Instead, most treated it as something they had to adjust to: if they wanted to play soccer they had to risk playing on the concrete parking lot or drive to Franklin, North Carolina (25 miles), or south to Cornelia (47 miles). Given that a majority of our respondents did not have a driver's license, driving was a particularly risky proposition that further limited their freedom of recreation.

The traces of this league, and the spatial politics of exclusion reflected in its demise, are still visible in the landscape. Behind the civic center the field still sits, covered largely in two-foot high switch grass.[4] Next to the empty grassy expanse there is a sign, which reads:

> Noticia: Este campo es para usarse por medio de reservación. Para reservar: Llamar 706–212–2149 o 706–982–9432. Uselo bajo su propio riesgo. *No bebidas alcoholicas *Por favor no tire basura *Remueva o levante toda la basura cuando se retire del campo. No envasas de vidrio.

> [Notice: This field is only for use with prior reservation. To reserve, call: 706–212–2149 o 706–982–9432. Use at your own risk. No alcoholic beverages allowed, please do not leave garbage, remove all garbage when you leave the field. No glass containers allowed.]
>
> (*Author's translation*)

Rather than being a sign of the league's historical *presence*, it is a sign of its exclusion, and the ways this exclusion is racialized. There is no English version of this sign at the site. This might make sense to white locals, as there is really no reason to tell English speakers they cannot use the field. White, presumably "legal" subjects are vested with rights to the ample sports fields and recreational facilities maintained by the County and so would not be looking to play on an uneven, weed-filled space with no lighting. It is clearly directed at an(other) audience. Although the sign performs a gesture of bureaucratic rationality – you simply need to call this number to reserve the field – it had stood for nearly a decade on a site that was in fact not available for reservation. Permission to play soccer had been revoked, so calling that number would not lead to access to that space. The sign instead marked racialized exclusion, broadcasting to any immigrant considering playing on that field that it is not allowed.

By 2004, most adult Latino soccer players who wanted to play in a formal soccer league travelled the 25 miles north to Franklin, North Carolina, where a Latino soccer league continues to thrive. Despite the dangers of driving the distance, a number of Latino men make the trip on a weekly basis. One of these men is Victor, age 30, whom I interviewed on a return research trip in 2015. Victor described the day that he started playing soccer again after a long time away from the sport:

> One day they [co-workers] said, "What are you doing on Sunday? Join us to play soccer!" Oh, man! It had been three years since I touched a ball. I was very emotional. I went to buy the equipment, with anticipation I got dressed. I got to play with a good team, all Mexicans. But they saw I could play well, and they said "please play with us on Sundays." This for me was a luxury. My life then was work, work. Soccer for me was a passion in my own country, but I had left it behind because of the commitment I had to work, to send money to my family. For me soccer was a dream and nothing else.

Victor had migrated from Guatemala to Los Angeles in 2009 and later moved to Georgia. He worked in masonry, usually building stone walls for wealthy clients in the hinterlands of Rabun County and into North Carolina. He described the suffering he experienced crossing through Mexico and then over the U.S. border, as well as the exploitation he experienced in California and his escape from those difficult conditions by coming to the U.S. South. He spent the first three years in California "working, working, working" because his motivation for leaving his Guatemalan home was to get his father out of debt. In the beginning, Victor's wages were meager – often just $60 per week – forcing him to work long hours in order to live and send a little money home. In that situation, he said, "I forgot all about soccer," even though he had once played for a semi-professional team.

After his move to Georgia, he continued to struggle, but eventually landed steady employment in masonry, earning more money and Sundays off. He said that the day his coworkers invited him to play soccer was "a dream come true."

For Victor and other adult Latino men, soccer and a space to play is key to their sense of well-being and masculinity. But because there is no space to play league soccer in Rabun County, they regularly risk getting pulled over by the police on the drive. Driving that distance is a risky proposition given the new authority accorded to local police under the "Secure Communities" program to check the immigration status of any person pulled over or booked into jail (see Coleman 2012). Yet the men we interviewed do this week after week because it is their only break from work and it feeds their body and soul. Those respondents in Rabun County who played in Franklin regularly were often living without their families in the United States, whereas soccer players with families were more likely to resort to playing in the concrete parking lot in Figure 9.2 – a site more dangerous in terms of injuries during play, but safer in terms of avoiding the risks of driving without a license.

Discussion

In *Immigrant Farmworkers and Citizenship in Rural California: Playing Soccer in the San Joaquin Valley*, anthropologist Hugo Santos-Gómez (2014) explores local struggles over a space to play for a Latino soccer league as an entry-point for considering the shifting parameters of citizenship and civil society in a community with a long history of farmworker settlement. He argues that farmworkers' success in building a league and getting access to fields – despite strong resistance from many white residents who fought them using local school fields for their games – embodied a shift locally toward acknowledging "farmworkers as legitimate members of the community, i.e., entitled to certain rights and obligations" (Santos-Gómez 2014: 13). This public battle, in which they threatened to launch public protests if excluded from the school fields where they had been playing (with permission of the school board), crystallized an unprecedented sense of political agency on the part of Latino residents, many of whom were farmworkers or had parents who had been farmworkers when they arrived in the community.

This compelling ethnography of soccer among immigrant men in central California testifies to the ways the local and mundane politics of sports can shed insight into identity, politics, and belonging in the context of globalization as global migration flows of labor deterritorialize and reterritorialize labor markets and cultural markers of difference. His approach is important given that the literature on sport geographies has often taken as its focus professional leagues, national or global federations involved in sporting competition (e.g., Conner 2014; Huish and Darnell 2014; Shobe 2008), stadiums and the politics of urban space (Bale 1993, 2001; see Friedman, Lee, Chapters 12 and 10 this volume), or the reading of sports as a cultural performance or landscape (Bale and Vertinsky 2004). Santos-Gómez (2014) points the way toward a scaling down sports geographies. His ethnographic approach takes on sports as a critical dimension of social relations and identity formation, as they are embedded in broader political-economic dynamics, regional histories, and embodied cultural politics (see also, Wise, Chapter 15 this volume).

The research presented in this chapter builds on this work in two ways and contributes to the revitalization and rethinking of sports geographies as articulated by contributors to this volume. First, the case from Rabun County, Georgia, is about the politics of soccer in the rural US South, a context quite distinct from Central California and one that sheds light on the *uneven* politics of soccer and belonging for Latino immigrant communities in the United States. The Central California location is one with a much longer history of in-migration and settlement of Latino immigrant workers and Mexican-American residents (both US-born and naturalized citizens), tied to the political economy of farm-work, as well as a long history of organizing for farmworker rights. The community where Santos-Gómez conducted research is over 50 percent Latino, which creates its own dynamics even though the power structure remains predominantly white (elected leaders, etc.) and racial hierarchies are still profound. The Latino community there is not averse to threatening public protests if the school district were to revoke its permission to play on the fields. Santos-Gómez tells a story of the struggle over soccer as representing an achievement of the expansion of Latino citizenship and civic involvement.

The soccer players in Rabun County, in contrast, are recent immigrant arrivals in a "new destination" community with little history of Latino presence prior to the early 1990s, and within a regional racial formation quite distinct from the US West. Immigrants in rural northern Georgia are racialized as "illegal" and undeserving subjects at a level not apparent in Santos-Gómez's analysis (on regional racial formations in the South, see Winders 2005, 2007). In fact, Santos-Gómez hardly mentions race or legal status in his otherwise in-depth investigation, nor are these concepts theorized in relation to citizenship and the spatial politics of soccer raised in his book. That Santos-Gómez (2014) does not focus on narratives of legality/illegality in the struggle over a space to play is not surprising given that the regional politics of illegality is distinct in the Central Valley. A significant percentage of Latino/Latina residents in central California are US born or documented (the latter due to the legacy of the 1986 Immigration Reform and Control Act). That enfranchised population, in conjunction with the legacy of Chicano and farmworker movements of the 1970s, produces a politics in which "illegality" as justification for exclusion is unacceptable.

The majority of Latino immigrants in Rabun County are undocumented and struggling to move safely about the community on a daily basis, leaving little possibility to imagine protesting against white political authorities denying them access to formal sports fields. What the case of soccer politics in Rabun County highlights is the need to consider regional racial formations and political economic contexts of reception as we explore how spaces of play operate as mechanisms of inclusion or exclusion in immigrant-receiving communities. In this respect, the story of soccer in California is nearly opposite that of "new destination" Georgia, where local communities' proscription of immigrant bodies playing soccer on maintained sports fields was not just about denying them a (humane) space of play, but a process intimately constituted by, and reflective of, broader spatial architectures of daily life that solidified processes of racialized social-civic exclusion.

My second contribution to Santos-Gómez's work, and advancing critical geographical analyses of sports, is to call for more conceptual attention to race and illegality as constitutive of the mundane spatial politics of sport. The important and critical work on race and professional sports notwithstanding (Hylton 2009), this literature has tended to focus on media representations of race and the cultural politics of professional athletes. It examines cultural representations of sport visible at broader scales to consider how they are constituted by and reaffirm existing racial formations and white hegemony. This research accords less attention to more informal spaces of play and recreation at the local scale, within the embodied politics of everyday life, local histories, and regional political economies. Geographers drawing on ethnographic and feminist methodologies have important contributions to make in expanding our approach to "sports geographies" that attends to the local, embodied (racialized, gendered, sexualized) spatial politics of sports and recreation. It is a move that expands conceptually and methodologically the kinds of questions being asked by sports scholars.

Finally, while we are rethinking the boundaries, theories, and methodologies used to study the geography of sport, it is important to recognize how sports represent important and unique entry points into a range of other debates in geography – in this case over space, territory, and nation. My research treats soccer as a way *into* the spatial and deeply racialized politics of exclusion directed at low-wage immigrants living in the United States, processes often studied at broader scales or in relation to more visible geographies of violence and exclusion. The militarization and hardening of the actual border between the US and Mexico has been accompanied by a hardening of the discursive rhetoric of illegality and the assumed criminality of low-wage Latino immigrants. As Joseph Nevins (2002: 147) writes:

This is because the "illegal" is someone who is officially out of place – in a space where he does not belong. Thus, the official relationship of the "illegal alien" to the particular national space in which he finds himself defines his status. The practice of territoriality – the effort to exert influence over people and/or phenomena by asserting control over a defined geographic area – reinforces the designation of the "illegal."

How do the dynamics identified by Nevins become refracted at the local scale, once these "illegal" subjects are deep within the territory of the nation? Complementing work on the local policing of national boundaries for undocumented immigrants (e.g., Coleman 2012), soccer provides an important way into considering how the spatial politics of national bordering are refracted in daily life. National discourses of normalized exclusion provided a logic for the exclusion of certain bodies and activities from formal sports fields in Rabun County. The brief window of opportunity for a soccer league to arise in the community in the early 2000s was shut quickly, as groups of immigrants gathered and socialized in public yet unsanctioned space for sport. The sign barring use of their old field signifies this exclusion, lying in stark contrast to the deep dependence and need for immigrant labor in these locales.

Notes

1 Acknowledgements. I am grateful to the women and men in Rabun County who shared their stories and perspectives during the course of this research, as well as their friendship and hospitality. The broader rural gentrification project, from which this analysis emerged, was developed in collaboration with co-investigator Peter B. Nelson (Middlebury College, Vermont). I am also appreciative of the work of two graduate research assistants, Laurie Trautman (now of Western Washington University) and Graciela "Meche" Lu (University of Oregon). The rural gentrification and Latino immigration project was made possible by funding from the National Science Foundation, Geography and Regional Science Program (BCS-0852104 and BCS-0851375).
2 All names used here are pseudonyms.
3 While a range of scholarship has been published on new destination communities, this work has centrally focused on new urban destinations (Massey 2008; Winders 2013), or rural areas shaped by industrial restructuring such as meatpacking plants (Broadway and Stull 2006; Marrow 2011). Our broader project was focused on gentrification as an important yet overlooked driver of new Latino immigrant rural settlement patterns in the 1990s and beyond.
4 The full space of the field used in the early 2000s was not *empty* by 2015. Approximately one-third of it is now used as a community garden, founded in 2010. Two-thirds of it remains empty and none of it has been made into a parking lot. The community garden project was spearheaded by a group of white, middle-class newcomers/gentrifiers enacting their relationship to nature and perceptions of rurality. Although also newcomers, their class, race, and presumed legality provided them the "right" to convert this public space to their own vision of leisure in a way that was not possible for the Latino immigrants.

References

Álvarez-Rivadulla, M. (2007). Golden Ghettos: Gated Communities and Class Residential Segregation in Montevideo, Uruguay. *Environment and Planning A* 39(1): 47–63.

Bale, J. (1993). *Sport, Space, and the City*. New York: Routledge.

Bale, J. (2001). The Changing Face of Football: Stadiums and Communities. *Soccer and Society* 1(1): 91–102.

Bale, J., and P. Vertinsky (2004). *Sites of Sport: Space, Place, Experience*. New York: Routledge.

Broadway, M., and D. Stull (2006). Meat Processing and Garden City, KS: Boom and Bust. *Journal of Rural Studies* 22(1): 55–66.

Clayton Tribune (2005). Editorial: Growth has Benefits. *The Clayton Tribune*, 8 September. A6.

Coleman, M. (2012). The "Local" Migration State: The Site-Specific Devolution of Immigration Enforcement in the U.S. South. *Law and Policy* 34(2): 159–89.

Conner, N. (2014). Global Cultural Flows and the Routes of Identity: The Imagined Worlds of Celtic FC. *Social and Cultural Geography* 15(5): 525–46.

Harrison, J., and S. Lloyd (2012). Illegality at Work: Deportability and the Productive New Era of Immigrant Enforcement. *Antipode* 44(20): 365–85.

Huish, R., and S. Darnell (2014). Cuban Sport Development: Building Capacity from *El Parque* to the Podium. In *A Contemporary Cuban Reader*, 2nd edn, eds. P. Brenner, M. Jiménez, J. Kirk, and W. Leogrande. New York: Rowman and Littlefield.

Hylton, K. (2009). *"Race" and Sport: Critical Race Theory*. New York: Routledge.

Kandel, W., and J. Cromartie (2004). *New Patterns of Hispanic Settlement in Rural America*. Washington, DC: United States Department of Agriculture Economic Research Service.

McCarthy, J. (2007). Rural Geography: Globalizing the Countryside. *Progress in Human Geography* 32(1): 129–37.

Marrow, H. (2011). *New Destination Dreaming: Immigration, Race and Legal Status in the Rural American South*. Stanford: Stanford University Press.

Massey, D. (2008). *New Faces in New Place: The Changing Geography of American Immigration*. New York: Russell Sage Foundation.

Nadel, J. (2014). *Fútbol!: Why Soccer Matters in Latin America*. Gainesville: University of Florida Press.

Nelson, L. and P. Nelson (2011). The Global Rural: Gentrification and Linked Migration in the Rural USA. *Progress in Human Geography* 35(4): 441–59.

Nelson, L., L. Trautman, and P. Nelson (2015). Latino Immigrants and Rural Gentrification: Race, "Illegality," and Precarious Labor Regimes in the United States. *Annals of the Association of American Geographers* 105(4): 841–58.

Nevins, J. (2002). *Operation Gatekeeper: The Rise of the "Illegal Alien" and the Making of the U.S.–Mexico Boundary*. New York: Routledge.

Paniagua, A. (2002). Counterurbanisation and New Social Class in Rural Spain: The Environmental and Rural Dimension Revisited. *Scottish Geographical Journal* 118(1): 1–18.

Rutheiser, C. (1996). *Imagineering Atlanta: The Politics of Place in the City of Dreams*. London: Verso.

Santos-Gómez, H. (2014). *Immigrant Farmworkers and Citizenship in Rural California: Playing Soccer in the San Joaquin Valley*. El Paso: LFB Scholarly.

Shobe, H. (2008). Football and the Politics of Place: Football Club Barcelona and Catalonia 1975–2005. *Journal of Cultural Geography* 25(1): 87–105.

Smith, D. (1998). The Green Potential of West Yorkshire. *Regional Review* 14: 6–7.

Winders, J. (2005). Changing Politics of Race and Region: Latino Migration to the US South. *Progress in Human Geography* 29(6): 683–99.

Winders, J. (2007). Bringing Back the (B)order: Post-9/11 Politics of Immigration, Borders and Belonging in the Contemporary U.S. South. *Antipode* 39(5): 920–42.

Winders, J. (2013). *Nashville in the New Millennium: Immigrant Settlement, Urban Transformation and Social Belonging*. New York: Russell Sage Foundation.

Zuñiga, V., and R. Hernández-León (2005). *New Destinations: Mexican Immigration in the United States*. New York: Russell Sage Foundation.

Chapter 10

Competing visions for urban space in Seoul

Understanding the demolition of Korea's Dongdaemun Baseball Stadium

Jung Woo Lee

Introduction

Baseball is arguably the most popular sport in South Korea. In understanding the historical and cultural meaning of the game, the collective memories and emotions associated with the Dongdaemun Baseball Stadium (DBS) are of paramount importance. Built in 1925 by the Japanese imperialists and the oldest modern sporting ground in the country, the DBS hosted numerous culturally and historically significant competitions (Son 2003). Notably, it was the venue where the inaugural Korean professional baseball match took place in 1982, in addition to hosting a series of the East Asian baseball derbies between Japan and South Korea in the 1960s and 1970s. More importantly, it was regarded as the home of South Korean amateur baseball for more than 30 years, including a number of annual nationwide high school baseball competitions (B. S. Lee 2007). The DBS was, in short, a place imbued with collective sporting memories, nostalgia, and, to some extent, a post-colonial Korean national identity.

In spite of the cultural and historical values that the DBS signifies, the baseball stadium was demolished in 2008 as part of Seoul's revitalization plan. In 2006, the Seoul Metropolitan Government (SMG) announced an inner city redevelopment policy that included constructing an iconic building, the Dongdaemun Design Plaza, to represent a new urban identity (SMG 2007). The newly elected mayor of Seoul, Mr. Se-hoon Oh, had a strong desire to transform the South Korean capital into a global city, and his municipal administration strategically fostered a fashion and space design industry within the frame of this globalizing policy (Hwang 2014). This plan prioritized the construction of iconic architecture as a way to denote the city's new post-industrial identity (Kriznik 2011). The place where the old baseball stadium had been standing was chosen to be a site where a new geographical landmark, the Dongdaemun Design Plaza (DDP), was to be built (Chung 2009). Although a large number of social activists and intellectuals, as well as the baseball community, protested against this mega construction project, the municipality carried out the building work as scheduled while promising to build an alternative base-ball stadium on the outskirts of Seoul. In addition, the SMG agreed to create a sport history museum near the DDP in order to commemorate the old stadium's 83 years at that site. In 2014, the DDP finally opened to the public and the following year, the construction of the new baseball arena, the Gocheok Sky Dome, was also completed. Currently, traces of the col-lective memories related to the DBS can only be found in a corner of a small museum, in rather fossilized form, without a geographical connec-tion to the actual sporting place.

This chapter critically examines the SMG's recent inner city redevelop-ment policy in relation to these demolition and construction projects. While being careful not to overly romanticize the sporting past, I argue here that the demolition of the baseball stadium and its subsequent reloca-tion, together with the construction of the new iconic Design Plaza, consti-tute the annihilation of a public place and its associated collective memories. Further, the Seoul municipality's desire to become a global city works to destroy certain local histories through its urban rebranding strategy. In this analysis, I emphasize the meanings of the now demolished DBS, as well as the implications of building the Dongdaemun Design Plaza and the Gocheok Sky Dome stadium for their surrounding areas. I will first briefly introduce the notion of the global city and the role of neoliberal globalization, which are necessary to explain Seoul's aspiration to con-struct a new urban identity through its architecture.

Global cities, neoliberalism, and architecture

The current wave of globalization has been dominated by the logic of neo-liberal capitalism and consumerism, which penetrates into almost every aspect of sociocultural and political life all around the world (Harvey 2006; Lash and Lury 2007; Ritzer 2010; Sklair 2002). One notable aspect of these processes is the changing role of the state as an autonomous polit-ical and economic actor, and the rising importance of the metropolis as a node of global economic, cultural, and technical networks (Castells 2010; Ritzer 2010; Sklair 2005). Major global cities, such as New York, London, and Tokyo, now operate as key nodes of political, economic, and cultural affairs – attracting both foreign investments and international tourists (Friedman 1986; Sassen 2001). Consequently, many cities aspire to achieve such global status and become a hub of these networks (Short 2004).

Many aspirant "global cities" have sought to reposition themselves by strategically fostering the creative culture industry (Pratt 2009; Taylor 2009; Zheng 2011). To do so, city planners have argued for the need to reimage, or "brand," their urban identity to correspond with this new cul-tural industry (Ward 1998). This process, city planners have argued, demands overhauling the shape of inner cities – often including diffuse forms of gentrification, but also including large-scale redevelopment projects. Yet, the process of rebranding a city is often directed by the logic of entrepreneurism, which involves the commodification of public spaces and the devaluation of non-profitable components of urban settings (Harvey 1982, 1989; Weber 2002). Paradoxically, then, these cultural branding exercises within the paradigm of neoliberalism are often undertaken at the expense of local, cultural, and historical traditions and the lived experience of long-term residents. The resulting repression of this organic dimension of urban life inevitably weakens local communality and civic involvement, which hinge on the strong interpersonal relations that are lost with the sacrifice of public space (Amin 2008; Watson 2013). Nevertheless, the project of selling cities and urban spaces to transnational power elites continues in many different areas of the world – Seoul included (Goodwin 1993; Kriznik 2011; Ward 1998).

Large-scale iconic architecture is one of the key urban reimaging strategies favored by city planners to gain global attention (Grubbauer 2014; Smith 2005). Such projects are often closely associated with urban rebranding efforts because iconic buildings can be used as a tool that symbolically represents a new city image (Zukin 1991). Leslie Sklair (2010:138) further argues that iconic buildings "are famous for those in and around architecture and/or public at large and have special symbolic/aesthetic significance." Iconic architecture is also thought to attract more tourists to a city, which suits urban planners' redevelopment policy within the paradigm of neoliberal globalization, insofar as they are understood to generate both symbolic and economic benefits (Urry and Larsen 2011).

In many cases, cities seek out a celebrity architect, or "starchitect," to design new urban icons (Lewis 2007; Ritzer 2010; Sklair 2010). Not only does international name-recognition make it more likely that a building will develop into a globally recognizable icon, but from the standpoint of an architectural firm, their involvement in mega-construction projects is an important way to promote their own global reputation (Sklair 2005). Hence, while any architectural masterpiece in itself may display artistic and aesthetic values with a state-of-the-art engineering technology, it is doubtful that it always can be harmonically articulated with the local cultural tradition and with the surrounding areas. Moreover, as Harvey (1990) notes, as a form of spectacle, iconic architecture both mediates and reifies the logic of consumerism and neoliberal globalization. Ultimately, such urban icons rarely signify anything but global standardization, with a minimum use, if any, of local elements (Castells 2010; Urry and Larsen 2011). With these challenges, then, how can we explain the Seoul Metropolitan Government's recent urban redevelopment policy and its accompanying mega construction projects?

Redeveloping Seoul: "a clean and attractive global city"

In 2006, with a newly elected mayor in power, the SMG implemented an urban redevelopment policy, entitled *Seoul, A Clean and Attractive Global City*. The SMG's promotional pamphlet notes that while the city observes excellent economic growth, Seoul as an industrial "hard city" has thus far relied heavily on manufacturing, civil engineering, and construction industries, which require a high level of energy consumption (Kwon 2010). The redevelopment initiative thus aims to transform the South Korean capital to a post-industrial "soft city," where information technology and creative industries serve as a driving force for sustainable and eco-friendly economic development (Kwon 2010).

This new urban policy is closely related to the SMG's ambition to join the ranks of the world's leading global cities – a status it has not been accorded despite its importance as a regional economic hub. So far, Seoul has been grouped as an "emerging" global city or "semi-peripheral" city (Shin and Timberlake 2006). For many Western audiences, Seoul is still considered as an East Asian industrial city, in spite of the fact that the metropolis has accumulated various regional cultural capitals and has accomplished technological innovation (Oh 2009). Working against this reputation and hoping to transform the image of Seoul, SMG planners have seen the need to foster an internationally recognized culture industry.

From 2006, Seoul's newly elected leadership turned to the fashion and design industry in particular, as a vehicle for transforming the urban economic structure and ultimately upgrading the international reputation of the city (Y. S. Lee and Hwang 2012). To accelerate this process, the SMG initiated two especially high-profile projects: (1) achieving UNESCO's "City of Design" status and eventually joining UNESCO's "Creative Cities Network," and (2) constructing an iconic building that represents Seoul's new urban identity. The first project met with success in July 2010 when Seoul was awarded the City of Design title, after an inner city renovation campaign focused on fostering a creative urban environment. With regard to the second, the SMG was also successful – and this project is the reason that the Dongdaemun Baseball Stadium no longer stands today.

In deciding on a location for Seoul's new urban icon, the SMG strategically chose the northern downtown area of Seoul because of its relative underdevelopment, as compared to the southern region of the capital. The economic disparity between the two districts has been a major concern that planners wished to address (Kriznik 2013; Watson 2013). Although the northern downtown site appears a rational choice, the SMG faced a problem in securing a spacious construction site within this densely populated area. In the end, the SMG concluded that the only viable option for siting the new iconic building was to demolish the Dongdaemun Baseball

Stadium. Given the cultural and historical significance of the stadium, a number of civic societies, activists, and academics, together with a group of amateur and professional baseball players, protested against the SMG's decision, claiming the structure to be an important piece of modern cultural heritage (Chung 2009; B. S. Lee 2007). However, their collective voices were not politically powerful enough to alter the SMG's globally oriented urban redevelopment plan (Hwang 2014; Kriznik 2013). So despite their protests, the ballpark was demolished in 2008 and, six years later, the completed Dongdaemun Design Plaza stood in its place.

The Dongdaemun Baseball Stadium: collective memory and Korean national identity

A detailed account of the Dongdaemun Baseball Stadium's (DBS) history and cultural value is necessary to properly evaluate the SMG's urban redevelopment policy, and specifically its iconic architecture agenda. The DBS was the first modern sport facility in Korea. Because it was built by the Japanese imperialists in celebration of the Japanese royal wedding in 1925, and because the Korean people experienced relatively short but harsh Japanese colonial domination (1910–45), the historical meaning of the DBS can be controversial. This colonial legacy was one of the major rationales developers used to justify their position on demolishing the nation's oldest stadium, which they deemed a humiliating form of cultural heritage. While the DBS, to some extent, reflected Korea's unfortunate past, a close examination of the actual use and the function of this sporting venue reveals equally meaningful, if not more important, cultural values surrounding Korean national identity and the development of modern sport in the country.

During the colonial period, sport and physical education played a significant role in fostering Korean national consciousness against Japanese imperialism (Ok 2005). In fact, sporting grounds were one of the few public places where Korean people displayed their national identity relatively freely (H. R. Lee 2000). The Dongdaemun stadium hosted a number of nationwide Korean baseball tournaments and friendly matches between Korean school clubs, and these sporting occasions offered a rare opportunity for the Korean people to come together and express otherwise repressed nationalist affinities, such as through singing the Korean national anthem and waving the national flag *en masse* (Ok and Park 2014). As a purpose-built sporting facility, the DBS could accommodate a large number of spectators at the same time. The gathering of the colonized Korean population within such a confined space was uncommon and often caused a sudden surge of nationalistic feelings at the stadium – a mood that easily turned into an ad hoc political protest against Japanese imperial domination. Having observed several such incidents, the Japanese imperial police banned a number of baseball matches they thought might result in the eruption of anti-colonial Korean nationalism at the baseball field (H. R. Lee 2000).

After Korea's liberation in 1945, the DBS hosted a series of international baseball competitions. Among others, these included the 1963 and the 1971 Asian Baseball Championships, which were particularly significant with regard to the expression of post-colonial Korean nationalism. Since 1945, Korean and Japanese baseball teams had encountered one another in various events, but until 1963 the Korean team had never beaten the Japanese. Japan took up baseball much earlier than Korea, and Japan had a modern professional league starting in 1937, while Korean baseball was still in a developing stage. By the mid-twentieth century, then, there was a noticeable gap between the two national teams in terms of skills and competitiveness. Hence, it was no easy task for Korean players to defeat the Japanese baseball team at that time.

However, at the 1963 Asian Baseball Championship, a miraculous event unfolded in the Dongdaemun stadium. For the first time in history, the Korean team won the championship title, beating the Japanese delegates twice, 5–2 and 3–0 respectively. As a recently liberated post-colonial society, a strong sense of anti-Japanese feeling was still prevalent in Korea in the 1960s. In this circumstance, the victory over Japan provided a cathartic moment for many Korean people – it was as if the Korean players took symbolic revenge on their former colonizers in front of a huge audience of their compatriots. Eight years later, the two teams faced each other once again at the DBS. The Korean players again prevailed, defeating the old foe 8–3 and winning the 1971 Asian Championship title. These two victories were particularly memorable because the Korean side defeated a better-equipped and much stronger Japanese team, by all standards. On both occasions, the matches were highly emotionally charged for both Korean audiences and players due to the colonial experience, while the players themselves were imbued with a stubborn spirit and willpower to beat the Japanese team on Korean soil at any cost. The collective memory of these victories over the Japanese gave rise to a sense of nationalist pride and fervor that the DBS long symbolized.

The DBS also became the heart of Korean amateur baseball (B. S. Lee 2007). Until the sport's professionalization in Korea in 1982, high school baseball tournaments were arguably the country's most popular spectator sporting events. The tradition of school baseball started in the colonial period, but its golden age was in the 1960s and 1970s. There were four major tournaments in this period: the Golden Lions Championship, the Blue Dragon Championship, the Phoenix Championship, and the Presidential Championship. The DBS, as the only proper baseball stadium in Seoul at that time, hosted almost every one of these inter-school matches. Given that teams from various regions and provinces in South Korea participated in the championships, it attracted nationwide attention. High school teams came to be seen as a delegation of their regions or cities, so, whenever the baseball championships began, fans from different regions travelled to the DBS to support their locale. Reflecting the people's demands for high school baseball, many of the matches were also broadcast live on television. In the 1960s and 1970s, at a time when the media industry was not overly developed in South Korea, these televised games offered one of the few sporting spectacles that drew South Korean people's interest on a national scale. With the increasing popularity of high school baseball tournaments, the status of the DBS as the home of Korean amateur baseball was reaffirmed, as it remained the primary venue for the games.

In 1982, a professional baseball league commenced in South Korea, and the DBS hosted the inaugural professional matches. However, the relationship between Korean professional baseball and the DBS did not last long. A new baseball stadium was to be opened in July 1982 on the east side of Seoul, and it was this new baseball park that served as a home field for the Seoul Blue Dragons Baseball Club. Also, while the popularity of professional baseball was continually on the rise, public interest in high school matches was noticeably in decline. It appeared that the newly launched professional league was coming to replace the amateur school tournament in popular sporting culture in Korea. When construction of the new baseball stadium was completed in 1982, the vast majority of professional matches were held there. Consequently, the DBS saw a precipitous decline in the number of visitors until its closure in 2007. Even though the DBS continued to be the main stadium for the high school matches until then, the old stadium became a less popular sporting venue in comparison with other baseball parks where professional games took place.

Although the DBS's use value may have declined, it by no means became obsolete or meaningless. Indeed, the stadium's symbolic value cannot be underestimated – especially with respect to its historical role in Korean nation-building through the collective experience of watching baseball games. Moreover, the feelings of nostalgia for the golden age of high school baseball tournaments in the 1960s and the 1970s represent invaluable cultural assets for those who observed these amateur baseball events. Additionally, the organization of these high school baseball competitions at that time, to some extent, paved the way for the introduction of the Korean professional baseball league in 1982 (Hong 2013). Invested with these collective memories and nostalgic sentiments, a sporting space like the Dongdaemun stadium is not a neutral place, but a site through which these emotions and values are invoked at a societal scale, reflecting the people's lived experience and histories (Bairner 2014; Carmona *et al.* 2010; Charleston 2009; Gaffney and Bale 2004; King 2004). With the DBP's demolition, then, much more was lost than a simple architectural structure.

The Dongdaemun Design Plaza: iconic architecture in isolation

In March 2014, the Dongdaemun Design Plaza (DDP) officially opened. As part of the government-promoted city branding program, the DDP has been positioned as the cornerstone of Seoul's inner-city restructuring agenda (Hwang 2014). More importantly, the structure was built with the purpose of illustrating Seoul's new cultural identity as a hub of design and creative industry (Kriznik 2011). The building's exterior, which has a unique futuristic design, potentially functions to represent the new image of Seoul, and perhaps to attract tourists, but it should be borne in mind that architecture never stands alone – it influences and is influenced by people and their buildings nearby (Amin 2008). This is especially so when the building is located in a busy urban area with a deep history. As we have already seen, the site of the DDP took the place of a stadium that had been standing for more than 80 years. Unable to match the cultural and historical values of the ballpark, the DDP's development feels to many who reside and work nearby as a structure out of sync with local context and traditions.

The DDP project is a clear case of how the logic of neoliberalism and global capitalism can overpower local culture and history. Critics may be correct in arguing that the old Dongdaemun stadium no longer produced desirable economic values, given the decreased game schedule and correlating reduced spectator numbers. Yet this exclusively financial reasoning cannot account for the cultural values associated with the DBP. In justifying the stadium's demolition as part of their urban regeneration plans, planners simply devalued these less tangible values and historical legacies represented in the stadium. And, by instead prioritizing the construction of the DDP, officials worked to further financialize Seoul's urban landscape and reshape the inner city property market around more economically lucrative activities (Chung 2009; Kriznik 2011). Equipped with such neoliberal market rationales, combined with the SMG's push to transform Seoul into a major global city, these planners were able to overcome civic opposition and renarrate the cherished baseball stadium as nothing more than an unworthy, rundown structure in need of bulldozing.

Notably, urban decision-makers received further support in realizing their visions from the celebrity architect, Zaha Hadid, who designed the Dongdaemun Design Plaza. Her recent projects have included the Guangzhou Opera House and the London Aquatic Center. As indicated earlier, the involvement of a "starchitect" like Hadid is often a crucial part of urban reimaging campaigns aimed at advancing aspiring global cities to the next level (Lewis 2007; Sklair 2010). A close examination of the process by which the Seoul Metropolitan Government selected Hadid's architectural firm reveals an uneasy relation between the global and the local, and how planners ultimately prioritized the desire to be a global actor at the expense of local cultural legacies.

In order to construct an internationally recognizable iconic building, the SMG nominated eight elite architectural engineering firms, four domestic and four international, to submit their construction designs. The invited firms included those of celebrity architects such as Steven Holl and Zaha Hadid. The SMG also organized a panel of architectural experts, consisting of four foreign and three Korean specialists, to review the submitted designs. As part of the selection process, the competing firms were asked to present their designs and engineering plans before the panel. The candidates were required to explain their work in English only, since more than the half of the evaluation panel members were non-Korean speakers. In this respect, one of the four Korean architects, Seung Hyo. Sang, noted in an interview that:

> While presenting the construction plan in English is in itself not necessary a bad decision, I was somewhat skeptical about the review process because most panel members had no geo-cultural and historical understanding of the building site. After the interview, I immediately felt that I won't be able to win the work as the questions I received from the panel were all about the building itself. I soon realized that they did not consider geo-cultural issues at all.
>
> (quoted in SBS 2012)

In fact, every Korean designer's drawings reflected the sporting memories and the local history of the Dongdaemun site as part of their proposed iconic works. Another Korean architect, Choi Moon Gyu, recollected that "our generation watched the Korea and Japan Derby at the DBS, also watched the high school tournaments. If the stadium needed to be demolished, I think at least the sporting memories should be preserved through the new icon" (quoted in SBS 2012). Zaha Hadid's architectural design proposal, by contrast, contained no element commemorating the site's sporting history and collective memories. Nonetheless, acting on the advice from the panel, the SMG finally awarded her the DDP project.

It is difficult to identify the panel's criteria for its final decision. Yet, the overall review process indicates that neoliberal norms of globalization – manifested in a sort of standard, Westernized global culture – were major considerations. This is evident in part by the number of Western panel members, the invited, internationally famous Western architects, as well as the use of English as an official language during the interview and presentation process. And the fact that the project was ultimately awarded to the architectural firm whose building design did not consider the local factors at all, and instead only focused on constructing the futuristic architectural spectacle, is further proof. Consequently, a place that once served as a local repository for the collective sporting memories and feelings of national pride associated with sport has now disappeared without a trace. Instead, only a new image of the South Korean capital, "Design Seoul," is highlighted through Hadid's Dongdaemun Design Plaza. As Chi (2008) argues, the combined logic of neoliberal development and the desire to be a global city killed the cultural and historical legacies of the local.

The Gocheok Sky Dome: a true replacement?

The Gocheok Sky Dome (GSD) is the replacement for the Dongdaemun Baseball Stadium, offered by the Seoul Metropolitan Government as a concession to the Korean baseball community and others protesting about the old stadium's demolition. Built on the city's outskirts, the GSD's construction has also engendered a range of controversial issues. First, as an alternative venue for amateur baseball, the GSD was originally designed to be an open-field baseball park. However, nearby residents objected on the grounds that games would generate too much noise and negatively affect living conditions in the area. Since the site for the new field is located in one of the most densely populated areas in the city, surrounded by schools and residential apartments, local people's concern is fair and understandable (Park 2015). Aiming to tackle this problem by containing the noise, the SMG changed the initial design to a dome.

The baseball community, however, did not welcome the new plan because it would triple the building cost and waste too much public money. Furthermore, critics pointed out that it was not practical to build a dome stadium mainly used for amateur baseball games – especially when no professional club at that time had a dome (Bae 2015). The SMG's decision was not only surprising, but seemingly inconsistent, since it had previously rejected a number of professional clubs' plans to construct a fully roofed baseball stadium in the city. So, while it was not necessarily a bad idea to construct a dome, in consideration of the high construction cost relative to an open-field ballpark Seoul's baseball community argued that it was not pragmatic to build an amateur-only dome stadium. In spite of these concerns, the SMG went ahead with its plans.

Given the high construction costs, and the more expensive maintenance and operating fees, the SMG realized that the Gocheok Sky Dome would have to be commercially viable in order to prevent unnecessary spending of taxpayer money (Kyunghyang Shinmun 2014). Eventually, the local government dropped the idea of the GSD hosting only amateur games and, as a result, the venue has now been hired to a professional baseball club (Park 2015). This means that the main rationale for building a new stadium – to replace the old Dongdaemun Baseball Stadium as a hub for amateur teams – has now been abandoned. As a result, both culturally and functionally, the GSD is hardly a replacement for the old DBS.

In the wake of the Dongdaemun stadium's demolition, the cultural place of amateur baseball seems to be in jeopardy in South Korea. As the Sky Dome's managers seek more commercial opportunities, and as the city's planners turn again to neoliberal rationales, the new stadium has rapidly become another way for the SMG to financialize the urban landscape and boost the local economy through attracting a large number of spectators to the area (Ham 2015). In the end, public concern becomes marginalized once more, and the profit-making motive emerges at the forefront of the GSD's management, whether originally intended or not. The logic of neoliberal development again prevails, even in the supposed reincarnation of the demolished Dongdaemun stadium.

Conclusion

The Dongdaemun Baseball Stadium is now dead and buried. The old field's cultural and sporting legacies have passed with it, replaced materially and symbolically by the Dongdaemun Design Plaza – a tribute to Seoul's newly globalized identity and the neoliberal values of the city's planners. In contrast to the standardization of hyper-modern architecture, sporting stadiums are sites that preserve collective memories and thereby provide a source of local and national identities, cultural and historical importance (Bairner 2014; Bale 1993; Charleston 2009; Gaffney and Bale 2004; Maguire 1995; Nielsen 1995). As discussed in this chapter, the Dongdaemun Baseball Stadium is one such site of cultural and historical significance in relation to the development of Korean baseball, post-colonial nationalism, and the collective memories and emotions of the country's population. In spite of this national significance, the Seoul Metropolitan Government bulldozed the old stadium to build a globally oriented icon of architectural spectacle.

The Dongdaemun Design Plaza redevelopment project, promoted by Seoul's municipal government but ultimately envisioned by internationally renowned architect Zaha Hadid, exemplifies the processes characteristic of globalization in many cities around the world: the devaluation of locally defined values, lived experiences, and urban histories so that land can be turned into more economically profitable space, with iconic architecture used to promote these financial flows (Castells 2010; Harvey 1982). In addition, even the Dongdaemun's replacement stadium, the Gocheok Sky Dome, shows that, in contrast to initial attempts to inherit partial legacies of the old baseball stadium, the logic of development and profit-making motives prevailed. This case is just one of a series of demolition and construction processes that have been associated with Seoul's "clean and attractive global city" reimaging campaign, but it clearly shows that fitting the city into the paradigm of neoliberal capitalism is the foundational principle of the SMG's urban redevelopment policy. Unfortunately for the

Korean baseball community, and the country's posterity more generally, this has also entailed the destruction of culturally and historically meaningful local cultures, including those mediated through sport.

The new Design Plaza may successfully play its iconic role in displaying the South Korean capital's new "Design Seoul" identity. As the architecture of spectacle, it may also promote Seoul's tourism and thereby attract more international visitors and capital to the city, helping boost the local economy. Eventually, as a center for the creative industry, the DDP may also accelerate the SMG's initiative to make Seoul a leading global city. Yet, as Ritzer (2010) aptly points out, the processes of globalization that discount local cultural issues are more likely to be the globalization of nothing. This means that with an overemphasis on standardized global culture, the interface between the local and global quickly becomes the mere Westernization of urban culture, rather than promoting a diversification of culture. Likewise, Hwang (2014) argues that SMG's global city project through cultivating design and creative industry, however intricate it may be, simply imitates other aspiring global cities, and therefore lacks an idiosyncratically identifiable cultural identity. This is particularly so in relation to the DDP because this structure contains no component commemorating the site's hallowed sporting past. While the DDP can be seen as a unique building, which boasts a futuristic and atypical design, it is nonetheless a cliché insofar as it is an attempt to promote and reimagine urban identity through iconic architecture designed by a world-famous architect – a pattern that can be found in many different global metropolises (Sklair 2005). In this sense, Seoul's urban redevelopment project merely adopts a standardized formula.

At the time of this writing, it is too early to evaluate whether the DDP has successfully acted as Seoul's new icon, thereby helping the SMG transform the city into a place of global flow. For the local people, though, this new building is already seen as a meaningless structure, standing anonymously in the inner city area without cultural connection to the surrounding areas. From a cultural geographical perspective, then, the Design Plaza is clearly another case whereby elite planners justify the financialization of the urban landscape and with it, the annihilation of public space and erasure of collective sporting memories that the Korean people long associated with the Dongdaemun Baseball Stadium – all in the name of development.

References

Amin, A. (2008). Collective Culture and urban Public Space. *City* 12(1): 5–24.

Bae, W. K. (2015). Gocheok Dome-e Anin Dongdaemun-ae Ya-goo-jang-eul Jee-ut-da-myun [What if We Built a Baseball Stadium in Dongdaemun Area, Not in Gocheok]. *Sport Seoul*, September 24. Available at: www.sportsseoul.com/news/read/295726 (accessed October 1, 2015).

Bairner, A. (2014). Emotional Grounds: Stories of Football, Memories, and Emotions. *Emotion, Space and Society* 12: 18–23.

Bale, J. (1993). *Sport, Space, and the City.* London: Routledge.

Carmona, M., S. Tiesdell, T. Heath, and O. Taner (2010). *Public Places, Urban Spaces: The Dimensions of Urban Design.* Oxford: Architectural Press.

Castells, M. (2010). *The Rise of the Network Society.* Oxford: Wiley-Blackwell.

Charleston, S. (2009). The English Football Ground as a Representation of Home. *Journal of Environmental Psychology* 29(1): 144–50.

Chi, H. (2008). What is the Cultural City? Criticism on the Dongdaemun Stadium Redevelopment Project. *Munhwagwahak* 53(1): 538–47.

Chung, H. (2009). A Critical Review on Regenerating a Place's Economic Value Through Landscape Restructuring: The Case of Dongdaemun Stadium. *Journal of the Korean Geographical Society* 44(2): 161–75.

Friedman, J. (1986). The World City Hypothesis. *Development and Change* 17(1): 69–83.

Gaffney, C., and J. Bale (2004). Sensing the Stadium. In *Sites of Sport: Space, Place, Experience* eds. P. Vertinsky and J. Bale. London: Routledge, 25–38.

Goodwin, M. (1993). The City as Commodity: The Contested Spaces of Urban Development. In *Selling Places: The City as Cultural Capital, Past and Present* eds. G. Kearns and C. Philo. Oxford: Pergamon Press, 145–62.

Grubbauer, M. (2014). Architecture, Economic Imaginaries and Urban Politics: The Office Tower as Socially Classifying Device. *International Journal of Urban and Regional Research* 38(1): 336–59.

Ham, T. S. (2015). Gocheok Dome, Joo-byun Sang-in-eun Wha-sek. Joo-min-eun Guk-jung [Local Businesses Welcome the GSD while Local Residents Worry About It]. *Sport Chosun*, September 17. Available at: http://sports.chosun.com/news/ntype.htm?id=2015092101002302700016162&servicedate=20150920 (accessed October 15, 2015).

Harvey, D. (1982). *The Limits to Capital.* London: Verso.

Harvey, D. (1989). From Managerialism to Entrepreneurialism: The Transformation in Urban Governance In late Capitalism. *Geografiska Annaler* 71(B): 3–17.

Harvey, D. (1990). *The Condition of Postmodernity: The Enquiry into the Origin of Cultural Change.* Oxford: Blackwell.

Harvey, D. (2006). *Spaces of Global Capitalism: Toward a Theory of Uneven Geographical Development.* London: Verso.

Hong, S. I. (2013). *The Chronicle of Korea Baseball 1896–1979.* Seoul: Korea Baseball Organization.

Hwang, J. T. (2014). Territorialized Urban Mega-Projects Beyond Global Convergence: The Case of Dongdaemun Design Plaza and Park Project, Seoul. *Cities* 40(A): 82–9.

King, A. (2004). *Spaces of Global Cultures: Architecture, Urbanism, Identity.* London: Routledge.

Kriznik, B. (2011). Selling Global Seoul: Competitive Urban Policy and Symbolic Reconstruction of Cities. *Revija Za Sociologiju* 41(3): 291–313.

Kriznik, B. (2013). Changing Approaches to Urban Development in South Korea: From "Clean and Attractive Global Cities" Towards "Hopeful Communities." *International Development Planning Review* 35(4): 395–418.

Kwon, Y.-G. (2010). Designing Seoul: Hierarchy. *Design Seoul*, 7: 5–9.

Kyunghyang Shinmun (2014). *Gocheok Dome, Noo-goo-rul wi-han goo-jang-in-ga?* [The GSD, a stadium for whom?]. *The Kyunghyang Shinmun*, December 17. Available at: http://news.khan.co.kr/kh_news/khan_art_view.html?artid=201412 172357595&code=980101 (accessed September 5, 2015).

Lash, S., and C. Lury (2007). *Global Culture Industry*. Cambridge: Polity.

Lee, B. S. (2007). Dongdaemun Stadium Should be Conserved as a Modern Cultural Heritage. *Sport Science*, Winter: 100–107.

Lee, H. R. (2000). *Hankook Chaeyook Backnyunsa* [The 100-year history of Korean sport]. Seoul: KAHPERD.

Lee, Y. S., and E. J. Hwang (2012). Global Urban Frontiers Through Policy Transfer? Unpacking Seoul's Creative City Programme. *Urban Studies* 49(13): 2817–37.

Lewis, M. J. (2007). The Rise of the "Starchitect." *New Criterion* 36(4): 4–9.

Maguire, J. (1995). Sport, the Stadium and Metropolitan Life. In *The Stadium and the City* eds. J. Bale and O. Moen. Keel: Keel University Press, 45–57.

Nielsen, N. K. (1995). The Stadium in the City: A Modern History. In *The Stadium and the City* eds. J. Bale and O. Moen. Keel: Keel University Press, 21–44.

Oh, S.-H. (2009). *UNESCO City of Design Seoul: Application: Design Seoul Story*. Available at: www.unesco.org/new/fileadmin/MULTIMEDIA/HQ/CLT/images/CNN_Seoul_Application_en.pdf (accessed August 15, 2015).

Ok, G. (2005). The Political Significance of Sport: An Asian Case Study: Sport, Japanese Colonial Policy and Korean National Resistance, 1910–1945. *The International Journal of the History of Sport* 22(4): 649–70.

Ok, G., and K. Park. (2014). Cultural Evolution and Ideology in Korean Soccer: Sport and Nationalism. *The International Journal of the History of Sport* 31(3): 363–75.

Park, D. H. (2015). Gocheok Dome 'Sun-mul-in-ga, Jae-ang-in-ga' [The GSD, 'Gift or Disaster']. *Naver Sports*, September 4. Available at: http://sports.news.naver.com/kbo/news/read.nhn?oid=295&aid=0000001416 (accessed October 5, 2015).

Pratt, A. (2009). Policy Transfer and the Field of the Cultural and Creative Industries: What Can Be Learned From Europe. In *Creative Economies, Creative Cities: Asian–European Perspectives* eds. L. Kong and J. O'Connor. London: Springer, 9–23.

Ritzer, G. (2010). *Globalization: A Basic Text*. Chichester: Wiley-Blackwell.

Sassen, S. (2001). *The Global City: New York, London, Tokyo*. Princeton: Princeton University Press.

SBS (2012). *Design Seoul eui gu-nul* [The Dark Side of Design Seoul]. Directed by Seoul Broadcasting System. Korea: Seoul Broadcasting System.

Shin, K., and M. Timberlake (2006). Korea's Global City: Structural and Political Implications of Seoul's Ascendance in the Global Urban Hierarchy. *International Journal of Comparative Sociology* 47(2): 145–73.

Short, J. R. (2004). *Global Metropolitan: Globalizing Cities in a Capitalist World*. Abingdon: Routledge.

Sklair, L. (2002). *Globalization: Capitalism and Its Alternatives*. Oxford: Oxford University Press.

Sklair, L. (2005). The Transnational Capitalist Class and the Contemporary Architecture in Globalizing Cities. *International Journal of Urban and Regional Research* 29(3): 485–500.

Sklair, L. (2010). Iconic Architecture and the Culture Ideology of Consumerism. *Theory, Culture, and Society* 27(5): 135–59.

SMG (2007). *Seoul, a Clean and Attractive Global City: Four Year Plan of the Fourth Elected City Administration, 2006–2010.* Seoul: Seoul Metropolitan Government.

Smith, A. (2005). Conceptualizing City Image Change: The "Re-Imaging" of Barcelona. *Tourism Geography* 7(4): 398–423.

Son, H. (2003). A Study on the Korean Modern Sports Facilities During the Japanese Colonial Rules with Reference to Gyungsung Ground. *The Korean Journal of Physical Education* 42(4): 33–43.

Taylor, C. (2009). The Creative Industries, Governance and Economic Development: A UK Perspective. In *Creative Economies, Creative Cities: Asian-European Perspectives* eds. L. Kong and J. O'Connor. London: Springer, 153–66.

Urry, J., and J. Larsen (2011). *The Tourist Gaze 3.0.* London: Sage.

Ward, S. V. (1998). *Selling Places: The Marketing and Promotion of Towns and Cities 1850–2000.* London: Spoon Press.

Watson, I. (2013). (Re)Constructing a World City: Urbicide in Global Korea. *Globalizations* 10(2): 309–25.

Weber, R. (2002). Extracting Value From the City: Neoliberalism and Urban Redevelopment. *Antipode* 34(3): 519–40.

Zheng, J. (2011). "Creative Industry Clusters" and the "Entrepreneurial City" of Shanghai. *Urban Studies* 48(16): 3561–82.

Zukin, S. (1991). *Landscapes of Power: From Detroit to Disney World.* Berkeley: University of California Press.

Chapter 11

Running order

Urban public space, everyday citizenship, and sporting subjectivities

Simon Cook, Jon Shaw, and Paul Simpson

Introduction

> "Virtually all sports are, in essence, struggles over space."
>
> (Bale 2003: 11)

In his seminal text *Sports Geography*, John Bale underscores the power-laden relationship between sport and space. This chapter probes this relationship of struggle and the complex interplays between sport, space, and power through the sport of running. We focus on sporting bodies themselves, their *in situ* struggles for space in the shared urban realm, and their implications for how citizenship is practiced and understood. This is a case study of running in Plymouth and specifically the mundane micro-movements involved in passing pedestrians in the street. We have already presented some of this work elsewhere (Cook *et al.* 2015), but here we further unpack the conceptual ideas involved in analyzing such everyday encounters to shed light on sport's place in contemporary cities and how sporting bodies fit into public spaces in England.

Admittedly, this is not the context Bale had in mind when he penned the opening statement. Rather, he is referring to the struggle to master space: to neutralize, specialize, and rationalize space in order to establish the spatial limitations and spatial rules of sports (Bale 2003). This was the foundation of his pioneering arguments about the critical relationship between sport and space, and the need for a sport geography prepared to study it. Sporting spatialities, he argued, govern and define. A game of doubles lawn tennis, for example, is not a game of tennis unless the ground is flat; a court of 23.77 meters long and 10.97 meters wide is demarcated; halves, services boxes, center-marks, baselines, side-lines, and centerlines are marked in the proper width (AELTCC 2014). Sport requires a permissible geography to take place and this, in turn, requires a particular mastery of space.

Our appropriation of Bale's statement may then seem a little awry, but at their core, his arguments demonstrate how space is involved in the production and organization of sport and how, likewise, sport is involved in the production and organization of space. For him, sport geography is about the symbiotic relationship between the spaces of sport and those who participate in it, and the socio-political significance of such sport-spaces. These are our interests too, which we extend beyond achievement sport to everyday sport, from dedicated sport-spaces to appropriated shared spaces, and from macro-politics to micro-politics. Ultimately, though, this chapter is concerned with the same co-constitutive entanglement of sport, space, and power laid out in Bale's vision of sport geography. Taking these themes out of specialized sport-spaces and into the "wild" running spaces of public streets raises new questions about this entanglement in terms not only of where runners fit spatially and socially into the streetscape, but also with regard to the wider notion of their citizenship.

Sport, space and everyday citizenship

Rather than a mastery of space, the struggle for urban runners is finding and belonging in space. As Wood and Waite (2011: 201) explain, "belonging is a dynamic emotional attachment that relates people to the material and social worlds that they inhabit and experience. It is about feeling 'at home' and 'secure' but it is equally about being recognized and understood." There exists then a dialogical nature to belonging (Antonsich 2010). The pressing questions for urban runners are whether they feel they belong while running on the streets, and to what degree those they encounter concur. Differing perceptions about this "belongingness" (or sense of belonging) in such encounters can translate into runners having their right to space denied or withheld in practice by those they pass on the streets. Probing this further brings into focus questions of transgression – to have broken the social norms of a place (Cidell 2014; Cresswell 1996): Is running on the city streets a transgressive act? Is the runner a deviant urban subject? These questions tie into to a wider notion of citizenship (Yarwood 2013).

Citizenship has typically been conceived as place-bound. As organized through the state system, the status of being a citizen (Chouinard 2009) conventionally denotes a set of political, civil, and social rights and obligations for members of a particular, territorially delineated political community (Anderson *et al.* 2008; Painter and Philo 1995). Recently, however, scholars have argued that citizenship need not be bound to a particular place, treating it instead as a flexible practice pertaining to an individual or group's ability to partake fully in society at a range of scales (Cheshire and Woods 2009; Painter and Philo 1995; Smith 2000). Citizenship establishes the social order of everyday life, entwining legal statuses with mundane doings. It is enacted in daily life with personal rationalities, politics, perceptions, emotions, and values all agents in its production: "The geography

of ordinary citizenship … is really the geography of sociospatial relationships" (Staeheli *et al.* 2012: 641). Viewed in this manner, a runner's (in)
ability to run on the city streets is a question of citizenship regarding his or
her access to public space, rights to health and desired forms of movement,
convivial social relations, mobile hierarchies (i.e., the relative status of different mobile forms in particular spaces), and more.

In this chapter, we explore the complex negotiation of citizenship
between different agents in everyday life. What insights into citizenship
practices can we gain by exploring an incredibly commonplace and
mundane act in the practice of urban running – that of passing pedestrians? What implications do these fleeting moments of encounter hold for
understanding rights of way, mobile hierarchies, the belongingness of
sporting bodies, and street citizenship? Our emphasis on the mundane is
crucial: the moments discussed here are inevitable occurrences in running
practices, but are seldom thought about or discussed explicitly. It is difficult to overstate the importance of taking seriously the "background stuff"
of practices and places. There is much at stake in the everyday, for our
micro-social lives are co-constitutive of wider social, cultural, economic,
and political processes/practices (Castree *et al.* 2013; Neal and Murji
2015). The everyday speaks about how we live and what makes our lives
livable (Back 2015).

Methods

The broad study on which this chapter is based examined some geographies of running by considering the ways in which abstract movements are
pervaded by a range of embodied experiences, social interactions, and co-
constituted meanings that come together to produce running as a mobile
practice (for a full methods discussion, see Cook *et al.* 2015). The study
was based in Plymouth, England, and engaged 14 runners in two different
forms of mobile interview. First, six participants were joined on one of
their runs for a "go-along" (GA) interview. Participants were asked to
suggest a convenient time, location, and route for a joint run of between
30 to 90 minutes to take place. The run was then completed at "conversa-
tional" pace and dialogue was very loosely structured to allow for the
adaptation of topics to changing situations, and for questions to evolve
from spontaneous exchanges or encounters on the run. Going the "extra
mile" (Vettenniemi 2012) like this, scholars have argued, can generate
richer data as participants are prompted by meanings, connections, and
memories relating to the surrounding environment and passing events, as
well as building deep rapport with the researcher (Anderson 2004; Evans
and Jones 2011).

Second, eight participants undertook mobile-video-ethnography (MVE)
elicitation interviews. This method has been utilized in research on cycling,

on the basis of its ability to "capture the moment" (if only partially) and reveal the humdrum and banal aspects of mobile practices. A major advantage of employing MVE, Simpson (2014) has argued, is the ability to retain the context and detail of practices to allow researchers to scrutinize them in a more comprehensive fashion. In this project, encounters with pedestrians were the center of analysis, and such an approach allowed participants to relive the encounters and talk through them on the minute scale. The MVE interviews were based on unaccompanied runs recorded via a head camera (see Brown *et al.* 2008). The unedited footage was watched separately by both participant and researcher, the latter drawing up a specific interview schedule for each participant. The interviews then involved rewatching the video whilst working through the interview schedule. Through these methods, as well as our emphasis on running in public spaces, this chapter marks a break from traditional sport geography which has tended to focus on more formal methodologies and more serious "achievement" sports and their associated spaces (Bale 2004). Since there are important differences between such sports and spaces, the analytical and methodological refocusing go together to shed light on the mundane encounters experienced by runners and their implications for citizenship.

Running spaces and encounters

As a space of achievement sport, the British running track is subject to rigorously enforced spatial parameters as set out in the UK Athletics' *Rules for Competition* (UKA 2014). Ever since the first cinder athletics track was laid in London in 1837, the track has become increasingly rationalized, artificial, and homogeneous. It is a synthetic, technological, and predictable monoculture designed to produce a near laboratory setting, offering controlled conditions and neutralization from some of the vagaries of nature. It is designed to be replicable anywhere in the world. The encounters had on the athletics track are also highly controlled. Runners are kept separate from spectators and often from other runners, via lanes. During longer races when lanes are not in use, interactions are only unidirectional (mostly parallel and anticlockwise) and are governed by the rules laid out by the UKA (the governing body for athletics in the UK). The track is an unmistakable sportscape, dedicated to the competitive runner and set outside of the everyday happenings of social life (Bale 1994, 2000a, 2003).

Running in the street might be considered the track's absolute antithesis. Everything offered by the track is lacking when running in the urban environment. Public streets are not monocultures, but shared arenas in which runners must appropriate space for their own purposes. No sporting-spatial parameters are enforced on running in the urban environment – a space more open to nature's "noise" and one often lacking predictability. In contrast to the track, streets can be irrational, unspecialized, and heterogeneous spaces, better understood as ephemeral running "taskscapes" than sportscapes (Howe and Morris 2009; Ingold 1993). Due to these characteristics, some commentators have conceptualized running in public as transgressive. Bale (2000b, 2004, 2008), for example, underscores how urban running transgresses the norms of modern achievement sport by literally stepping outside its territorial confines in the synthetic, Fordist running track, and by performing anti-sport gestures through embodying motivations beyond just performance enhancement. Winters (1980) also positions running in the streets as a reaction to, and an attempt to fit into, a landscape designed for the automobile. From this perspective, running can be a way to reclaim the street for human locomotion, contesting the dominance of motorized mobility, and reinhabiting urban space (Bale 2003, 2004, 2011).

Street running's transgressions are not ubiquitous however, and they have a temporality. Drawing particularly on road-races as a form of sanctioned transgression, Cidell (2014) demonstrates how mass participation events can temporarily appropriate spaces that are usually off-limits, allowing people to run without the usual risks involved with transgression. Here, the activities and subjectivities that otherwise prevail must cede primacy in certain spaces for a period of time. Yet, once such events are over, the normal order of things returns; the temporarily sanctioned transgressions again risk the social and physical repercussions of deviance. The degree to which these resistances are deliberate or simply a by-product of everyday running practices is very much up for debate and very much a question of an individual's positionality.

Most crucially for the purposes of this chapter, urban running also involves different encounters from those of the track. Rather than being set apart from everyday life, running on the street is in the thick of it – it involves intermingling with others and the rhythms of a city. Runners face an onslaught of social and physical encounters with pedestrians, cyclists, loiterers, children, cars, dogs, etc., and must negotiate this shared space on the move. In analyzing their own running practices, Hockey and Allen-Collinson (2013) suggest that there is no consensus among runners about how best to negotiate such encounters. There is no code or UKA *Rules for Competition* to govern this space. Examining the encounters between runners and pedestrians, then, can offer insights into how and why shared space is negotiated in the ways that it is. Focusing on these socio-spatial encounters, we ask what forms of everyday citizenship emerge from them, and how a micro-political order develops through such fleeting experiences.

Encountering pedestrians

Within geography and related fields, *the encounter* has been established as a critical site for understanding the social, cultural, and political processes of everyday life (Amin 2002; Jensen 2013; Leitner 2012; Valentine 2008; Wilson 2016). Encounters are not simply micro-sociologies of face-to-face contact but acts of citizenship relating to the capacity of groups/individuals of difference to live together harmoniously. Encounters are bound up in distinct histories and geographies, and are guided by uncodified regulatory frameworks. These frameworks are influenced by statutory laws and social norms, as well as social expectations (Cresswell 1996; Waldron 2006). This analytical approach stresses identities as citizens above those of individuals because encounters are at the frontline of belonging; it is in these micro-meetings that someone's at-homeness is both displayed and affirmed or rebutted. The encounter has also opened new research inquiries about how urban public space is shared amidst diversity (Amin 2002). Scholars have largely studied difference through traditional delineations of identity – gender, ethnicity, nationality, sexuality, age, and (dis)ability. Yet recent work on the messiness and intersectionality of identities has opened up the scope of research on geographies of difference (Noble 2009; Valentine 2007).

A person's mobility is exemplary of how intersectional identities and urban space come together to produce political geographies of difference. As Patton (2004: 21) argues, people adopt particular subject positions, which are "mediated by their habitual activities in moving about the city," and facilitate the construction of mobile subjects (Jensen 2013). This creates room for running to become a significant part of someone's identity and the status of being a "runner" to come to the fore at particular moments (Ronkainen *et al.* 2014; Skinner 2015). When on the run, a passing encounter with someone of a different subjectivity/mobility/activity becomes an important window into the profound everyday processes which establish social order on the street. In such encounters, two or more actors have to pass by each other in public space, often requiring someone (or everyone) to change their course or halt their passage. As acts of citizenship, they can either legitimize or delegitimize a person's right to movement – ultimately producing a form of mobile hierarchy founded on perceived or actual claims to space. Scholars have examined such encounters between cyclists and drivers (Aldred and Jungnickel 2012), mountain bikers and walkers (Brown 2012), and snowboarders and skiers (Edensor and Richards 2007), and this section now brings such analysis to the encounters between runners and pedestrians.

Perspectives on encounters

Many runners are accustomed to running in public spaces and with the challenges of managing the wide range of obstacles and momentary meetings with pedestrians routinely generated in shared space. As one participant in this study put it, the intensity of such interactions are commonplace to the extent that they become an integral experience of running:

> I don't really like it when it comes to running on the pavements ... and sharing it with other people because you have to get out of their way and they have to get out of your way and they don't see you and crossing the road rather too frequently. It is quite dangerous because I think drivers expect runners to get out of the way, not to be there.
>
> (MVE)

For this participant, street running is unpleasant because of the absence of rules or codes of conduct for negotiating encounters with others. So, while runners may not have a consensus about how best to approach sharing space with differently mobile subjects, out of this ongoing competition for/ over space a mobile order is established (Binnie *et al.* 2007). Most of these struggles are resolved in split-second decisions taken to negotiate the encounter.

Due to their higher speed (and momentum) than other pedestrians, as well as public notions about the "normal" use of a pavement, runners are typically deemed the ones responsible for avoiding pedestrians (Hockey and Allen-Collinson 2013). However, the runners interviewed here suggested a more complex situation, expressing contrasting views on how runners should pass pedestrians in shared spaces. Many runners felt that responsibility to pass others safely should rest with themselves. These individuals argued that, since they are a minority with regard to how they use the streets, this carries with it a responsibility to ensure passing encounters are handled successfully. For them, it is just more practical and convenient for runners, as the minority, to make the effort to avoid pedestrians rather than expect the majority to avoid them:

> No, I see it as my responsibility. I think everybody else is trying to use the environment in a relaxing way and there is me trying to use it in a more, probably, productive but personal way. So I think it is my job to not interrupt their free time in the way that because ... I can do that but I wouldn't expect a hundred people to move out of their way to avoid me and my free time ... I think that would be selfish because clearly there aren't as many runners as there are dog walkers for example.... We are probably inconveniencing their space.
>
> (GA)

Here, streets are understood as predominantly a space for walking and the general rhythms and tempos that characterize it. Movements and paces straying from this "norm" are thus seen as out of place (See Cook, forthcoming). Although some of the respondents were happy to assume responsibility for avoiding collisions with others in shared spaces, based on their minority status, none would have gone so far as to conceive of themselves as engaging in a deviant act. As one participant argued, albeit with regard to park pathways rather than city streets, running may not have been the originally preferred or anticipated activity, but it is now a pervasive fact of urban space:

> I think these places were built for it! I think these days, perhaps not originally, obviously this is a manor house park, but at some point somebody went, "we'll turn that into a public park" and they must have known that people that want to go for a run are gonna use that. And if they didn't, they weren't thinking.
>
> (GA)

In the UK these days, the runner is, or at least should be, an expected urban subject (Latham 2015).

The principal line of disagreement among respondents about who is most responsible for avoiding collisions centered on the issue of speed. Those who stressed runners' obligations claimed that the speed at which they are moving, which is probably greater than might be anticipated by many on the streets, makes it incumbent on them to bear the responsibility: "I think I would take responsibility because I'm the one moving faster" (GA). Or in the words of another participant: "It is my responsibility to make sure we don't hit each other because I'm going faster" (MVE). Other respondents, however, used an identical argument – that runners are moving more quickly than other pedestrians – to impose this responsibility upon pedestrians. As one noted: "Because they're walking and I'm running, they can get out of my way" (MVE). Differences in speed here form the basis of two antithetical arguments: on the one hand, runners learn to be more attuned to the chances of a collision and are thus more likely to be vigilant against such occurrences. On the other hand, pedestrians' relative slowness means they are more agile than runners, able to stop or hastily change direction than runners in the event that they are surprised by a potential collision.

Most participants in the study took a more diplomatic stance, however, advancing the view that the task is a shared one. In one interview, the participant commented simply: "I always think it is our responsibility as much as anyone else's" (GA). Another remarked: "It [the responsibility] would be both of ours'" (MVE) and "I think it's a joint effort" (MVE). Although never offering a lengthier analysis of the matter, these runners felt that since both parties have an equal claim to space, both they and pedestrians should take responsibility in negotiating their fleeting but important encounters.

Passing pedestrians

The differing views about who should assume responsibility for avoiding conflict when pedestrians are passed raises the question of how passing-by is actually accomplished. Although a number of approaches were demonstrated by our participants, they were all in some way or another related to three in particular – choosing a side, stepping down, and slaloming. Each of these three approaches is aided by particular "tools" of encounter. Runners' subjective desires to maintain flow, speed and momentum (basically, not to stop running) are aided primarily by the body as a tool for signaling intent and actualizing movements. At the same time, runners' attunements to the potential of, and potential solution to, encounters are facilitated by a wider arsenal of bodily senses and distinct micro-geographical sensibilities – enrolling feeling, rhythm, speed, sight, hearing, memory, spatial calculations, and intuition into the negotiation of encounters.

The tactic of choosing a side is predicated on the assumption that both runners and pedestrians share some responsibility for preventing a collision from occurring and thus are equals in the mobility hierarchy. Here, runners use bodily movements to signify their intention but rely on pedestrians responding appropriately (or at least as the approaching runner expects them to). As one participant explained: "My strategy is I pick a side I am going on first ... I choose a side of the pavement first so they can see that I am on that side of the pavement" (MVE). Another more stridently reported that they used overt bodily gestures to show their planned movements: "I kind of like duck to one side as an indication saying, 'I'm leaving you space to get past this side – kind of take the hint or I will run into you!' " (MVE). Although the action of physically moving is a strong indication of the way a runner would like to negotiate the situation, it is generally at its most effective in relatively straightforward scenarios, where the direction of the pedestrian being passed is evident and does not run in parallel to the direction of the runner.

More complex situations – such as when space is narrow, there are large groups of pedestrians, or the runner is approaching from behind – frequently rely not only on the runner taking more (and often complete) responsibility for avoiding collision, but also on using the body far more actively than simply indicating intent and following a pre-determined course. To navigate these complexities, participants used two further tactics – stepping down and slaloming. Stepping down refers to when a runner steps off the sidewalk, choosing to run in the separated space of the road to avoid conflict with pedestrians. This can be seen in Figure 11.1 where the runner, in approaching the dog walker, takes a very wide berth, including moving onto the road (Image C), despite there appearing to be enough space on the pavement. The unpredictable nature of the dog and the risk of tripping over it or becoming entangled with its leash resulted in this precaution. To some, this notion of "stepping down" is unfathomable given the risks involved in entering the roadway. Yet, to others, the danger from potentially erratic or perhaps encumbered space-sharers is greater than that from cars, whose movements somehow "flow" more reliably, or who might have more room for maneuver. As one respondent pointed out, if the momentary meeting of runner and pedestrian occurs in limited space, inevitably something must give:

> I would much rather be the person who got in the road than move somebody else into the road because I would feel like that would be my responsibility. I mean they are not going to die but say if something happened in that second, that would be my fault.

(GA)

Figure 11.1 "Stepping down" (source: Author).

Others came from a slightly different perspective, revealing a sense of duty toward fellow space-sharers in the sense of not wishing to endanger them as a result of being on a run:

> Yesterday there was a guy walking his dog up towards Plymstock [an area of Plymouth] and he went to go in the road and I went "no no, I'll go in the road, mate" and I think he appreciated that. But I appreciated his gesture but he had two little dogs on a leash and it's easier for me to stay narrowly in the road than it is for two dogs.
>
> (GA)

The final tactic is the slalom, which involves weaving the body around and past other space-sharers, and indeed space-sharing objects, often in response to unexpected obstacles or movements made by others. As with stepping down, slaloming requires runners to take responsibility for creating their own route through a shared space. As one participant noted in explaining the sequence of events in Figure 11.2:

> RESEARCHER: So here you are just about to overtake some people but you do so in quite a strange fashion. You seem to be going to the left and then all of a sudden change your mind?
>
> PARTICIPANT: Yeah, because that guy, he didn't seem to be too aware of me and started to move further to the left, so I thought if he is moving further across, I don't want him to just step into the path I was going so I thought I would just take that out of the equation completely.
>
> (MVE)

Although it is the most difficult and potentially disruptive means of passing, there are occasions when it may be a preferred option. In such situations, runners find it useful to have some opportunity to survey a situation before actually deciding what to do. One respondent chose a slalom because, "I saw it from a while off. I just squeezed through. It would take less time to squeeze through then go around to the left and I won't have to go back on myself" (MVE). For another:

> Well, I knew what pace I was going at and what pace they were going at and I worked out that instead of going in the road and around the car, that if I just waited for half a second I could just squeeze through a gap between them.
>
> (MVE)

It is clear from these passages that decisions about whether to choose a side, step down, or slalom have to be made in an instant. This does not

Figure 11.2 "The slalom" (source: Author).

necessarily mean they are random or that they are straightforwardly habit-ual or mindless. Rather, urban runners become adept at making quick and calculated judgments to inform them about which spatial tactic would be the best, most appropriate, and plausible in any given encounter. Such an attunement brings to light differences not only in terms of how particip-ants believe encounters should be negotiated, but also how they actually happen. While most participants suggested some shared responsibility with pedestrians, the burden of negotiating such encounters generally falls solely upon the runners. The urban runners in this study felt that they belong in public space, claiming an equal right as pedestrians and overwhelmingly agreeing that the negotiation of space should be a shared task. Despite this, the physical movements of both runners and pedestrians would suggest that walkers top the mobile hierarchy, with runners most often breaking their passage, changing their route, and conceding their mobile/sporting subjectivities.

Toward a running order

Understanding the actual taking place of sport is necessarily a question for critical geographers of sport. It is at the level of the everyday that geographies happen, get made, and remade – that speed, space, power, and difference play out on any city's street. Yet the everyday is also a level that has tended to fall outside of sport geography's purview and the methodological tools used here, including go-along and mobile-video-ethnography interviews, suggest one solution for capturing these mundane and momentary experiences, and for visualizing runners' situational subjectivities on the streets.

This chapter thus underscores the need for more research into the everyday of sporting practices and the wider socio-political perspectives on the place of sport they reveal. The case study demonstrates how an analytical focus on fleeting encounters can enrich our understanding of how social order is created and everyday citizenship is produced on the go (Brown 2012). Here, citizenship is a deeply embodied and physical practice; it is something done, not just given/received from the state. The unscripted-encounter choreographies enlist the bodily capacities, sensory receptors, subjective desires, and communicative mediations of those involved, pitting them against one another until a solution is reached. If taken as emblematic, this study suggests that sporting practices and subjectivities are more widely subordinate in urban public spaces than other mobile practices.

Of course, the research for this chapter focused on particular individuals, in one particular city, in one particular country. As an everyday sport enjoyed by many people around the world, there are undoubtedly plural running cultures and norms between countries and cities, with implications for how people understand and negotiate personal encounters with pedestrians. The thoughts of pedestrians are sorely lacking here also. Considering the way in which non-runners encounter runners in the shared spaces of the city has the potential to add significantly to the analysis of the place of sport in urban public space.

Many sports have clear territories – a purpose-built site for it to take place. Moving these sports into a city's shared spaces introduces new questions about primacy of use. Perhaps it is precisely because sports are imagined to have a dedicated territory – the field, the track, the stadium – that sports and sporting bodies become marginalized as "out of place" (see Nelson, Chapter 9 this volume). Whatever the reasons, what is clear is that such subordination is certainly tolerable – and, in cases, actively embraced – by those engaged in everyday urban sports. Whilst many participants enthused in sharing their opinions on pedestrians, none were too irate or emasculated by the outcome of encounters to have changed their practices radically (barring the avoidance of particular pedestrian black spots). These are, after all, moments in the background.

References

AELTCC (2014). Grass Courts. *Wimbeldon.com*. Available at: www.wimbledon.com/en_GB/atoz/grass_courts.html (accessed November 12, 2015).

Aldred, R., and K. Jungnickel (2012). Constructing Mobile Places between "Leisure" and "Transport": A Case Study of Two Group Cycle Rides. *Sociology* 46(3): 523–39.

Amin, A. (2002). Ethnicity and the Multicultural City: Living with Diversity. *Environment and Planning A* 34(6): 959–80.

Anderson, J. (2004). Talking Whilst Walking: A Geographical Archaeology of Knowledge. *Area* 36(3): 254–61.

Anderson, J., K. Askins, I. Cook, L. Desforges, J. Evans, M. Fannin, D. Fuller, H. Griffiths, D. Lambert, R. Lee, J. MacLeavy, L. Mayblin, J. Morgan, B. Payne, J. Pykett, D. Roberts, and T. Skelton (2008). What Is Geography's Contribution to Making Citizens? *Geography* 93(1): 34–9.

Antonsich, M. (2010). Searching for Belonging: An Analytical Framework. *Geography Compass* 4(6): 644–59.

Back, L. (2015). Why Everyday Life Matters: Class, Community and Making Life Livable. *Sociology* 49(5): 820–36.

Bale, J. (1994). *Landscapes of Modern Sport*. Leicester: Leicester University Press.

Bale, J. (2000a). The Rhetoric of Running: Representation of Kenyan Body Culture in the Early Twentieth Century. In *Sports, Body and Health* eds. J. Hansen and N. K. Nielsen. Odense, Norway: University Press of Southern Denmark, 123–31.

Bale, J. (2000b). Sport as Power: Running as Resistance. In *Entanglements of Power: Geographies of Domination and Resistance* eds. J. S. Sharpe, P. Routledge, C. Philo, and R. Paddison. London: Routledge, 148–63.

Bale, J. (2003). *Sports Geography*. London: Routledge.

Bale, J. (2004). *Running Cultures: Racing in Time and Space*. London: Routledge.

Bale, J. (2008). *Anti-Sport Sentiments in Literature: Batting for the Opposition*. Abingdon: Routledge.

Bale, J. (2011). Running: Running as Working. In *Geographies of Mobilities: Practices, Spaces, Subjects* eds. T. Cresswell and P. Merriman. Farnham: Ashgate, 35–50.

Binnie, J., T. Edensor, J. Holloway, S. Millington, and C. Young (2007). Mundane Mobilities, Banal Travels. *Social & Cultural Geography* 8(2): 165–74.

Brown, K. (2012). Sharing Public Space Across Difference: Attunement and the Contested Burdens of Choreographing Encounter. *Social & Cultural Geography* 13(7): 801–20.

Brown, K., R. Dilley, and K. Marshall (2008). Using a Head-Mounted Video Camera to Understand Social Worlds and Experiences. *Sociological Research Online* 13(6): Article 1.

Castree, N., R. Kitchin, and A. Rogers (2013). *Oxford Dictionary of Human Geography*. Oxford: Oxford University Press.

Cheshire, L., and M. Woods (2009). Citizenship and Governmentality, Rural. In *International Encyclopedia of Human Geography* Vol. 2 eds. R. Kitchen and N. Thrift. London: Elsevier, 112–18.

Chouinard, V. (2009). Citizenship. In *International Encyclopedia of Human Geography* Vol. 2 eds. R. Kitchen and N. Thrift. London: Elsevier, 107–12.

Cidell, J. (2014). Running Road Races as Transgressive Event Mobilities. *Social & Cultural Geography* 15(5): 571–83.

Cook, S. (forthcoming). Running in a station: everyday emergencies and the design of mobilities. In *Mobilising Design, Designing Mobilities: Intersections, Affordances, Relations* eds. J. Spinney, S. Reimer, and P. Pinch. London: Routledge.

Cook, S., J. Shaw, and P. Simpson (2015). Jography: Exploring Meanings, Experiences and Spatialities of Recreational Road-Running. *Mobilities* DOI: 10.1080/17450101.2015.1034455.

Cresswell, T. (1996). *In Place/Out of Place: Geography, Ideology, and Transgression*. London: University of Minnesota Press.

Edensor, T., and S. Richards (2007). Snowboarders vs Skiers: Contested Choreographies of the Slopes. *Leisure Studies* 26(1): 97–114.

Evans, J., and P. Jones (2011). The Walking Interview: Methodology, Mobility and Place. *Applied Geography* 31(2): 849–58.

Hockey, J., and J. Allen-Collinson (2013). Distance Running as Play/Work: Training-Together as a Joint Accomplishment. In *Ethnomethodology at Play* eds. P. Tolmie and M. Rouncefield. London: Ashgate, 211–35.

Howe, P., and C. Morris (2009). An Exploration of the Co-Production of Performance Running Bodies and Natures Within "Running Taskscapes." *Journal of Sport & Social Issues* 33(3): 308–30.

Ingold, T. (1993). The Temporality of the Landscape. *World Archaeology* 25(2): 152–74.

Jensen, O. (2013). *Staging Mobilities*. Abingdon: Routledge.

Latham, A. (2015). The History of a Habit: Jogging as a Palliative to Sedentariness in 1960s America. *Cultural Geographies* 22(1): 103–26.

Leitner, H. (2012). Spaces of Encounters: Immigration, Race, Class, and the Politics of Belonging in Small-Town America. *Annals of the Association of American Geographers* 102(4): 828–46.

Neal, S., and K. Murji (2015). Sociologies of Everyday Life: Editors' Introduction to the Special Issue. *Sociology* 49(5): 811–19.

Noble, G. (2009). 'Countless Acts of Recognition': Young Men, Ethnicity and the Messiness of Identities in Everyday Life. *Social & Cultural Geography* 10(8): 875–91.

Painter, J., and C. Philo (1995). Spaces of Citizenship: An Introduction. *Political Geography* 14(2): 107–20.

Patton, J. W. (2004). Transportation Worlds: Designing Infrastructures and Forms of Urban Life. Unpublished PhD thesis. Rensselaer Polytechnic Institute.

Ronkainen, N., M. Harrison, and T. Ryba (2014). Running, Being, and Beijing: An Existential Exploration of a Runner Identity. *Qualitative Research in Psychology* 11(2): 189–210.

Simpson, P. (2014). Video. In *The Routledge Handbook of Mobilities* eds. P. Adey, D. Bissell, K. Hannam, P. Merriman, and M. Sheller. London: Routledge, 542–52.

Skinner, S. (2015). Mothering, Running, and the Renegotiation of Running Identity. *Qualitative Sociology Review* 11(3): 18–39.

Smith, S. (2000). Citizenship. In *The Dictionary of Human Geography*, 4th edn, eds. R. Johnston, K. Gregory, G. Pratt, and M. Watts. Oxford: Blackwell, 83–4.

Staeheli, L., P. Ehrkamp, H. Leitner, and C. Nagel (2012). Dreaming the Ordinary: Daily Life and the Complex Geographies of Citizenship. *Progress in Human Geography* 36(5): 628–44.

UKA (2014). UKA Rules for Competition. *British Athletics*. Available at: www. britishathletics.org.uk/EasysiteWeb/getresource.axd?AssetID=126114&type=full &servicetype=Attachment (accessed November 12, 2015).

Valentine, G. (2007). Theorizing and Researching Intersectionality: A Challenge for Feminist Geography. *The Professional Geographer* 59(1): 10–21.

Valentine, G. (2008). Living with Difference: Reflections on Geographies of Encounter. *Progress in Human Geography* 32(3): 323–37.

Vettenniemi, E. (2012). Epilogue: Going the Extra Mile. *The International Journal of the History of Sport* 29(7): 1090–95.

Waldron, J. (2006). Cosmopolitan Norms. In *Another Cosmopolitanism* ed. R. Post. Oxford: Oxford University Press, 83–101.

Wilson, H.F. (2016). On geography and encounter Bodies, borders, and difference. *Progress in Human Geography*. DOI: 10.1177/0309132516645958.

Winters, C. (1980). Running. *Landscape* 24(2): 19–22.

Wood, N., and L. Waite (2011). Editorial: Scales of belonging. *Emotion, Space and Society* 4(4): 201–12.

Yarwood, R. (2013). *Citizenship*. London: Routledge.

Chapter 12

Mallparks and the symbolic reconstruction of urban space

Michael Friedman

Located in Bloomington, Minnesota, the Mall of America (MoA) is the busiest and second largest shopping mall in the United States. Covering 2.5 million square feet and welcoming 40 million visitors per year, MoA features more than 500 stores over four levels, 20 full service restaurants, an aquarium, a comedy club, exhibition space, a wedding chapel, and the seven-acre Nickelodeon Universe® with 17 amusement park rides (MoA 2016). Toward making this enormity navigable, MoA is divided into four distinct shopping areas, each with its own theme and design palate (Goss 1999).

Before becoming a shopping mall qua theme park, the site was occupied by Metropolitan Stadium ("The Met"), the home of the Minnesota Twins baseball team and the Minnesota Vikings football team between 1961 and 1981. A plaque embedded in the floor within Nickelodeon Universe marks the location of home plate and a red seat paneled on a distant wall identifies the landing point of The Met's longest home run by Harmon Killebrew. There is a Minnesota Vikings Locker Room Official Team Store, ten stores sell Twins' gear, and the Field of Dreams shop sells certified memorabilia from The Met. However, echoes from cheering masses, great athletes, and legendary managers faded long ago. A shopping mall has replaced a ballpark.

Twelve miles to the north sits Target Field, the Twins' home since 2010. Located on eight acres in downtown Minneapolis, the 39,504-seat stadium has welcomed an average of 2.9 million visitors annually. Three concourses lined with shopping kiosks and concession stands sell food, drink, and merchandise. In addition to the traditional ballpark fare of peanuts, hot dogs, and beer, the Twins offer an 80-item menu, including Cuban sandwiches, burritos, walleye fish and chips, vegetarian options, craft beers, and Killebrew cream soda. Six permanent retail shops and numerous portable stands peddle Twins' souvenirs, including clothes, novelty items, and memorabilia. A 5,757 square foot high-definition video board and several smaller scoreboards show replays, statistics, out of town scores, entertainment, and advertisements. Eight ATM machines facilitate further consumption (Target Field 2010).

As MoA marks the landing point of Killebrew's 520-foot clout, Target Field celebrates it with the 70 square foot Golden Glove art installation located an identical distance from home plate on Target Plaza outside the Kirby Puckett gate. Other artwork decorating Target Field include bronze statues of team legends (Puckett, Killebrew, and Rod Carew), murals celebrating Minnesota, oversized vintage baseball cards, and photographs from baseball history. The Twins further celebrate these histories by naming concession stands, food offerings, entry gates, and lounges for former players, exhibiting significant artifacts within the Delta 360 Lounge, honoring state champion baseball teams in the Town Ball Tavern, and displaying items from past stadiums in the Metropolitan Club. Thus, the 41-minute light rail trip between the Mall of America and Target Field connects baseball's past, present, and future. At the line's Bloomington origin, time has separated a ballpark from the shopping mall and theme park. At its Minneapolis terminus, the ballpark, shopping mall, and theme park have been successfully melded together to create a new type of consumption site: a mallpark.

The journey from Metropolitan Stadium to Target Field also represents the evolution toward what Ritzer (2010) calls the "new means of consumption." Ritzer's (2011) work on McDonaldization discusses the rationalization of consumption, while his work on enchantment (Ritzer 2010) focuses on the spectacularization of consumption environments toward countering the alienating aspects of rationalization. Mallparks display these tensions through the fusion of rationalized revenue-generating processes with spectacular thematic environments. Yet, the concept of the mallpark does not suggest a radical change in stadium design toward emphasizing economic activity. Baseball spaces have been commodified since the 1850s and economic considerations have always been central to designers (Gershman 1993). This generation is different, however, in the sophistication of efforts maximizing economic activity both within and around stadiums and the prominence of aesthetic elements.

Examining mallparks as consumption spaces still captures only part of their symbolic importance. Henri Lefebvre (1970) stated that the social relations of power are abstract, but tangibly expressed within the built environment. For this reason, spaces can be read as products of power relations, but also dialectically for the ways in which they produce, reproduce, and challenge those power relations. As will be discussed, mallparks are particularly representative of the culturally driven, postmodern capitalism of the early twenty-first century (Harvey 1989; Jameson 1991). They are concrete manifestations of abstract ideologies and social relations that elevate commercial exchange over other forms of social interactions, require economic resources to participate in community life, and reduce history to a sanitized source of meaning-rich aesthetic material. This research examines the material and symbolic aspects of mallparks to develop a deeper understanding of the contemporary moment.

Producing the consumption spaces of late capitalism

Since the 1970s, the economies of Western Europe and North America have restructured as manufacturing has largely relocated to lower-wage, lower-regulation areas on the global periphery (Harvey 1989). As industrial employment has declined, the service sector has expanded with the consumption of goods, cultural products, and experiences taking a more prominent position within economic life. In this new economic order, "aesthetic production has become integrated into commodity production generally" (Jameson 1991: 4) as products are consumed as much (if not more so) for their novelty, image, and meaning as much as for their functionality.

With production practices central to analyses of political economy, the processes facilitating consumption have received less attention. Ritzer's (2011) theory of McDonaldization describes the rationalization of service industry practices through efficiency, calculability, predictability, and control. While these processes increase profitability, they also standardize consumer experiences and can create "disenchanted" spaces that alienate consumers through homogenization and dehumanization (Ritzer 2010). Producers of leisure sites, including shopping malls, amusement parks, retail stores, casinos, restaurants, sports facilities, and museums attempt to "enchant" consumption spaces by creating spectacular environments using meaning-rich aesthetic elements, utilizing extravaganzas and simulations, and collapsing barriers between different types of consumption (Ritzer 2010). Las Vegas casino-hotels exemplify enchantment efforts with elaborate stage productions, magnificent architecture simulating buildings from distant times and places, and with around-the-clock offerings of concentrated and diverse consumption opportunities (Gottdiener *et al.* 1999).

Although Lefebvre's theories can be used to analyze built environments, space was not the focus of his research. Rather, Lefebvre used space, along with everyday life, rural life, politics and the state, and fascism, as entry points into studying exploitation, alienation, and mystification (Shields 1999). Framed in this way, the built environment represents a material expression of inequitable power relations within the dominant mode of production (Lefebvre 1991). Toward eliminating inequalities, Lefebvre (1996) proposed a "Right to the City" that would provide all residents with access, use, and the ability to shape urban space. This right further demands that inhabitants not be excluded from urban spaces, but, rather, be fully involved in governance regardless of citizenship status or economic resources.

However, within the conditions of post-industrial urban governance, hopes of inclusivity remain unfulfilled and seem more unlikely to be realized as cities are being transformed into consumption spaces. Since the 1970s, many cities in North America and Europe have invested substantial public resources to create amenities – such as hotels, museums, festival marketplaces, restaurants, bars, clubs, sports facilities, convention facilities, and casinos – to attract spending from tourists and business travelers (Judd 1999, 2003). These facilities are concentrated into clearly defined "tourist bubbles" that are "cordoned off and designed to cosset the affluent visitor, while simultaneously warding off the threatening native" (Fainstein and Gladstone 1999: 26). As such, the urban poor tend only to be present in low-wage service jobs, especially with their limited ability to engage in consumption activities and as vigorously enforced rules limit other possibilities (Flusty 2001).

Lefebvre (1991) suggested a framework of spatial practice, representations of space, and spaces of representation as one way to analyze power relations within space. Spatial practice (or perceived space) encompasses the physical environment, people's everyday activities and routines, and the interpersonal interactions. Representations of space (or conceived space) exist at the intersection of knowledge and power as dominant groups design space to promote their interests. Spaces of representation (or lived space) encompass the ways in which people invest a space with meaning through use. Although "lived spaces" offer potential for resistance against dominant conceptions of space, people often conform to expectations and reinforce narratives that dominant groups seek to inscribe in space.

While a full Lefebvrean analysis would involve all three moments of production, this chapter is limited to exploring spatial practices, which regulate and structure social relations in three ways:

- spatial practices help determine the specific functions, meanings, and distinctive elements found within a space;
- spatial practices impact access to and the availability of space to groups; and
- spatial practices define boundaries between areas (Lefebvre 1991).

Specifically, this chapter examines the rationalization and spectacularization of mallparks as reenchanted consumption sites, and the use of baseball stadiums within the transformation of urban areas into landscapes of consumption. This analysis is based on materials collected between 2013 and 2015 through qualitative research methods, including ethnographic site visits to stadiums, archival research at the Baseball Hall of Fame, interviews with stadium designers, and textual analyses of newspapers, books, team websites, and other media sources.

Mallparks as sites of consumption

A baseball stadium's basic purpose has always been to sell the opportunity to attend a baseball game. No matter the era or building material, stadiums are designed to control access by admitting only ticketholders and excluding everyone else. While this function has not changed, stadiums have become more effective and efficient revenue generators through sales of ancillary products, better management of ticket inventories, and the development of premium experiences. Competing in a cluttered entertainment marketplace, baseball stadiums have improved the quality of their entertainment product with diverse experiences enhanced by immersion in a meaning-rich, themed environment. This section considers the evolution of stadium design and examines the themes and consumption offerings within mallparks.

The history of baseball stadium design

Within 20 years of the first recorded game, William Cammeyer opened the first enclosed baseball diamond in 1862 with bleachers seating 1,500 (Shannon and Kalinsky 1975). First-generation baseball facilities generally were wooden structures that were inexpensive to build, but unsafe and susceptible to fire. They lacked concession facilities, but employed independent vendors to sell food, drinks, and souvenirs. Facilities were mostly unadorned, though Cincinnati's Palace of the Fans was built in a Beaux-Arts style with Corinthian columns, concrete opera boxes, and elongated bars along the base lines (Gershman 1993).

Ritzer and Stillman (2001) describe the next generation as "early modern stadiums." Built between 1909 and 1930 from brick, steel, and reinforced concrete, ballparks were designed for durability and constructed in stages, with renovations adding new sections, upper levels, and lights. Ballparks which had capacities of 25,000–50,000 included three types of seats: box seats, wooden grandstands, and bleacher benches (Gershman 1993). Team owners built their own facilities, which were rented to other baseball tenants and for boxing matches, football games, and civic events (Ritter 1992). Concessions and souvenirs were tertiary revenue sources that often made the difference between profit and loss (Shannon and Kalinsky 1975). Chicago's Wrigley Field built the first permanent concession stands in 1914 and menus were generally limited (Gershman 1993).

Despite designs emphasizing functionality, some ballparks featured aesthetic embellishments such as the cupola of Philadelphia's Shibe Field and the rotunda at Brooklyn's Ebbets Field (Gershman 1993). However, the most distinctive features tended to be practical responses to specific site problems. Property lines necessitated asymmetrical outfields and teams constructed oversized outfield walls to make home runs more difficult and prevent neighbors from watching games for free. Fenway Park's Green Monster was built because the City of Boston would not sell Lansdowne Street during the ballpark's 1934 renovation (Ritter 1992). Piecemeal construction obstructed views from lower deck seats with support columns and created anomalies like the home run porch in Detroit's Tiger Stadium, which overhung the field by 10 feet (Gershman 1993).

Ritzer and Stillman (2001) describe these ballparks as "enchanted" and note that the last two in operation, Fenway Park and Wrigley Field, are considered among the best places to watch games as century-long histories, players, events, and fan interactions provide a patina of meaning. Ritter (1992: 3) attributes strong emotional connections to intimacy as ballparks were "built on a human scale that allowed spectators and players to share a common experience." However, by the 1950s, many early modern stadiums were considered obsolete as they needed age-related repairs and were located in changing neighborhoods with poor highway access and insufficient parking.

Late modern stadiums (1930s–80s) were generally large, round concrete structures that had minimal adornment. Designs offered comfort, convenience, cleanliness, and unobstructed views as cantilevered designs eliminated support posts. Excellent highway access and large parking lots accommodated automobiles. Artificial turf surfaces, large seating capacities, and occasional domes allowed municipal owners to maximize uses and provided parity to professional football tenants (Ritter 1992; Ritzer and Stillman 2001). Stadiums included many revenue-generating features with better-equipped concession facilities, permanent souvenir stands, and new innovations, including luxury boxes, private clubs, and restaurants. Technology helped to enhance game experiences by replacing hand-operated scoreboards with electronic scoreboards providing game information, pictures, statistics, and entertainment. During the 1980s, scoreboards were upgraded further with video screens capable of showing replays, pre-produced videos, and advertisements (Gershman 1993).

Although stadiums promised to improve viewing experiences, they were disenchanted with symmetrical outfields, artificial turf, and generic designs offering few distinguishing characteristics (Ritter 1992). Fully enclosed seating rings and domes exacerbated feelings of placelessness by sealing off stadiums from the surrounding city. Stadiums also undermined the quality of the baseball experience with capacities that were too large and seats with poor sightlines and distant from the field. Just as stadiums addressed the perceived deficiencies of ballparks, Ritzer and Stillman (2001) suggest "postmodern stadiums" (described here as mallparks) responded to the disenchanting aspects of late-modern stadiums. Retro aesthetics, asymmetrical outfields, smaller capacities, and connections to surrounding cities offer better experiences and suggest irrationality and unpredictability.

Despite appearances, mallparks are actually more rationalized with teams generating higher revenues through market segmentation, upscale amenities, and more diverse consumption environments. Within this context, aesthetic elements act as an essential façade that obscures increasing rationalization (Friedman *et al.* 2004). Thus, in order to understand their built environments, it is necessary to examine both the consumption and symbolic landscapes of mallparks.

The consumption landscape of the mallpark

In their attempts to spectacularize mallparks, architects and team officials have experimented to find a mix of amenities to attract corporate spending, draw wealthy consumers, appeal to families, and satisfy long-term fans. Catering to different market segments, teams offer diverse consumption opportunities that have monetized virtually the entire facility. Architectural critic Philip Kennicott (2008) described Washington's Nationals Park as a "machine for baseball and for sucking the money out of the pockets of people who like baseball." Seemingly hyperbolic, Kennicott's observation recognizes the highly commercialized design of mallparks.

Historically, teams sold three types of tickets: box seats, grandstands, and bleachers, with minor price variations based on distance to home plate. The 1985 Baltimore Orioles were typical in selling tickets in Memorial Stadium at five prices between $3.50 and $8.50. In mallparks, computerized ticketing programs allow teams more flexibility in setting prices. In 2015, the Orioles divided Camden Yards into 22 different seating areas and sold tickets at 12 prices between $10 and $224. Dynamic pricing further calibrates tickets on a game-to-game basis by charging more for weekend dates and popular opponents (Baltimore Orioles 1985, 2015).

At the top price tier, teams sell luxury suites and premium club seats with superior views of the game. The very best box seats, some of which are closer to the batter than the pitcher, demand the highest prices. New York's New Yankee Stadium sells season tickets in its "Legends Suite" for $125,000 and luxury suites for as much as $800,000 (Kane 2012). Ushers and security guards strictly control access to premium areas, which are also protected by special entrances, express elevators and escalators, physical barriers, and moats. Premium tickets also include upgraded amenities, including gourmet restaurants and buffets, bars with premium liquor, exclusive shops, and less crowded restrooms. Furnishings include more comfortable and spacious seats, marble and carpet-covered floors, air-conditioned lounges, and hardwood-appointed walls. Decorations include fine artwork and authentic team artifacts. Ticket holders receive valet parking, in-seat waiter service, and concierge and business services. Some teams offer special experiences; buyers in the Yankees Legends Suite can watch batting practice from the field, attend pregame press conferences, enjoy events with retired players, and go on an all-expense paid trip to a road game (New York Yankees 2015).

Fans without premium tickets do not lack consumption opportunities: concourses provide diverse dining, shopping, museum, amusement park, theater, and recreation experiences. Mallpark dining has gone well beyond traditional stadium fare, as hot dogs and peanuts are served alongside sushi, tacos, cheesesteaks, barbeque sandwiches, funnel cakes, churros, and vegan offerings. Several mallparks feature signature items, such as the $26 "Boomstick," a 24-inch all beef hot dog covered in chili, cheese, onions, and jalapenos at the Rangers Ballpark in Arlington. National chains, such as Panda Express, Hooters, Outback Steakhouse, and Waffle House, operate concession stands, while TGI Friday's offers full table service in Milwaukee's Miller Park and Phoenix's Chase Field. Patrons can satisfy their thirst with much more than soda, water, and beer as mallparks also offer craft beers and sodas, margaritas, frozen daiquiris, and hard liquors from portable carts, atop party decks, or in full service bars. Tropicana Field in St. Petersburg, Florida even has a cigar bar.

Mallparks provide many shopping opportunities. At concourse kiosks, attendees can buy team merchandise, including shirts, hats, replica jerseys, and sundry items. Central team stores offer broader product selection and specialty shops exclusively sell hats or retro clothing. Several mallparks have children's stores, including five with Build-a-Bear Workshops, in which patrons can make their own stuffed toys of the team mascot. Women can buy designer fashions at Alyssa Milano's Touch boutique in New York's Citi Field or at the Pink by Victoria's Secret stand at Rangers Ballpark. Many mallparks sell sport art and collectibles, customize bats and jerseys for fans, and offer game-used and player-autographed items guaranteed as authentic by Major League Baseball (MLB).

Most mallparks offer museum experiences. In concourse displays and dedicated areas, Halls of Fame celebrate team history by recognizing important players, displaying trophies, memorabilia and photographs, and showing videos of significant events. The Tampa Bay Rays, who only began play in 1998, borrow from baseball's broader history by hosting the Ted Williams Museum and Hitters Hall of Fame at Tropicana Field. Legacy Square in Pittsburgh's PNC Park commemorates the Negro Leagues with statues, interactive touchscreens, and a film in the 25-seat Legacy Theater. Beyond history, many mallparks curate extensive baseball-themed art collections, and Tropicana Field offers a 10,000-gallon touch tank full of rays.

For young children, mallparks provide playgrounds with climbing equipment, slides, baseball diamonds, and special areas to meet the team mascot. Older children can test their baseball skills in speed pitch machines and batting cages, and video gaming skills in areas sponsored by EA

Sport's Baseball 2K series. Tropicana Field offers a carnival midway and Detroit's Comerica Park has a Ferris wheel and carousel. At San Diego's Petco Park, visitors can relax in the "Park at the Park," 2.7 grassy acres beyond the centerfield concourse or hang out at "The Beach" below the centerfield bleachers. People can enjoy an outdoor shower at Chicago's US Cellular Field. At Chase Field, the Diamondbacks sell a field level swimming pool suite, complete with hot tub, beach, pool towels, and lifeguards. Many mallparks offer convention facilities and Toronto's Rogers Centre is attached to a 348-room hotel. Once patrons exhaust themselves dining, shopping, learning about baseball history, appreciating art, supervising playing children, enjoying carnival rides, brushing sand from their feet, and feeding sea creatures, they can even watch a baseball game.

The symbolic landscape of the mallpark

As mallparks have become thoroughly commodified, theming helps obscure rationalized consumption processes and intensify people's experiences by using recognizable symbols to create an overarching "motif that defines an entire built space" (Gottdiener 2001: 3). To do so, designers use symbolically rich aesthetic elements which derive meanings from shared cultural narratives within national discourses, history, geography, religion, literature, film, sport, theater, and music with the intention of eliciting positive affective responses from consumers as they associate the space with these broader narratives (Gottdiener 2001; Lukas 2007). Disney theme parks epitomize this process by using distinctive architecture, rides, foods, music, and employee attire to refer to such themes as fantasy and small-town America (Bryman 1999).

Baseball is unique within American sports for the resonance of mythology, history, and the characteristics of place, which may help to explain the exalted status of Wrigley Field and Fenway Park and the popularity of retro aesthetics within mallpark design (Bale 1994). To provide "baseball with a baseball theme" (Ritzer and Stillman 2001: 110), mallparks reuse historic buildings, showcase local foods, honor past players, and simulate architectural features of ballparks. These elements help to enchant mallparks by instilling meanings drawn from baseball and the surrounding urban environment into their consumption spaces. Four main themes stand out: baseball history; baseball architecture; baseball as a cultural form; and the local context. Themes are not mutually exclusive as aesthetic elements are multivalent:

- Baseball history: Beyond the Halls of Fame contributing to their consumption mixes, mallparks represent team and baseball history through art and stadium decorations, on flags displaying titles won and player numbers retired, and in video packages. Teams often bestow special honors upon their greatest players by erecting statues, naming stadium gates, and representing them in other ways. For example, PNC Park features a statue of Roberto Clemente and its 21-foot-high right field wall honors Clemente's position and uniform number. Mallparks also celebrate the local connections of baseball greats with the New York Mets naming Citi Field's rotunda for Jackie Robinson, although he never played for the franchise. Beyond these iconic players, teams also recognize popular players from the past in the names of bars, concessions stands, picnic areas, parking lot zones, and in their entertainment packages.

- Baseball architecture: Mallpark architecture reinforces feelings of pastness by reusing items from previous stadiums and simulating structural and aesthetic features from ballparks. However, these features are used without regard for their original contexts. Distinctive architectural structures that were practical solutions to problems posed by property lines (e.g., Fenway Park's Green Monster) have been reproduced as aesthetic choices in mallparks lacking similar site constraints. Mallpark designers have also decontextualized and reproduced hand-operated scoreboards, Forbes Field's sunshade, Wrigley Field's ivy-covered outfield wall, Ebbets Field's rotunda, Tiger Stadium's home run porch, and the knotholes of St. Louis's Sportsman's Park. Beyond these reproductions, many mallparks reuse items from previous stadiums in attempts to convey some of the meaning associated with the old facility to the new site. For example, in a small war memorial outside its gates, Baltimore's Camden Yards has recycled the art deco letters from the inscription that dedicated Memorial Stadium to the city's war dead.
- Baseball as a cultural form: With its special status within American culture, baseball's language and iconography goes beyond the sport and is evident within art packages and decorations around mallparks. Outside Chase Field, "Based on Balls" is a $10 \times 10 \times 41$-foot kinetic installation complete with miniatures of players, baseballs, hot dogs, and a xylophone playing "Take Me Out to the Ballgame" (Creative Machines n.d.). Baseball equipment is featured in artwork and reproduced to decorate functional items ranging from wooden door handles to concrete anti-terrorism barriers. Baseball references are also used to name concession stands and restaurants, with Anaheim's Angels Stadium selling food from "The Grand Stand," Camden Yards offering "Baseline Burgers," and Rangers Stadium featuring the "Dublin Up Irish Pub."
- Celebrating the local: Whereas stadiums were often perceived as placeless, mallparks are designed to be distinctively local by following local architectural styles, adapting on-site buildings, and using locally sourced materials. In Nationals Park, architect Joseph Spear sought to

represent "the transparency of democracy" through a limestone façade reminiscent of buildings along Washington's National Mall and by using glass (Friedman 2010). Mallparks also showcase cities by offering picturesque views of downtown buildings, landmarks, and surrounding environment, as, for example, the Gateway Arch rises just outside St. Louis's Busch Stadium and AT&T Park borders San Francisco Bay. Referring to local iconography, Coors Field signifies Denver's mile-high altitude with a row of differently colored seats at 5,280 feet above sea level, while home runs light a neon Liberty Bell at Philadelphia's Citizen Bank Park. Local food cultures are also highlighted as prominent local restaurants operate concession stands and mallparks sell local specialties, such as cheesesteaks in Philadelphia and crab cakes in Baltimore.

Mallparks and the symbolic reconstruction of urban space

While mallpark designs concretize ideologies emphasizing consumption, the economic challenges faced by urban governments impact the ways in which mallparks have been built into urban environments. Since the 1950s, cities in the US have been caught in an accelerating spiral of decline due to disinvestment from suburbanization, deindustrialization, and Federal government retrenchment (Friedman *et al.* 2004). Seeking to break this spiral, many urban planners have sought to transform downtown areas from centers of production into landscapes of consumption by directly investing tax revenues, offering subsidies, and providing other incentives and public resources for developers to build infrastructure and operate businesses related to the retail, entertainment, and travel industries.

Substantial public investments in tourist bubbles have resulted in intense competition for tourist and business-travel spending and present two additional problems:

- Tourist areas have become homogenous as a result of risk-averse planners and developers replicating amenities proven successful elsewhere. During the 1980s, many cities built their own versions of Baltimore's Harborplace festival marketplace. Flagship convention center hotels proliferated during the 1990s, and developers now lease space to the same national retail, hotel, dining, and entertainment corporations (Harvey 2001; Zukin 1998).
- The ability of sites to attract consumers is constrained by the limited duration of novelty and spectacle (Ritzer 2010). As once new and exciting amenities age and become mundane and other cities update their consumption offerings, competition forces cities to add amenities to spectacularize their tourist bubbles yet again.

Mallparks promise solutions to these dilemmas by enabling cities to differentiate themselves through marketing. As games are transmitted to local, national, and global television audiences, mallparks become the centerpieces of three-hour advertisements for the city. During games, viewers see flattering views of downtown, active waterfronts, and monuments, and hear complimentary banter discussing local history, cultural activities, music, and food. Thus engaged, civic leaders believe viewers would be more likely to visit their city.

In contrast to contemporary practices, construction of ballparks in the early twentieth century was a private sector concern. Team owners built ballparks within the confines of surrounding neighborhoods and in relation to their other business interests, seen, for example, with Ebbets Field in Brooklyn being located near an underused trolley line controlled by the team's owners (Riess 1999). At this time, local governments' minimal interest in ballpark development was paired with marginal public accommodations for team owners. Beginning in the Great Depression, however, municipal stadiums received more public investment, and, by the 1950s, new facilities enticed many MLB teams to relocate and encouraged the League's expansion (Gendzel 1995). For emerging cities in the South and West, MLB teams signified their growing importance, while cities with existing teams built new stadiums to retain them and anchor downtown revitalization (Danielson 1997; Lipsitz 1984). However, renewal efforts often failed as stadiums were surrounded by large parking lots and poorly integrated into broader redevelopment plans (Chapin 2002).

By the 1990s, planners recognized the failure of stadiums to spur redevelopment and began designing mallparks to fit better into tourist bubbles. Several cities pair mallparks with arenas to create "Sports Districts," which regularly attract large crowds and supposedly make areas desirable locations for restaurants, bars, and other shops. San Diego's Petco Field, for example, anchors a comprehensive plan that includes retail, hotel, office, and residential uses and is near the Gaslamp Quarter entertainment district (Chapin 2002). Despite improvements in planning practices and promises of substantial economic benefits, retrospective economic analyses have found minimal, if any, impact (Coates and Humphreys 2008). Chapin (2004) suggests that positive economic impacts are highly localized as sports districts relocate consumption activity from other areas in the city rather than attract new spending.

While mallparks seem to differentiate cities from one another, they also contribute to growing homogenization as their spatial practices are very similar to those of the highly McDonaldized consumption spaces inhabited by the national chains populating tourist bubbles. On the surface, mallparks celebrate the local community with attractive urban vistas, local designs, and local foods, and through the hometown team. These aesthetic presentations make mallparks seem unique, but, as a type, mallparks are *different from one another in the exact same way.* The above formula is replicated in city after city – with appropriate substitutions – but underlying consumption-oriented structures are essentially identical. This homogenization could be explained by several factors. One architectural firm, Populous (formerly HOK Sport), has been involved in 18 of 23 mallparks and has refined its approach based on experiences at other facilities and responses from teams, cities, and consumers. Teams also learn from one another as they request similar amenities from cities and architects during construction and renovation processes, and hire consultants with experience in other mallparks.

Conclusion

The spatial practices of mallparks have broader implications for understanding the production of consumption spaces and urban spaces more generally within the United States. Similar to many other consumption sites, mallparks are highly exclusionary as ticket costs have risen and price-differentiated experiences have proliferated. Although their retro aesthetics suggest historic authenticity, themed environments offer superficial and Disneyfied versions of the past (Bryman 1999). More broadly, the exclusionary tendencies of mallparks are representative of those found in downtown areas due to their transformation into consumption landscapes.

Through much of its history, baseball has been supported by the working-class (Riess 1999). Ballparks were usually built within or near working-class neighborhoods and were accessible by public transportation. Although stadiums were designed to be convenient for middle-class suburban residents, large capacities generally ensured the availability of inexpensive tickets with the average cost for a family of four to attend a game, park a car, eat, and buy souvenirs at $78 in 1991 – the year before the first mallpark opened (Pappas 2001). However, as smaller capacities of mallparks limit the number of affordable tickets and teams have become more sophisticated in maximizing revenues, this cost had risen to $211 by 2015 (Team Marketing Report 2015). With the Bureau of Labor Statistics (2014) estimating the monthly entertainment budget for the average American household to be $207, middle-class consumers are consigned to watch baseball from distant areas, while traditional working-class fans probably cannot afford to attend.

With average costs exceeding the monthly entertainment budget of average American middle-class families, the experiences and amenities associated with premium clubs are generally affordable only to corporations and the wealthy. Most fans are denied access to the exclusive clubs where many mallparks exhibit World Series trophies and other important artifacts of team history. Seats behind home plate were once always filled, but now these areas may be sparsely occupied with corporate season tickets going unused or as patrons luxuriate in their premium benefits. As premium seats have become more luxurious, the experiences and comfort of other areas have been degraded. In ballparks, less expensive upper deck seats were frequently as close to the field as those in the lower deck. The cantilevered designs of stadiums moved upper decks away from the field, while mallparks have further increased the distance with club and suite levels. Bess (2000) estimated the last row of Comiskey Park's (opened in 1910) upper deck was 150 feet from home plate, but in its mallpark replacement, U.S. Cellular Field, the *first* row of the upper deck is 160 feet from home plate. In Nationals Park, non-premium seats are one inch narrower and provide three fewer inches of tread space than seats in RFK Stadium, which opened in 1961 (Levin 2005).

Moving beyond issues of access and amenities, the symbolic elements within mallpark themes can be highly problematic. In general, managers of heritage sites wrestle with questions about whose stories are told, whose are not, and how stories are expressed. While mallparks are not heritage sites, their substantial and decorative use of historical elements promotes a selective version of the past that becomes commonly understood as "authentic." Mallpark art may represent fans of different classes, races, and genders sitting together in ballparks, but this egalitarian myth functions in a similar fashion to the failure of mallparks to acknowledge MLB's systematic racism of the early twentieth century while celebrating Negro League history. Eschewing historical complexity in favor of a gauzy nostalgia that distracts and comforts consumers, this sanitization of the past ultimately serves commercial purposes (Bryman 1999).

Within the broader urban context, mallparks contribute to the growing exclusion of the poor from cities valuing visitors over residents. Supporters promote public investments in consumption sites as ways of attracting suburbanites, tourists, and business travelers – whose spending increases economic growth, land values, and tax receipts and provides employment for urban residents (Friedman *et al.* 2004). However, these projects rarely return sufficient revenues to recover public costs, much less compensate the public for assuming substantial financial risks that otherwise would have been borne by the private sector. Moreover, tourist bubble jobs tend to be low-wage service sector employment that provides few opportunities for economic advancement (Flusty 2001). Both of these problems are evident within mallparks, which require on-going subsidies and expensive upgrades and renovations, and, due to cost of attendance, limits the presence of the working-class to low-wage, no-benefit, seasonal jobs.

The issues of inclusion and exclusion within mallparks raise much deeper questions in regards to societal priorities. Lefebvre's (1996) "Right to City" offers a model of urban democracy in which all people could enjoy the space of the city and actively participate in its governance.

Symbolically, mallparks may celebrate the values of democratic inclusion, but spatial practices devoted to consumption provide a very different reality. Like the working-class residents excluded from the city, many fans are excluded from the mallpark. In both places, they have been devalued by policy makers, urban designers, architects, and amenity operators and have been replaced by consumers.

References

Bale, J. (1994). *Landscapes of Modern Sport*. Leicester: Leicester University Press.

Baltimore Orioles (1985). *1985 Media Guide*. Baltimore: Baltimore Orioles.

Baltimore Orioles (2015). Oriole Park Seating Map. *Baltimore Orioles*. Available at: http://baltimore.orioles.mlb.com/bal/ticketing/seating.jsp (accessed June 15, 2015).

Bess, P. (2000). Mallpark: New Comiskey Park and the State of the Art. In *Inland Architecture: Subterranean Essays on Moral Order and Formal Order in Chicago* ed. P. Bess. Oxford, OH: Interalia/Design Books, 83–98.

Bryman, A. (1999). The Disneyization of Society. *The Sociological Review* 47(1): 25–47.

Bureau of Labor Statistics (2014). *Consumer Expenditures: 2013*. Available at: www.bls.gov/news.release/cesan.nr0.htm (accessed June 22, 2015).

Chapin, T. (2002). Beyond the Entrepreneurial City: Municipal Capitalism in San Diego. *Journal of Urban Affairs* 24(5): 565–81.

Chapin, T. (2004). Sports Facilities as Urban Redevelopment Catalysts: Baltimore's Camden Yards and Cleveland's Gateway. *Journal of the American Planning Association* 70(2):193–209.

Coates, D., and B. Humphreys (2008). Do Economists Reach a Conclusion for Sports Franchises, Stadiums, and Mega-events? *Econ Journal Watch* 5(3): 294–315.

Creative Machines (n.d.). Based on Balls. *Creative Machines*. Available at: http://creativemachines.com/ballmachines/based-on-balls (accessed June 20, 2015).

Danielson, M. (1997). *Home Team: Professional Sports and the American Metropolis*. Princeton: Princeton University Press.

Fainstein, S., and D. Gladstone (1999). Evaluating Urban Tourism. In *The Tourist City* eds. D. Judd and S. Fainstein. New Haven: Yale University Press, 21–34.

Flusty, S. (2001). The Banality of Interdiction: Surveillance, Control and the Displacement of Diversity. *International Journal of Urban and Regional Research* 25(3): 658–64.

Friedman, M. (2010). "The Transparency of Democracy": The Production of Washington's Nationals Park as a Late Capitalist Space. *Sociology of Sport Journal* 27(4): 327–50.

Friedman, M., D. Andrews, and M. Silk (2004). Sport and the Facade of Redevelopment in the Postindustrial City. *Sociology of Sport Journal* 21(2): 119–39.

Gendzel, G. (1995). Competitive Boosterism: How Milwaukee Lost the Braves. *Business History Review* 69(4): 530–66.

Gershman, M. (1993). *Diamonds: The Evolution of the Ballpark from Elysian Fields to Camden Yards*. Boston: Houghton Mifflin.

Goss, J. (1999). Once-Upon-a-Time in the Commodity World: An Unofficial Guide to Mall of America. *Annals of the Association of American Geographers* 89(1): 45–75.

Gottdiener, M. (2001). *The Theming of America: American Dreams, Media Fantasies, and Themed Environments*. Boulder: Westview.

Gottdiener, M., C. Collins, and D. Dickens (1999). *Las Vegas: The Social Production of an All-American City*. Malden: Blackwell.

Harvey, D. (1989). *The Condition of Postmodernity: An Enquiry into the Origins of Cultural Change*. Oxford: Blackwell.

Harvey, D. (2001). From Managerialism to Entrepreneurialism: The Transformation in Urban Governance in Late Capitalism. In *Spaces of Capital: Toward a Critical Geography* ed. D. Harvey. Edinburgh: Edinburgh University Press, 345–68.

Jameson, F. (1991). *Postmodernism, or, The Cultural Logic of Late Capitalism*. Durham: Duke University Press.

Judd, D. (1999). Constructing the Tourist Bubble. In *The Tourist City* eds. D. Judd and S. Fainstein. New Haven: Yale University Press, 35–53.

Judd, D. (2003). *The Infrastructure of Play: Building the Tourist City*. Armonk: M. E. Sharpe.

Kane, C. (2012). Most Expensive Luxury Suites. *CNBC.com*, May 3. Available at: www.cnbc.com/id/47285181 (accessed June 16, 2015).

Kennicott, P. (2008). This Diamond Isn't a Gem. *Washington Post*, March 31. Available at: www.washingtonpost.com/wp-dyn/content/article/2008/03/30/AR2008033002216.html (accessed December 27, 2015).

Lefebvre, H. (1970). *The Urban Revolution*. Trans. R. Bononno. Minneapolis: University of Minnesota Press, 2003.

Lefebvre, H. (1991). *The Production of Space*. Trans. D. Nicholson-Smith. Oxford: Blackwell, 1992.

Lefebvre, H. (1996). Right to the City. Trans. E. Kofman. In *Writings on Cities* eds. E. Kofman and E. Lebas. Oxford: Blackwell, 63–181.

Levin, J. (2005). Rich Fan, Poor Fan. *Washington City Paper*, October 7–13. Available at: www.washingtoncitypaper.com/cover/2005/cover1007.html (accessed December 27, 2015).

Lipsitz, G. (1984). Sports Stadia and Urban Development: A Tale of Three Cities. *Journal of Sport and Social Issues* 8(2): 1–18.

Lukas, S. (2007). The Themed Space. In *The Themed Space: Locating Culture, Nation, and Self* ed. S. Lukas. Lanham: Lexington Books, 1–22.

MoA (2016). Facts: Mall of America® By The Numbers. *Mall of America*. Available at: www.mallofamerica.com/about/moa/facts (accessed January 23, 2016).

New York Yankees. (2015). Yankees Legends Suite Brochure. Available at: http://newyork.yankees.mlb.com/nyy/ticketing/sth_legendsbrochure.jsp (accessed June 15, 2015).

Pappas, D. (2001). 1991–2001 Ticket Prices and Fan Cost Index. Available at http://roadsidephotos.sabr.org/baseball/1991-2001tickets.htm (accessed May 23, 2015).

Riess, S. (1999). *Touching Base: Professional Baseball and American Culture in the Progressive Era*. Urbana: University of Illinois Press.

Ritter, L. (1992). *Lost Ballparks: A Celebration of Baseball's Legendary Fields.* New York: Viking Studio Books.

Ritzer, G. (2010). *Enchanting a Disenchanted World: Continuity and Change in the Cathedrals of Consumption.* Los Angeles: Sage.

Ritzer, G. (2011). *The McDonaldization of Society 6.* Los Angeles: Pine Forge.

Ritzer, G., and T. Stillman (2001). The Postmodern Ballpark as a Leisure Setting: Enchantment and Simulated De-McDonaldization. *Leisure Sciences* 23(2): 99–113.

Shannon, B., and G. Kalinsky (1975). *The Ballparks.* New York: Hawthorn Books.

Shields, R. (1999). *Lefebvre, Love, and Struggle: Spatial Dialectics.* London: Routledge.

Target Field (2010). Target Field: By the Numbers. *Twins Magazine: Special Commemorative Issue.* 50(1).

Team Marketing Report (2015). 2015 MLB Fan Cost Index. *Team Marketing Report*, April. Available at: www.teammarketing.com/public/uploadedP-DFs/2015 mlb fci (1).pdf (accessed December 27, 2015).

Zukin, S. (1998). Urban Lifestyles: Diversity and Standardisation in Spaces of Consumption. *Urban Studies* 35(5/6): 825–39.

Chapter 13

Sports and the social integration of migrants

Gaelic football, rugby football, and Association football in South Dublin

Neil Conner

Introduction

Despite the "crisis" rhetoric that characterized discussions about the sudden influx of asylum-seekers and other immigrants to Europe in 2015, immigration policy has actually been a top priority of the European Union (EU) since 1999 (European Commission 2015). Given the significance of migration in all EU member states, the Council of the European Union (CEU) has developed a series of mechanisms to promote member states' efforts to integrate their newest citizens and residents. *The Common Basic Principles for Immigrant Integration Policy in the European Union*, for example, sets out a series of guidelines and frames integration "a dynamic, long-term, and continuous two-way process of mutual accommodation, not a static outcome" (CEU 2004: 19; see also Niessen and Kate 2007). In researching this dual nature of integration, scholars have tended to focus on formal mechanisms as well as employment and other economic "pathways of integration" (Agner and Strang 2008; Gilmartin and Migge 2015). However, as I argue in this chapter, other societal forces besides work are equally, if not more, significant to the larger integration debate.

Everyday activities such as sports are central to how recent migrants are being integrated in their new European homes. Indeed, in 2010, the CEU formally recognized sports' role as an active component in the social integration process of migrants, arguing in a recent council document:

> Sport holds an important place in the lives of many EU citizens and plays a strong societal role with a powerful potential for social inclusion in and through sport, meaning that participation in sport or in physical activity in many different ways contributes to inclusion into society.
>
> (CEU 2010)

Following the line of reasoning articulated here by the Council, this chapter considers the relationship between sport and social integration in

Ireland. More specifically, I examine migrant participation in three popular sports in South Dublin: Gaelic football, rugby football, and Association football (soccer).

Over the past 20 years, the Republic of Ireland has seen a dramatic demographic shift as a result of increased global migration. Ireland has been a nation of emigrants and it was only during the mid-1990s that the country started to receive large numbers of immigrants (Fanning 2002; Gilmartin 2013, 2015). According to the most recent census data, Ireland has a foreign-born population of just less than 17 percent, a figure that puts its relative share of migrants above the majority of other European states (Central Statistics Office 2011; United Nations 2013). My research, conducted from 2012 to 2014, suggests that sports can serve as a bridge and/or a barrier in the social integration process in Ireland. Approached through this bridge/barrier construct, this analysis sheds light on the wider relationship between sport and geographies of inclusion and exclusion. This dichotomous relationship plays a fundamental role in the ways that a society attempts to define the socially constructed categories of "us" and "them" (O'Boyle and Fanning 2009; Sibley 1995).

> The challenge facing Ireland [according to Mike Cronin (2013: 163–4)] is whether native pastimes are open to outsiders, how far racism is an abhorrent but inevitable by-product of the initial stages of sporting integration, and whether sport should be the lens through which society judges if integration is working.

Accordingly, I show how specific sporting practices in South Dublin have facilitated the social integration of migrants by contributing to their sense of belonging but, also, how these sports have impeded this process by excluding migrants from certain everyday activities that are directly connected to national narratives and notions of "Irishness."

Sports and social integration: potential and practicalities

Sports, we are often told, are a microcosm of society (Brainard 2013; Clark 2013). Cliché as it may be, there is certainly some validity to this phrase. Sports occur within specific societal boundaries, meaning that "they are intimately bound up with community structure, culture and ritual" (Sugden and Bairner 1993: 23). Sports therefore offer a window into the world of a place, or, more accurately, a mirror reflecting the unique processes of constructing a place's identity. When approached as something far more than an "apolitical" form of recreation, sports offer geographers a compelling point of entry to critically engage with social issues such as migration, race, ethnicity, and numerous other identity characteristics and their intersections (Conner 2014a; see also Raento, Bohland, Crampsie, Nelson, Wise, Chapters 2, 3, 8, 9, 15 this volume).

Within the context of social integration, sports represent a vehicle for migrants as they "look for methods to assert their cultural heritage and identity abroad" (Conner 2014b: 530). Additionally, as Cronin (2013: 163) explains, it is "through participation in sport, in playing the national games and becoming part of the nation's narrative, that the immigrant communities [have] marked their arrival and announced their success." However, sports also represent a powerful site of place-based collective identity construction for many domestic-born individuals as well (Bale 2001). But, while this certainly is a positive attribute in many cases, it also has the potential to become problematic, especially concerning the integration of migrants. Indeed, myriad examples from around the world confirm that sports often go hand in hand with chauvinistic sentiments of place-based pride and expressions of racism, and other forms of bigotry such as sectarianism become all too commonplace (Back *et al.* 1998; Bradley 1995; Burdsey 2011; Müller *et al.* 2007). Consequently, given the dual nature of the social integration process, sports and sporting spaces serve as a strategic venue where both domestic- and foreign-born identities are continually conceptualized, constructed, and contested on an everyday basis.

This chapter extends the nascent literature on sports and social integration within geography. Although sociologists, cultural anthropologists, and other social scientists have considered this connection in various studies, there is something unique about approaching it through the geographers' lens that encourages an analysis of human experiences with an emphasis on various spatial dimensions. Regarding the social integration of migrants through sports, the specific place where this process occurs and/or the scale that is examined are equally important to the overall narrative as the actors themselves. One example of this type of research is Paul Cuadros's (2011) article examining how the integration of migrants through sports participation occurs and how new identities are being created by Latina women playing organized soccer in the southeastern United States. Cuadros's research offers valuable insights into how, at the scale of the individual, soccer has empowered these women and given them the confidence to feel more comfortable in their new surroundings despite the many difficulties they face within their community as a result of being foreign-born. Although this article makes an important contribution in its analysis of an individual's identity construction through sports participation, social integration, as mentioned above, is a two-way process and Cuadros unfortunately omits a discussion from the domestic-born point of view. As I illustrate below, having an understanding from both groups is a crucial component when determining whether sports serve as a bridge and/or a barrier to the social integration process within a particular community.

Elsewhere, Nicholas Wise (2011) analyzes Haitian immigrant identity construction in the Dominican Republic through participation in football (soccer). He points to how the soccer pitch represents "a stage for [migrants] to express emotional attachments to home, belonging to a new place, and their national identity abroad" (Wise 2011: 260). Here the geographic scale is broadened from the individual to the community, but, again, the identity narratives and sporting participation of the Dominican nationals are not fully addressed. To be fair, Wise's focus is not explicitly on social integration, and, in a later article, he does contrast the Haitian minority's preference for soccer and Dominicans' preference for baseball and the impact this has on identity construction (Wise 2015). From a social integration perspective, however, it is necessary to understand how both groups (foreign- and domestic-born) conceptualize the same sport in order to more accurately determine that particular sport's role as a bridge and/or barrier in the social integration process.

To address this issue, I developed a mixed-methods research project in Ireland over a three-year period from 2012 to 2014. South Dublin was selected as a research site in part because it represents a microcosm of Ireland from a demographic standpoint: mirroring the national percentages, 83 percent of residents in South Dublin are Irish-born and 17 percent are foreign-born (Central Statistics Office 2011).[1] The primary method used in this study was a 20-question survey, conducted in June 2013 and June 2014 ($n = 176$). I administered the survey in various locations throughout South Dublin County, including recreational centers, public parks, libraries, restaurants/pubs, shopping centers, a multicultural non-denominational church, a Catholic church, and at various social gatherings in several neighborhoods within the county.

The choice of locations here speaks to two points:

- This research was conducted for a much larger study on social integration that examined additional topics beyond the role of sports in this process.
- The pervasiveness of sports within society extends beyond the locations where sports are being contested (e.g., field, pitch, court, etc.). For example, the viewpoint of a 62-year-old Irish-born man who has not actually played Gaelic football or stepped onto a pitch in decades is equally as important to that sport's perceived role within society as that of a 25-year-old who plays every day. Additionally, if a particular sport is considered to be a barrier by a foreign-born individual, the probability of connecting with that individual at the particular sporting space in question is unlikely.

Finally, and most obviously, not everyone likes sports. As such, it was important to visit multiple locations that are not directly connected to sports in order to diversify the results and thereby more accurately represent the beliefs of residents in South Dublin as a whole.

Table 13.1 provides a basic description of the survey respondents, including a list of the 28 states represented by the foreign-born participants. To supplement and inform the findings from the survey, I also conducted semi-structured interviews and participant observation. The interviews were informal with no specific set of questions and they were carried out after the survey was completed by those individuals who wanted to discuss the topic further. These discussions proved invaluable to this study as they provided much more breadth and depth than the survey had allowed. Within the context of the interviews, several of which are quoted below, the participants could speak directly to their personal experiences and more accurately share their understanding of the role that a particular sport plays in the social integration process.

Survey participants were asked to classify several popular sports within the Irish cultural landscape as representing either a bridge or a barrier in the social integration process in South Dublin. In the survey, the term "bridge" was defined as something within society that strengthens the bonds between migrants and members of the host community. The term "barrier" was defined as those societal features or activities that inhibit this relationship. As noted above, the bridge/barrier metaphor has been employed by many researchers when referring to societal features and activities that either facilitate or impede the integration process of migrants. Employing this metaphor allows for a more nuanced discussion concerning a person's sense of belonging, which is crucial to the social

Table 13.1 General results of survey in South Dublin, 2013–14 (n = 176)

Irish-born 95 total (54%)		Foreign-born 81 total (46%)	
Male 58 total (61%)	Female 37 total (39%)	Male 44 total (54%)	Female 37 total (46%)
AGE	18–20		5 total (2.8%)
	21–29		41 total (23.3%)
	30–39		53 total (30.7%)
	40–49		31 total (17.6%)
	50–59		34 total (19.3%)
	60+		11 total (6.3%)

Birthplaces of foreign-born respondents
AFRICA: Cameroon, Ghana, Kenya, Malawi, Nigeria, South Africa, Zimbabwe

AMERICAS: Brazil, Canada, Colombia, United States of America

ASIA: China, Iran, Iraq, Pakistan, Philippines, South Korea, Vietnam

EUROPE: Germany, Italy, Lithuania, Norway, Poland, Romania, Spain, Switzerland, Ukraine, United Kingdom

integration process. As Mary Gilmartin's (2015) work on migration in twenty-first-century Ireland shows, many migrants desire a sense of "place-belongingness" to their new home. She elaborates:

> Belonging occurs, and is experienced, in a range of spaces and scales, from the informal sense of being at home to the more formal belonging that is expressed through citizenship and legal status and the right to vote. For migrants, it can sometimes be difficult to feel a sense of belonging, and many migrants are conscious of the barriers to belonging that they encounter. Often, these barriers are expressed and experienced in more everyday, banal ways.
>
> (Gilmartin 2015:143)

It is important to acknowledge that this sense of belonging is "socially mediated," meaning that it is "related to the discourses and practices of socio-spatial inclusion and exclusion, a means of defining membership to a group and ownership of a place" (Alderman and Inwood 2013: 219). Because identity narratives are an important mechanism of socio-spatial inclusion and exclusion, dominant social groups often seek to "consciously define the terms of belonging as they seek to impose cultural coherence and fix the boundaries of identity of 'us' and 'them'" (Alderman and Modlin 2013: 9). Such identity boundaries formed through the politics of belonging become the frontiers where the social integration process occurs. Stressing the importance of everyday activities such as sports as one such frontier, the remainder of this chapter examines how migrants perceive three particular sports: Gaelic football, rugby football, and Association football.

These three sports were specifically selected based on their popularity in South Dublin and their perceived importance to notions of "Irishness," albeit uniquely so. The first sport discussed is Gaelic football, which is one of the three main Gaelic games organized by the Gaelic Athletic Association (GAA). Gaelic football was chosen to be the representative sport of the GAA in this research, as opposed to handball or hurling/camogie, as this is the Gaelic game that I most regularly witnessed being played and discussed on an everyday basis in South Dublin. And, while it is commonly understood that "hurling has the purest Irish pedigree" of all the GAA sports, Gaelic football is the most popular GAA sport in Ireland and it "is played and defined in opposition to non-indigenous forms of football (rugby and soccer) as if it were the chosen sport of ancient Hibernia" (Sugden and Bairner 1993: 24–5).

The second sport in this study, rugby football, has been an organized sport in Ireland since 1854, when it diffused from England through the participation of students attending Dublin University (IRFU 2016). Today, the Irish national rugby union team is recognized as one of the best teams in the world and it is arguably Ireland's most successful sporting team on an international level. Finally, the third sport examined in this study, Association football (or soccer), is, like rugby football, not a native sport to Ireland. While FIFA, the international governing body of the sport, correctly claims that Britain is the birthplace of contemporary football, the truth is that elements of the sport are found in various sporting cultures around the world (FIFA 2015). Additionally, Association football is by far the most popular sport in the world and, thus, it is considered by many to be a global sport as opposed to a national game (Gaelic football) or one that was popularized based on colonial histories (rugby football).

Gaelic football

The Gaelic Athletic Association, or GAA, is an amateur sporting organization in Ireland whose declared aim is to strengthen "National Identity through the preservation and promotion of Gaelic Games and pastimes … and other aspects of Irish culture" (GAA 2013: 5). The GAA was established in 1884 as part of a nationalist reaction against British influence in Ireland. A thorough history of the organization is beyond the scope of this chapter (but for an overview, see Crampsie, Chapter 8 this volume), though it should be noted that the GAA has played a significant role in the construction of Irish identity throughout the twentieth century. During its formative years, the GAA was connected to several pro-independence, anti-British paramilitary/political groups including the Irish Republic Brotherhood, Sinn Féin, and the Irish Republican Army. Following Irish independence in 1921, and the subsequent Irish Civil War until 1923, Gaelic sports started to be viewed as "neutral territory" for developing a sense of national identity and unity (Sugden and Bairner 1993). As scholars of the GAA have noted, the institution eventually came to define "Irishness and a sense of place like no other organization on the island" (Cronin 2013: 159–60).

This unifying potential aside, the GAA's definition of "Irish identity" has been problematic in that it "creates its own exclusions, claiming authority over the expression of an authentic Irish identity that is highly gendered and racially and ethnically exclusive" (Gilmartin 2015: 115). Historically working with a narrow or "essentialist" understanding of Irish culture, the GAA's sports and cultural programs have contributed to a more general romanticization of "Irishness." This dynamic has certainly strengthened Gaelic football's popularity in Ireland, but the ethnocentric chauvinism that can be associated with such narrow visions of Irish identity has also caused problems for the GAA in the twenty-first century. Incidents of racism directed at foreign-born players of Gaelic football have been occurring with much more frequency in recent years (Breheny 2014;

Fogarty 2015), and many of this study's foreign-born respondents felt that the GAA has not done nearly enough to stop the rampant racial abuse within the sport.

Working to respond to these challenges, the GAA has started to enforce harsher penalties for acts of racial abuse. They have also introduced club "family days," during which the "New Irish," or foreign-born individuals, are invited to the clubs, "introduced to the games, and have the whole phenomenon of the GAA explained to them" (Cronin 2013: 167). Despite these efforts, the survey results in Table 13.2 indicate that the vast majority (over 80 percent) of foreign-born respondents believe that Gaelic football represents a barrier to social integration. Moreover, Gaelic football was not only the highest "barrier" percentage of the three sports discussed in this chapter, but it was also the highest out of all of the societal features presented in the survey. The sense of exclusion attached to Gaelic football by foreign-born respondents becomes clearer through their qualitative responses provided after they had completed the survey. Many of their personal comments about the sport contain graphic examples of the racist abuse that they have either personally experienced or have heard about from friends and family members. Here, the vast majority of the foreign-born respondents associate Gaelic football and the GAA more with xenophobia and racism than "Irish culture."

The sentiment that Gaelic football is more of a "barrier" to social integration was confirmed and elaborated upon by a 42-year-old Nigerian-born man and current Irish citizen who said:

> Several years ago, my young nephew was practicing GAA football when a group of teenage boys approached him, stole his ball, called him a f***ing n***er and told him to "Go back to Africa. This is our sport!" My nephew was born in Dublin and was only 12 years old at the time and he has never played the sport since. I understand why GAA football is important [in Ireland] because of its anti-English history and links to ancient Irish culture. But I will not play it and I will not allow my son or daughter to play it – or any other GAA sport – because of the discrimination and racism I fear they would likely encounter. I see no logic participating in something where you are clearly not welcome.

Table 13.2 Perceptions of Gaelic football in South Dublin survey (n = 176)

	Irish-born only	Foreign-born only	Combined
Bridge	48 (50.5%)	15 (18.5%)	63 (35.8%)
Barrier	37 (39.0%)	66 (81.5%)	103 (58.5%)
Both	10 (10.5%)	0	10 (5.7%)

This statement is telling of the deep-seated racial issues running through Gaelic football and is indicative of how the majority of foreign-born respondents feel about the sport and, indeed, the GAA more generally. Perceiving its importance in an ethnocentric Irish identity narrative, participants in this study typically wanted no association with it at all, as evident in the quote above.

From the Irish-born perspective, the survey data on Gaelic football is not as straightforward. Only a slight majority of these respondents expressed a sense that Gaelic football is a bridge to social integration. Yet this statistic is a bit misleading: the majority of those Irish-born respondents that chose "bridge" on the survey believe Gaelic football *should be* a bridge for migrants to socially integrate into Irish society. However, because of the perceived ethnocentrism tied to the GAA, these respondents did not think that this would be possible for several generations, if at all. This particular insight was acquired during the post-survey interviews and several of these respondents discussed how Irish migrants throughout history have embraced the national sports of their new country thereby opting for what Cronin (2013) terms "sporting integration."

In the words of a 58-year-old Irish-born man: "Gaelic Football is OUR national sport. It helps to define who we are as a people. If immigrants want to become Irish then it is up to them to conform to our society." Although not addressing the problems that many foreign-born residents have with the GAA, this mentality was a common theme across the responses from the Irish-born. According to them, for immigrants to successfully integrate, migrants themselves need to adapt. But, if we understand integration as a two-way process, requiring adaptation from both foreign- and domestic-born residents, it becomes clear that this is a highly political narrative in which the dominant group is defining the "terms of belonging" (Alderman and Modlin 2013). If the Irish-born are not willing to eliminate such expressions of ethnocentric chauvinism from the sport, then Gaelic football will most likely continue to be viewed as a barrier to integration by the foreign born.

Rugby football

Unlike Gaelic football, rugby football is not native to Ireland, but arrived from England during the mid-nineteenth century. Despite this, some individuals in Ireland, particularly those aligned with specific Gaelic notions of Irish identity, believe that rugby may actually stem from an ancient Irish sport known as Cad (Sugden and Bairner 1993: 54). Today, Irish rugby is organized to include teams/clubs/schools from all of Ireland, including both the Republic of Ireland and Northern Ireland. Consequently, rugby is viewed by many in Ireland as a sport designed to "widen friendships and unite" people across the island thereby providing "a different definition of

Irishmen from the acrimonious sterile political one" (Diffley 1973: 14). Yet the notion that somehow rugby is apolitical is a bit naïve according to Sugden and Bairner (1993: 54), who point to the development of the sport and its contemporary character to emphasize that rugby is actually "deeply implicated in the cultural politics of division." These cultural divisions are made clearer when the discussion includes immigrants. Historically, rugby developed in Ireland at fee-paying schools and because these "schools are unlikely to have a large cohort of New Irish students ... the game remains largely unchanged in terms of class and ethnic background" (Cronin 2013: 165).

As indicated in Table 13.3, both the Irish-born and foreign-born respondents consider rugby to be a barrier to integration at approximately the same percentages: 66 percent and 65 percent respectively. Many of the comments from respondents confirm Cronin's suggestion that rugby is tied to fee-paying schools. For example, a 38-year-old Brazilian man explained: "Rugby [in Ireland] is for rich white people at private Catholic schools. For those of us poorer non-Catholics, our children are not exposed to the sport at a young enough age to appreciate it." Similarly, a 42-year-old Irish-born man said:

> While I enjoy watching rugby union, I did not attend a private school, so I do not have much experience playing the sport. I would expect that this is the case with most immigrants here in Ireland. Unless of course, those immigrants are from countries where rugby is a popular sport.

This man's assertion did, in fact, hold up in my own research findings. All of the respondents from South Africa, France, Romania, and the United Kingdom – as well as more than half from Zimbabwe and Kenya – considered rugby as a bridge to integration. For many of them, the fact that they were already familiar with rugby allowed them to easily participate in the sport. A 34-year-old Italian-born woman explained that she actually met her Irish-born husband through her participation with rugby:

> When I first arrived in Ireland ten years ago, I spoke only a small bit of English. This made it very tough for me to make friends. Then, one

Table 13.3 Perceptions of rugby football in South Dublin survey (n = 176)

	Irish-born only	Foreign-born only	Combined
Bridge	22 (23.2%)	20 (24.7%)	42 (23.8%)
Barrier	63 (66.3%)	53 (65.4%)	116 (65.9%)
Both	10 (10.5%)	8 (9.9%)	18 (10.3%)

day I saw an advertisement on a bulletin board in my apartment complex that was looking for women who were interested in playing rugby. I never played rugby when I lived in Italy, but my two older brothers did so I knew the rules and the general atmosphere associated with the sport. After a particular tough match when I was covered in mud and bleeding from a small cut, the man who eventually would become my husband approached me and told me that I played well.

This particular story notwithstanding, rugby's history in Ireland suggests that there may be too many obstacles for it to ever have the same success concerning social integration as other sports. However, this could change in the future, as the Irish Rugby Football Union (IRFU) has recently created several new urban clubs around the country (Cronin 2013: 165). Additionally, the Irish national rugby team has been very successful in recent years. In August 2015, for example, it was second in the world – the highest rank ever achieved (Rees 2015). Ireland also currently holds the Six Nations Championship, an annual international tournament that includes Ireland, England, Scotland, Wales, France, and Italy. This success on the international level has ramped up the popularity of the sport in Ireland, and rugby may now be poised to overtake Gaelic football in terms of popularity (Hughes 2015).

Association football (soccer)

When referring to Association football in Ireland, both "soccer" and "football" are used widely, depending largely on personal preference. For some individuals who hold Gaelic football or rugby football in higher regard, Association football is typically called soccer. In this discussion, the term soccer will be used in reference to Association football in order to differentiate the various types of "football" that are played in Ireland (i.e., Gaelic and rugby). Regardless of which name is used, soccer is not only the most popular spectator sport in the Republic of Ireland, but it also has the highest levels of participation (Neville 2014; O'Brien 2014). Because of its international appeal, Cronin (2013: 165) explains that "many of the New Irish arrive with experiences of the game and are keen to continue their involvement.... Since it is familiar, soccer lends itself to a degree of integration." Despite its clear potential for social inclusion and integration, acts of discrimination and racial abuse have been prevalent in Irish soccer throughout its history (Hassan and McCue 2011).

Responding to these troubling issues, a Dublin-based organization called Sports Against Racism Ireland (SARI) was established in 1997, with the aim to promote "cultural integration and social inclusion through sport. SARI works closely with the major Irish sports bodies and has involved 50,000 New Irish people in various sports at different levels" (Cronin 2013: 164).

Since its creation, SARI has strategically employed soccer, and other sports more generally, as vehicles to confront various forms of discrimination such as xenophobia, sectarianism, and racism within Irish society (Hassan and McCue 2011: 60). Throughout the year, SARI hosts several soccer tournaments, including the SARI Soccerfest, which annually attracts approximately 4,000 people, and the Fair Play Football Cup that celebrates World Refugee Day (SARI 2015). Additionally, the organization also hosts Soccernites, which are free soccer practices organized weekly in Dublin.

SARI was clearly important for many of the foreign-born respondents included in this research. The group's effort to promote an inclusive soccer environment has been instrumental to these individuals' integration experiences in Ireland – either on the basis of their own participation in games, or through their children's and/or their extended family members' involvement. The survey results presented in Table 13.4 indicate that over 92 percent of foreign-born respondents consider soccer to be a bridge to integration. This is not only the highest "bridge" percentage of the three sports discussed in this chapter, but soccer also trumped all of the other societal features presented in the survey, including obtaining Irish citizenship and having the ability to speak English or Irish. A 42-year-old Iranian-born woman explained that:

> Soccer has been a blessing for my two boys. When we first moved here they had a difficult time making friends with the Irish children in the neighborhood where we live. But because of their participation with soccer they now love it here and have so many new Irish friends.

Similarly, a 25-year-old Polish man said that:

> I work at a nursing home so soccer has been important for me in terms of providing a way to interact with others my own age. Even though I do not speak English that well, I can communicate through my play on the pitch.

These two quotations highlight how soccer has the potential power to bridge the socio-cultural divide and provide a sense of belonging for migrants and their families. They illustrate how the dual-nature of social integration can operate through friendships, which begin to develop

Table 13.4 Perceptions of soccer in South Dublin survey (n = 176)

	Irish-born only	Foreign-born only	Combined
Bridge	80 (84.2%)	75 (92.6)	155 (88.0%)
Barrier	3 (3.2%)	4 (4.9%)	7 (4.0%)
Both	12 (12.6%)	2 (2.5%)	14 (8.0%)

between foreign-born and Irish-born individuals, and serve as an initial step in the long-term and continuous process of developing a sense of belonging to a new place.

What makes soccer unique within the Irish cultural landscape is that both groups consider it a bridge to integration, with the Irish-born "bridge" percentage at slightly over 84 percent. For many of the Irish-born respondents, soccer is already considered an international sport and this global aspect appears to lend itself very easily to the acceptance of others. According to a 32-year-old Irish-born man: "Soccer is *the* global sport and in Ireland it is the bridge that will eventually – hopefully – allow the Irish and the immigrants to come together as one nation. World Cup 2022 and beyond!!" While this is admittedly an optimistic comment, it represents a common thread found within many of the Irish-born responses concerning their high hopes for the future of soccer in Ireland. This is not to say that racism, xenophobia, and other forms of discrimination are absent in the sport. However, based on the research conducted for this study, it appears that soccer is understood by the residents in South Dublin as having the potential ability to transcend some of these detriments of society.

Conclusion

This chapter focused on three popular sports in South Dublin and how they are perceived as a bridge and/or a barrier in the social integration of migrants in Ireland. The research presented here demonstrates that sports are more than just frivolous endeavors or "apolitical" forms of recreation. Instead, sports are intimately tied to the processes and politics of place-based identity construction through various socio-spatial notions of inclusion and exclusion. Dominant groups, such as the GAA, Irish private schools, and even the Irish themselves on a more everyday level, actively define the boundaries of identity to these sports through the politics of belonging, thereby deciding who is included and, perhaps more importantly for this study, who is not.

As a national game with a particularly narrow ethno-cultural understanding of Irishness, Gaelic football, and the GAA more generally, appear to have significant work to do in terms of providing a more inclusive environment if they are going to attract migrants and their families. Similarly, rugby's historic link to private schools is somewhat problematic in its class-based exclusion, despite its broader appeal to recent immigrants familiar with the sport in their countries of origin. Soccer, on the other hand, appears to be moving in the direction of promoting a more inclusive vision of Irish society, with organizations such as SARI helping to facilitate this process. Additionally, the fact that soccer has the highest "bridge" percentage out of any of the societal features included in the survey is certainly important to consider.

Despite the generally positive results with the case of soccer, my research suggests that, in using sport as a metric, it may be too early to tell if integration is "working" in Ireland. Yet, if members of a receiving society and the migrants themselves both understand sport as a mechanism of social integration, then, moving forward, more research into the ways that sport is successful are necessary. The survey data and qualitative results provide only a brief snapshot of these various sports and their perceptions by foreign- and Irish-born residents of South Dublin today. In providing such a snapshot, this research and that of other sports studies scholars has the potential to provide sporting organizations, political decision-makers, and the broader public with an understanding of existing and future challenges to creating more inclusive societies. In this respect, perceptions about social institutions as bridges and/or barriers are important because they manifest in concrete actions. Even seemingly mundane decisions such as choosing to participate in one form of football versus another can have lasting effects on the social integration processes of immigrants. Perhaps if individuals advocating specific sports were aware of such perceptions, they might make a more concerted effort to provide safe and accommodating spaces for migrants and members of the receiving society to interact with one another, on a neutral playing field as it were.

However, it is important to keep in mind that integration through sport does not magically occur overnight. Integration, whether through sporting participation, economics, or religion is a long-term process that happens gradually over many generations and requires participation from both sides to be successful. It is also important to keep this all in context. Sports do not operate in a vacuum and therefore sports alone cannot solve racism, xenophobia, sectarianism, misogyny, and other forms of discrimination. Still, sports do provide us with a way to critically examine the dynamic power relations that come with all forms of social change, including but not limited to the integration of new immigrants. The significance of sports within society, in my opinion, is that they are a matter of choice. Seemingly small at first brush, an individual's sporting choices ultimately serve a major role in constructing a multicultural country – both in Ireland and beyond.

Note

1 The best estimates suggest that South Dublin's foreign-born population is comprised of individuals born in countries from the following regions: European Union (59.4%); Asia (17.6%); Africa (14.7%); Non-EU Europe (4.1%); Americas (3.3%); Australia and others (0.8%) (Breheny et al. 2013: 16).

References

Agner, A., and A. Strang (2008). Understanding Integration: A Conceptual Framework. *Journal of Refugee Studies* 21(2): 166–91.

Alderman, D., and J. Inwood (2013). Street Naming and the Politics of Belonging: Spatial Injustices in the Toponymic Commemoration of Martin Luther King, Jr. *Social & Cultural Geography* 14(2): 211–33.

Alderman, D. H., and E. A. Modlin, Jr. (2013). Southern Hospitality and the Politics of African American Belonging: An Analysis of North Carolina Tourism Brochure Photographs. *Journal of Cultural Geography* 30(1): 6–31.

Back, L., T. Crabbe, and J. Solomos (1998). Racism in Football: Patterns of Continuity and Change. In *Fanatics! Power, Identity and Fandom in Football* ed. A. Brown. London: Routledge, 71–87.

Bale, J. (2001). *Sport, Space and the City.* Caldwell: Blackburn Press.

Bradley, J. (1995). *Ethnic and Religious Identity in Modern Scotland: Culture, Politics and Football.* Brookfield: Avebury.

Brainard, K. (2013). Sports, A Microcosm of Our Society. *Ramona Sentinel,* January 3. Available at: www.ramonasentinel.com/news/2013/jan/03/sports-a-microcosm-of-our-society/ (accessed January 21, 2016).

Breheny, M. (2014). Zero Tolerance as GAA Vow to Get Tough on Racism. *Independent,* January 30. www.independent.ie/sport/gaelic-games/gaelic-football/zero-tolerance-as-gaa-vow-to-get-tough-on-racism-29963392.html (accessed January 21, 2016).

Breheny, A., I. McCafferty, P. Szlovak, and A. Mcilveen (2013). *An Inclusive County: South Dublin County Integration Strategy 2013–2017.* Dublin: South Dublin County Council, i–56. Available at: www.sdcc.ie/sites/default/files/publications/sdc-integration-strategy-2013-2017.pdf (accessed January 23, 2016).

Burdsey, D. (2011). *Race, Ethnicity and Football: Persisting Debates and Emergent Issues.* New York: Routledge.

Central Statistics Office (2011). *Census: Usual Residence, Place of Birth, Nationality and Foreign Languages.* Available at: www.cso.ie/en/census/census2011reports/census2011thisisirelandpart1/ (accessed January 23, 2016).

CEU (2004). *The Common Basic Principles for Immigrant Integration Policy in the EU, Brussels.* Brussels, Belgium: Council of the European Union, 1–34. Available at: www.consilium.europa.eu/ueDocs/cms_Data/docs/pressData/en/jha/82745.pdf (accessed January 24, 2016).

CEU (2010). Council Conclusions of 18 November 2010 on the Role of Sport as a Source of and a Driver for Active Social Inclusion (EN). *Official Journal of the European Union,* 3 December. Brussels, Belgium: Council of the European Union, 5–8. Available at: http://eur-lex.europa.eu/legal-content/EN/TXT/?uri=CELEX%3A52010XG1203%2804%29 (accessed January 21, 2016).

Clark, R. (2013). Sports Has Become a True Microcosm of Society. *Kinston Free Press,* August 17. Available at: www.kinston.com/article/20130817/News/308179992 (accessed January 21, 2016).

Conner, N. (2014a). *Geography of Sports.* New York: Oxford University Press.

Conner, N. (2014b). Global Cultural Flows and the Routes of Identity: The Imagined Worlds of Celtic FC. *Social and Cultural Geography* 15(5): 525–46.

Cronin, M. (2013). Integration Through Sport: The Gaelic Athletic Association and the New Irish. In *Race and Immigration in the New Ireland* eds. J. Ulin, H. Edwards, and S. O'Brien. Notre Dame, Indiana: University of Notre Dame, 157–74.

Cuadros, P. (2011). We Play Too: Latina Integration through Soccer in the "New South." *Southeastern Geographer* 51(2): 227–41.

Diffley, S. (1973). *The Men in Green: The Story of Irish Rugby.* London: Pelham.

European Commission (2015). Explaining the Rules. *EU Immigration Portal.* Available at: http://ec.europa.eu/immigration/who-does-what/more-information/explaining-the-rules-why-are-there-eu-rules-and-national-rules_en (accessed January 21, 2016).

Fanning, B. (2002). *Racism and Social Change in the Republic of Ireland.* Manchester: Manchester University Press.

FIFA (2015). History of Football: Britain, the Home of Football. Available at: www.fifa.com/about-fifa/who-we-are/the-game/britain-home-of-football.html (accessed January 21, 2016).

Fogarty, J. (2015). GAA Hit with Another Racist Abuse Claim. *Irish Examiner,* February 10. Available at: www.irishexaminer.com/sport/gaa/gaa-hit-with-another-racist-abuse-claim-311682.html (accessed January 21, 2016).

GAA (2013). *Official Guide: Part 1.* Dublin: Central Council of the Association, 1–224. Available at: www.gaa.ie/content/documents/publications/official_guides/officialguide-2013-part1.pdf (accessed December 20, 2015).

Gilmartin, M. (2013). Changing Ireland, 2000–2012: Immigration, Emigration and Inequality. *Irish Geography* 46(1–2): 91–111.

Gilmartin, M. (2015). *Ireland and Migration in the Twenty-First Century.* Manchester: Manchester University Press.

Gilmartin, M., and B. Migge (2015). European Migrants in Ireland: Pathways to Integration. *European Urban and Regional Studies* 22(3): 285–99.

Hassan, D., and K. McCue. (2011). Football, Racism and the Irish. In *Race, Ethnicity and Football: Persisting Debates and Emergent Issues* ed. D. Burdsey. New York: Routledge, 50–63.

Hughes, D. (2015). GAA Must Adapt if it's to Halt Rugby's Popularity Surge. *The Irish News,* October 21. Available at: www.irishnews.com/sport/opinion/2015/10/21/news/danny-hughes-300446/ (accessed January 23, 2016).

IRFU (2016). History of the Irish Rugby Football Union. Available at: www.irishrugby.ie/irfu/history/history.php (accessed January 21, 2016).

Müller, F., L. van Zoonen, and L. de Roode (2007). Accidental Racists: Experiences and Contradictions of Racism in Local Amsterdam Soccer Fan Culture. In *Football Fans Around the World: From Supporters to Fanatics* ed. S. Brown. New York: Routledge, 173–88.

Neville, C. (2014). If All Soccer Players and GAA Players in Ireland Went to War, Who'd Win? *Balls.ie,* 9 January. Available at: www.balls.ie/football/soccer-players-gaa-players-ireland-went-war-whod-win/108849 (accessed January 21, 2016).

Niessen, J., and M.-A. Kate (2007). *From Principles to Practice: The Common Basic Principles on Integration and the Handbook: Conclusions.* Brussels: Migration Policy Group. Available at: http://citiesofmigration.ca/elibrary/from-principles-to-practice-the-common-basic-principles-on-integration-and-the-handbook-conclusions/ (accessed January 21, 2016).

O'Boyle, N., and B. Fanning (2009). Immigration, Integration and Risks of Social Exclusion: The Social Policy Case for Disaggregated Data in the Republic of Ireland. *Irish Geography* 42(2): 145–64.

O'Brien, B. (2014). Rugby Closes on GAA as Soccer Still Most Popular Sport. *Irish Examiner*, December 17. Available at: www.irishexaminer.com/sport/rugby/rugby-closes-on-gaa-as-soccer-still-most-popular-sport-302892.html (accessed January 21, 2016).

Rees, P. (2015). Ireland Run in Five Tries to Crush Wales in World Cup Warmup. *Guardian*, August 8. Available at: www.theguardian.com/sport/2015/aug/08/wales-ireland-rugby-union-match-report (accessed January 21, 2016).

SARI (2015). Activities. Sport Against Racism Ireland. Available at: www.sari.ie/activities/ (accessed January 21, 2016).

Sibley, D. (1995). *Geographies of Exclusion*. New York: Routledge.

Sugden, J., and A. Bairner (1993). *Sport, Sectarianism and Society in a Divided Ireland*. London: Leicester University Press.

United Nations (2013). *International Migration 2013*. Department of Economic and Social Affairs, Population Division. Available at: www.un.org/en/development/desa/population/publications/pdf/migration/migrationreport2013/Full_Document_final.pdf (accessed January 21, 2016).

Wise, N. (2011). Transcending Imaginations through Football Participation and Narratives of the Other: Haitian National Identity in the Dominican Republic. *Journal of Sport and Tourism* 16(3): 259–75.

Wise, N. (2015). Maintaining Dominican Identity in the Dominican Republic: Forging a Baseball Landscape in Villa Ascension. *International Review for the Sociology of Sport* 50(2): 161–78.

Chapter 14

Spatial maneuvers

Geographies of power and labor practices in professional wrestling's territorial era

Bradley Gardener

Introduction

In 1948, powerful wrestling promoters met in Waterloo, Iowa, and formed the NWA or National Wrestling Alliance (originally called the National Wrestling Association). These promoters plotted a spatial strategy that profoundly shaped the business of professional wrestling in North America until the 1990s. Like European imperial interests carving up maps of Africa and Asia into spheres of influence, promoters at this meeting conspired to divide up the wrestling world into what they called "territories." The NWA turned the United States, Canada, and, to some extent, Japan, into a wrestling fiefdom, giving control to sponsored promoters over defined geographic areas in exchange for upholding the collectively determined best interests of the organization.[1] The primary purposes of this collective were twofold: to control wrestling talent and to protect the legitimacy of the business.

This chapter, in the spirit of this entire collection, explains the relationship between power and geography in shaping the business of professional wrestling in the mid to late twentieth century, or the so-called "territorial age" that lasted from the end of World War II to the 1990s. Specifically, I examine how promoters used space as a tool to make wrestlers do things they would not normally choose to do, such as travel thousands of miles per week, wrestle every day for months straight without a break, and work without retirement or injury/sick pay in a physically brutal profession. In this volume, we argue that power is not just an abstraction, but is manifested materially and geographically. Power *creates* material spaces – and vice versa (Harvey 1996). In sport, this is seen, for example, in the way that owners exert power over players through formal exchanges such as lockouts and contract negotiations, but also through more informal and seemingly mundane practices, for example in the way team facilities are run, the pattern of travel between cities, or who is allowed to participate in certain sporting spaces (Nelson, Chapter 9 this volume).

As I show here, the way the NWA divided up space into territories engendered the promoters' control over wrestlers, ensuring they would continue to exploit the fruits of these athletes' labor. This explicitly spatial strategy made the promoters' interests in the wrestling business concrete, and thus a normal part of everyday life for wrestlers. As a conceptual tool, space allows us to take a nuanced look at how one group conspires to control another, as well as how these efforts are variably negotiated or opposed. How did wrestlers encounter the set of places and movements that the promoters prescribed for them? What kind of strategies did they use to both fit in with and struggle against these spatial patterns? A close analysis of space also sheds light on how specific processes persevere over time. If space is indeed a fluid social process, always open to change (Harvey 1996), the relative longevity and stability of the NWA, and its strategy for special regulation, deserves special attention. This analysis thus offers insight into how spatial strategies of power persevere and ultimately change in other sports, in addition to wrestling, particularly in regards to conflicts between labor and owners.

While there is much to learn from the case of professional wrestling, it is also a relatively unique sport in that wrestlers and promoters during the territorial age attempted to hide the true nature of the business from fans and outsiders by creating the illusion that wrestlers were participating in fair athletic competition. Whether it was the desire to be world champion or to settle a score over a personal conflict, the audience was meant to believe that wrestlers' motivations for conflict were genuine. Professional wrestling not only involved fabricating violence, but also acting, both in and out of the ring, in a way that would spark fan interest. Professional wrestling's biggest secret was that the wrestlers were merely performing for an audience, and not actually trying to hurt their opponents. Instead of fighting against each other, the wrestlers, together with managers and referees, were cooperating with one another, both to make the match more entertaining and to prevent injuries. Both wrestlers and promoters feared that if the cooperative and planned nature of wrestling was revealed, fans would lose interest.

Protecting this secret was the key to wrestling's legitimacy. As a consequence, professional wrestling in the territorial age was a notoriously closed business, making research and investigations about it a challenge. Investigative reporters were threatened with violence if they asked the wrong questions (Shoemaker 2014). Television personality John Stossel was famously made partially deaf through repeated slaps to the ear from "Dr. D. David Shultz," when he asked too many question about the authenticity of wrestling. It has only been within the past 25 years that both wrestlers and promoters have openly admitted that wrestling is just for entertainment, and not a legitimate athletic competition. For example, in 2015, promoter of the WWE Vince McMahon openly spoke of the criteria he used to select champions on a popular wrestling podcast. Letting outsiders in on this secret was not a universal decision by the industry.

It occurred slowly, and largely took place through "shoot interviews," the main source of data for this chapter.

The shoot interview is a form of truth telling, in which wrestlers act out of character to reveal what happened behind the scenes at different times in the past. Shoot interviews in this form expanded in the late 1990s, when wrestling reached the peak of its popularity. Acting out of character, known to insiders as "exposing the business," could lead to wrestlers being blackballed during the height of the NWA's control. For this reason, disgruntled wrestlers, those who felt like they had nothing to lose, were the first to agree to shoot interviews. Since the 1990s, however, shoot interviews have been assimilated into the business of professional wrestling. For example, Stone Cold Steve Austin's podcast, *Unleashed*, is affiliated with the world's largest wrestling promotion company, the WWE (World Wrestling Entertainment). Austin's podcast and others like it typically feature one wrestler or wrestling personality interviewing another about what really happened in the past. Wrestlers are typically brutally honest about their own demons and struggles in these podcasts. They talk openly about drug addiction, injuries, and frustrations associated with the wrestling business. This chapter draws on these podcasts to reveal how promoters have historically used space as a mechanism to exert control over wrestlers.

Legitimacy and secrecy in the territorial age

As noted already, wrestlers and promoters worked hard to maintain the legitimacy of the business during the territorial age. They believed that if wrestling was exposed as planned or prefabricated, and, if fans found out that wrestlers were just men and not larger than life characters who fairly competed against each other, no one would pay to see them perform. Promoters have always been obsessed with bringing legitimate athletes into promotions for this reason (Shoemaker 2014). Mohammed Ali, for example, participated in several wrestling events. Football players and Olympic athletes have also been recruited by other wrestlers and promoters, with the explicit intention of bringing attention to the strength, endurance, and toughness required to perform in the ring.

This perceived need for legitimacy in the eyes of fans made injuries in the ring a regular part of professional wrestling. The wear and tear of working up to 300 days a year made injuries quite frequent (Hansen and Teal 2011). These injuries were often featured in professional wrestling's storylines and angles, as it painted the picture that wrestling was based on legitimate competition. In some storylines, wrestlers might seek revenge in reaction to injury, or use their hard plaster casts as a weapon. Rowdy Piper confidant Cowboy Bob Orton, for example, often used his cast to illegally club opponents. The steel chair, that foreign object that is synonymous with wrestling more than it is for sitting, was also introduced for this reason. A chair shot is usually applied with such strength that its impact makes an incredible sound. The audience feels the pain of the wrestler. After seeing and hearing such a spectacle, it is hard for some audiences to resist: they are likely to be sold on what they see and hear.

Wrestlers during this time were thus encouraged to be as brutal as possible in the ring, as the fans would be more engaged when they felt like the wresters were actually being hurt.[2] "Potatoes," or real shots, such as closed fist punches, were commonplace in the territorial era. A "receipt" was a similarly stiff blow, inflicted in response to a potato. Similarly, certain holds or maneuvers are favored over others because of the spectacle they provide fans, thus adding legitimacy to the business. For example, a knife-edge chop across the chest, often associated with Ric Flair, but originally perfected by former football player Edward "Wahoo" McDaniels, makes a great sound and leaves a visible mark on the recipient of the move (Austin 2014e). Obviously, leaving oneself vulnerable to another wrestler through such maneuvers, and getting hurt as a result, was a point of great concern for wrestlers, especially when an injury could ruin their livelihoods. Such vulnerability was required for wrestling holds that would be impossible to execute without the help of an opponent.

An overlooked necessity of keeping wrestling a closed business was the advantages it gave to promoters who sought to avoid regulation from the state. Unfair labor practices in professional wrestling were the norm, which included bilking talent (i.e., the wrestlers) out of the money owed to them at the end of a show, lying about gate receipts, and generally committing crooked accounting. Violence was often used to control wrestlers who refused to lose a belt, or threatened to jump to another promotion (*Legends of Wrestling* 2008, 2010, 2012; Shoemaker 2014). During this period (and still today), wrestlers were considered independent contractors. Nothing was guaranteed beyond the custom of giving a wrestler two weeks' notice before his termination. Unsafe working conditions and sexual harassment were also common occurrences.

Rowdy Piper, a wrestler famous for wearing a kilt and puffing on bag-pipes on his way to the ring, and the now-deceased host of the podcast "Piper's Pit," was fond of describing professional wrestling as the only business where you can kill someone in the ring and then go have lunch (Piper 2015c). The threat of violence from other wrestlers was real in this regard. For example, when Piper started wrestling as a skinny teenager, he was often stretched or put into submission holds and squeezed until he could not breathe. To work the audience, wrestlers needed to trust each other, to cooperate, and, in many instances, put each other's lives in someone else's hands. In some cases, Piper had to trust someone who had an economic incentive to injure him. He knew that power struggles between promoters and wrestlers could very well have led to serious injury or death in the ring – with no legal or institutional consequences (Piper 2015c). These realities often drove wrestlers to be paranoid. In those days, it was absolutely necessary for wrestlers to have some real fighting ability, as their lives were potentially in danger every time they stepped into the ring. The Iron Sheik, for example, was rumored to have been offered a significant sum of money by American Wrestling Association (AWA) promoter Verne Gagne to seriously hurt Hulk Hogan in a World Wrestling Federation (WWF) ring after Hogan unceremoniously left the rival AWA (*The Sheik* 2014).

The secrecy shrouding the business made it quite impossible for wrestlers to expose the injustices to which they were subjected by promoters. Even complaining within the business risked alienating fellow wrestlers, increasing the possibility of being blackballed. In the event of a wrestler turning his back on the business and speaking to a lawyer or the authorities, it was rare that others would corroborate his story. As in so many professional sports, such as cycling, where systematic doping is commonplace but publicly denied (Foot 2011), wrestlers knew the penalty for exposing business secrets was ostracization and being shut out from future career opportunities. Both wrestlers and promoters were afraid that one story or scandal could threaten the entire business. Since the NWA sought total control of the industry in North America, betraying their interests meant certain impoverishment for renegade wrestlers. The structure of wrestling under the NWA allowed promotions to exist in vacuum-like environments, and it is the relationship between these power dynamics and the specific spatial configuration of professional wrestling in the territorial era to which I now turn.

The NWA's spatial template: control and contest

Wrestling announcer Jim Ross once described the NWA as a "non-violent mafia group," adding: "They controlled their business and they controlled the people in their business. If you didn't play by their rules, they changed the game on you" (*Legends of Wrestling* 2008). Ross's description of the NWA as a cartel is apt. A cartel is an agreement between companies to fix prices and prevent new competition from entering the market. Promoters in this system acted like rational capitalists, competing and cooperating, challenging each other for geographic and economic supremacy, but also working together to preserve group interests. The NWA was initially created to address scalar issues, but, as this section illustrates, its spatial template facilitated its eventually becoming a powerful system of control within the industry.

With the growth of wrestling in the post-World War II era, unmediated competition over a large geographic area, such as the entire North American continent, created several problems for promoters that they could not address individually. First, a glut of uncoordinated promotions gave wrestlers an opportunity to work for different companies, and, with it, an increased ability to demand more control over the fruits of their labor. What if one promoter allowed wrestlers to unionize? Soon all wrestlers would demand the same privilege, or, worse, the best talent would pledge their allegiance to a promoter who provided superior benefits. Avoiding the costs of social reproduction for labor is what made wrestling a profitable business for promoters. Retirement, sick pay, and vacations were not available to the majority of wrestlers during the territorial age. From a spatial perspective, the NWA also needed wrestlers to be geographically flexible, to essentially live on the road, and visit other NWA territories for weeks or months at a time. On the other hand, promoters sought to trap wrestlers in place, preventing them from ever fully leaving a territory and thus management's grasp. Not unlike seasonal migrant workers, who pick fruit for a short period of time and are then asked to move on, wrestlers were needed to entertain spectators but expected to vanish when they became injured or could no longer draw fans, or what is known in the industry as "getting over" with the crowds.[3] For good guys or "baby faces," getting over meant being cheered or supported, even driving the audience to tears if they were unfairly assaulted.[4] For a bad guy or "heel," getting over with the crowd meant being hated or booed. They were successful if they inspired the crowd to throw objects at the ring.

The territorial system also allowed promoters to maximize profits by reshaping the characters of various wrestlers in different locales. At this time, promoters and wrestlers emphasized the idea that a wrestler was not an actor playing a character, but, instead, that the character was actually a real person. In practice, this was rather flexible, since different types of looks and characters worked better in different territories. The preferences of fans in different parts of the country would dictate changes in wrestler "psychology." Psychology in professional wrestling includes knowing how to move around the ring, interact with the fans, take a punch, and even enter the arena. For example, a sold-out Madison Square Garden in New York required a different approach than Homer Hesterly Armory in Tampa, Florida. This is seen in the case of Bruno Sanmartino, the hairy, barrel-chested Italian American who was a living legend in the northeast, a hero to European immigrants. He sold out Madison Square Garden on many occasions, but his character would have fallen flat in the U.S. South. Or as Stan "The Lariat" Hansen put it, "The bookers were well aware of that underlying psychology and tried to relate programs to the people in each area. What worked in New York might not mean anything to the sugar cane workers in Alexandria, Louisiana" (Hansen and Teal 2011). In fact, Sanmartino might have been a heel in other parts of the country. And, in some cases, if a promoter introduced a character incorrectly, or if the crowds did not immediately take to a wrestler's character, he might be sent to another NWA sponsored promotion where he could remake himself in a new character for a different storyline.

Responding to these geographic nuances, Vince McMahon Sr., the promoter of the WWF (located in the northeast where wrestling fans were highly diverse), insisted that each of his wrestlers have an ethnic origin. Hulk Hogan, for example, was given his last name, Hogan, because McMahon wanted him to appeal to Irish fans (Shoemaker 2014). In this system, it was advantageous for promoters to borrow wrestlers and temporarily repackage them based on the preferences of the local fan base: add a mask, change a look, alter geographical origins, and you have a new wrestler. Villains would even play heroes on occasion. In a 2015 podcast of *Stone Cold Steve Austin Unleashed*, "Triple H," former wrestler and current Executive Vice President of the WWE recalled, "You remember when we used to go to the towns, it would be different, some guys would be heels in some places [but] not others, in certain towns, the white meat baby face would get booed" (Austin 2015). However, when wrestling expanded to the national scale on basic cable television in the 1980s, this practice was threatened. For example, George Gray transitioned from the "One Man Gang," a biker from Chicago to "Akeem the African Dream," a shucking and jiving white man who claimed to be from "deepest, darkest, Africa." Without a developed storyline to explain why the same wrestler was playing a dramatically different character, the legitimacy of the business suffered.

More fundamentally, the territorial system allowed the NWA to spatially control wrestling-related activities in North America by creating a norm of conduct between promoters and labor. By creating the illusion of total control over the industry, promoters actively shaped the imagination of wrestlers and convinced them that there were no alternatives to the working conditions they experienced. If a wrestler was foolish enough to challenge one promoter, he would face the fury of the entire NWA. Control of the wrestling universe meant that wrestlers could not reasonably petition promoters for better pay, working conditions, or health care provisions. Any collective organizing could be snuffed out with the full force of the NWA. Wrestlers had to be careful about who they upset, lest they risk being universally denied making a living. Indeed, if wrestlers became too vocal about wanting more pay, or in any way threatened the dominance of the promoters in this system, they were swiftly punished. According to Rowdy Piper, promoters used a wrestler's family as leverage against him in negotiations. At the NWA's annual meeting in Las Vegas, promoters would conspire about how to handle wrestlers who were not playing by their rules. In such cases, a promoter from another territory might contact a mid-card wrestler and promise him big paydays and headline gigs in a far-away locale. The promoter would encourage him to buy a house in the new territory and to bring his family. Once the wrestler moved, the new promoter would refuse to book him. Having a host of financial obligations and newly incurred debts, the wrestler would thus be ruined (*Legends of Wrestling* 2012).

Travel distances in a territory represented another way that managers used space to regulate and otherwise manipulate wrestlers. The wrestling office, the seat of power where the promoter typically lived, was only one stop on a weekly or biweekly circuit, during which wrestlers would travel thousands of miles. Under these conditions, the only bargaining power a wrestler had vis-à-vis promoters was popularity with the fans. If a wrestler consistently drew crowds, they could be paid lavishly and often received special treatment compared to other wrestlers. In such cases, a wrestler was in a unique position of power, especially when they were billed in advance to appear at a particular place. For most, however, the strenuous schedule of continual travel from one town to another, combined with the physical absence of the promoter, meant that wrestlers had little time to formally protest about poor working conditions or inadequate pay.[5]

The geography of the territorial era, in its splinters at least, did have some potential to be advantageous to wresters in that they had multiple places to work. Although the NWA attempted to control unruly wrestlers by eliminating any unaffiliated promotions, internecine conflicts between promoters often produced cracks in the system and allowed, in certain situations, for wrestlers to move between promotions without penalty. Vince McMahon Jr., promoter of the WWE, violated these principles in the early 1980s by raiding other promotions for their best talent. The 1980s also saw the increased splintering of the NWA, particularly across international boundaries, which further jeopardized its spatial control of the sport at the end of the territorial era. This is exemplified in the case of certain wrestlers who competed in Japan. First, it should be noted that, although professional wrestling in Japan worked somewhat cooperatively with the North American territorial system, it has a different history and system of labor regulation than the NWA. Contracts in Japan were typically guaranteed, and, instead of heels and faces, the conflicts mainly took place between Japanese wrestlers and *gaijin*, or foreigners. In Japan, wrestling matches were also less performance based and involved more actual wrestling and fighting skill (Hansen and Teal 2011). Audience reactions and demands differed greatly in Japan and North America. Japanese fans were more reserved than Americans, often politely clapping when they were entertained. American wrestlers who regularly worked in Japan were in a particularly advantageous position (Hansen and Teal 2011; Matysik and Goodish 2007). This is clearly illustrated in the case of Stan "The Lariat" Hansen, who was a wrestling legend in Japan. Originally from West Texas, Stan Hansen's ability to get over with fans in Japan allowed him to pick and choose where and how he worked in the United States. His allegiances would be put to the test in the mid-1980s, when he became AWA champion.

Although the AWA formally broke off from the NWA, it still cooperated with other promotions in order to maintain legitimacy and regulate labor. Shortly before defending the belt, AWA promoter Verne Gagne asked Hansen to drop the belt to AWA mainstay Nick Bockwinkel. Before agreeing to wrestle, Stan Hansen called up his promoter in Japan, the Giant Baba, to ask for permission to lose the belt (Hansen and Teal 2011; *Legends of Wrestling* 2012; Ross 2014a). Baba had already billed him as AWA champion in an upcoming match in Japan, so he gave Hansen instructions to keep the belt. Hansen left for Japan very soon after this phone call, without wrestling Bockwinkel. The resulting dispute caused Gagne to threaten Hansen with legal action if he did not return the belt. Hansen eventually ran over the belt with his truck and mailed it back to Gagne in pieces. Hansen's popularity in Japan allowed him to deal with promoters in the United States on his own terms. If he felt he was being cheated out of money, he could simply refuse to work. Hansen also protected his reputation when he was in the United States. Afraid that a humiliating defeat would harm his image in Japan, losing to an inferior opponent in the United States was out of the question. With the advantage of multinational popularity, of getting over in multiple places, Hansen had much more control over his career – something that wrestlers trapped in one place lacked.

The late "Bruiser Brody," once a tag-team partner with Hansen, also leveraged the geography of the territorial system – and its demise – to his benefit when negotiating with promoters (Matysik and Goodish 2007). The mid-1980s represented the last days of the NWA fiefdom. The WCW and WWF, which by this time had jumped to the national scale, had already plundered the territories for their best talent. Struggling to survive, the fragments of the NWA and other smaller promotions were forced to feature independent headliners such as Bruiser Brody, a true larger than life character. Much like Stan Hansen, Brody also wrestled in Japan and refused to lose cleanly to most opponents, out of the fear that the toughness of his character would suffer. His reputation was what made him such a big draw. A promoter might deliberately undermine his future leverage by forcing him to lose a match by pin fall or submission – so Brody fought back. Accused of holding up promoters for a larger percentage of the gate, sometimes hours before a show started, Brody's style of negotiating most likely caused his death. During a show in Puerto Rico, promoter/wrestler Carlos Colon stabbed him to death in a dressing room (Hansen and Teal 2011; *Legends of Wrestling* 2012). Brody's murder may have been exceptional, but it was ultimately a symbol of the changing times and power dynamics between promoters and wrestlers at the end of the territorial era.

In the mid-twentieth century, promoters created a geography of wrestling territories to control the source of their wealth – the charisma and athleticism of wrestlers. Wrestlers found themselves in a similar position to other athletes, in that their physical gifts, fragile to injury, and the aging process, were the foundation of owners' profits. The inexact formula of creating a popular wrestler, coupled with the influence that top talent like Bruiser Brody had on selling out matches, made regulating the movement of wrestlers incredibly important for promoters. The NWA's spatial strategy was an important mechanism that allowed them to enforce such regulation, as well as to suppress wrestlers' ability to fight for better working conditions and pay. The NWA was thus an institutionalized effort to fix wrestlers into a time–space routine which ensured their compliance in a system that gave promoters unquestioned power over wrestlers. Promoters used the closed nature of the business and hardships associated with arduous travel schedules to take advantage of wrestlers, while the size of the territories ensured that if wrestlers were cheated, they had little recourse for changing their working conditions.

Conclusion

The territorial system that took shape under the NWA was flawed, but it remained strong for nearly 40 years. How did it stay intact for so long? In this chapter, I have shown how any attempt at collective action or opposition was brutally suppressed by the NWA. I have also highlighted how wrestlers found ways to work within in the system. Despite the hardships to their bodies, wrestlers often enjoyed life on the road. In today's podcasts, they fondly talk about drinking beer, telling stories, discussing their craft, and getting into trouble with the law. Playing larger than life characters made them regional superstars. Wrestlers became addicted to the high they got from getting a loud cheer from the crowd. And promoters knew that this feeling could not be easily replicated elsewhere.

Wrestlers could also work around their injuries by taking drugs to limit pain and learning new wrestling techniques, outlasting their physical primes by many years. If they were physically unable to perform in the ring, they could learn to speak better on the microphone and become a manager, or perhaps develop a new set of moves based on the limitations of their bodies. In retirement from in-ring action, some wrestlers became announcers or on-screen general managers. The star system of professional wrestling also helped keep the NWA afloat. Once a wrestler became a proven draw, they received preferential treatment from management, such as flying on a private plane, having access to subsidized health care, or working a smaller part of the schedule. This kind of preferential treatment was part of a "divide and conquer" strategy that separated wrestlers into classes.

The staying power of the NWA was costly, as the physical hardships associated with the road led to the premature death of many wrestlers. Those who survived still struggle with drug and alcohol addictions. Sadly, it was not these human costs that finally broke the NWA. Nor was it organized labor that buckled this spatial strategy. Rather, it was individual promoters acting in their rational self-interest that ultimately caused the splintering of this cartel and its eventual downfall. In the early 1980s, Vince McMahon Jr., the son of New York-based promoter Vince McMahon Sr., broke the spatial system the NWA used to regulate wrestlers. McMahon Jr. took the WWF to the national scale and, in the process, raided other promotions of television slots and talent.

What are the implications of this research for the study of the geography of sport? As we have seen, owners and promoters in professional wrestling's territorial era acted like rational capitalists to collectively pressure each other to keep labor in check, while still conspiring to out-compete each other individually. This contradiction is a key analytic to understanding the relationships between owners and labor. In other North American sports, owners have put salary caps in place to prevent individual owners from overspending and threatening the system. The National Football League, for example, has made sure that the Green Bay Packers will be the only team that is ever publically owned.

In the late 1980s, former wrestler, announcer, and governor of Minnesota, Jessie Ventura, sought to unionize the WWF. According to Ventura, the star of the WWF at the time, Hulk Hogan immediately informed promoter Vince McMahon Jr. of his plans (Shoemaker 2014). Until wrestlers are considered employees of a wrestling company, not just independent contractors, they have little legal basis to unionize or collectively bargain for better work schedules and health benefits. The plight of wrestlers is similar to college athletes today. In 2015, the National Labor Relations Board denied northwestern football players the right to unionize (Zirin 2015). The board decided that football players were student-athletes and not entitled to the rights of workers. Like wrestlers, college athletes must struggle to change the category in which their labor is categorized if they wish to unionize.

What kind of tension results from owners simultaneously working together while still being in competition with one another? While the spatial strategy of the NWA proved to be semi-permanent, creating a space that naturalized the power of promoters, it was ill prepared for inter-promotion competition. So, by examining the strategies that owners employed to drive down the price of labor, the case of the NWA suggests that their tactics were not only flawed, but also open to ruptures. More broadly, the case of wrestling and the NWA's spatial template suggests the importance of shifting our empirical focus from players to owners to gain a fuller understanding of the geographies of power at work in professional sport and beyond.

Notes

1 My interpretation of NWA and its origins are inspired from readings of Legends of Wrestling 2008; Shoemaker 2014.

2 Research about injuries, potatoes, and receipts are inspired from critical readings of: Austin 2013a, 2013b, 2013d, 2014c, 2014d, 2014e; Hansen and Teal 2011; Ross 2014a, 2014c.
3 My synthesis of spatial strategies of power comes from a critical reading of: Austin 2013b, 2014e, 2015; Hansen and Teal 2011; Legends of Wrestling 2008, 2009b, 2012; Matysik and Goodish 2007; Ross 2014a, 2014b; Shoemaker 2014.
4 My understanding of "getting over" is inspired by critical readings of: Austin 2013a, 2013b, 2013c, 2013d, 2014a, 2014b, 2014c, 2014d, 2014e; Hansen and Teal 2011; Hogan and Friedman 2002; Jericho 2015; Legends of Wrestling 2009a, 2009b; Piper 2015b.
5 Research about life on the road is inspired by critical readings of Austin 2013a, 2013b, 2014a, 2014b, 2014d, 2014e; Hansen and Teal 2011; Hogan and Friedman 2002; Legends of Wrestling 2008, 2009b, 2012; Matysik and Goodish 2007; Piper 2015a.

References

Austin, S. (2013a). Ep. 11: *Kevin Nash* (Part 2). The Stone Cold Steve Austin Show Unleashed [Podcast]. May 14. Available at: http://podcastone.com/pg/jsp/program/episode.jsp?programID=436&pid=260486 (accessed July 16, 2015).

Austin, S. (2013b). Ep. 36: *Razor Ramon Part 2*. The Stone Cold Steve Austin Show Unleashed [Podcast]. August 8. Available at: http://podcastone.com/pg/jsp/program/episode.jsp?programID=436&pid=313708 (accessed July 16, 2015).

Austin, S. (2013c). Ep. 60: *Bruce Pritchard Pt 2*. The Stone Cold Steve Austin Show Unleashed [Podcast]. October 31. Available at: http://podcastone.com/pg/jsp/program/episode.jsp?programID=436&pid=350006 (accessed 16 July 2015).

Austin, S. (2013d). Ep. 68: *Brian Knobbs*. The Stone Cold Steve Austin Show Unleashed [Podcast]. November 27. Available at: http://podcastone.com/pg/jsp/program/episode.jsp?programID=436&pid=360082 (accessed July 16, 2015).

Austin, S. (2014a). Ep. 92: *Zeb Coulter aka Dutch Mantell*. The Stone Cold Steve Austin Show Unleashed. February 20. Available at: http://podcastone.com/pg/jsp/program/episode.jsp?programID=436&pid=388454 (accessed July 16, 2015).

Austin, S. (2014b). Ep. 106: *Michael "P.S." Hayes*. The Stone Cold Steve Austin Show Unleashed [Podcast]. April 10. Available at: http://podcastone.com/pg/jsp/program/episode.jsp?programID=436&pid=406779 (accessed July 16, 2015).

Austin, S. (2014c). Ep. 122: *Big Van Vader Pt. 2*. The Stone Cold Steve Austin Show Unleashed [Podcast]. June 5. Available at: http://podcastone.com/pg/jsp/program/episode.jsp?programID=436&pid=417258 (accessed July 16, 2015).

Austin, S. (2014d). Ep. 142: *Mick Foley Pt1*. The Stone Cold Steve Austin Show Unleashed [Podcast]. August 14. Available at: http://podcastone.com/pg/jsp/program/episode.jsp?programID=436&pid=427755 (accessed July 16, 2015).

Austin, S. (2014e). Ep. 163: *The Nature Boy Ric Flair*. The Stone Cold Steve Austin Show Unleashed [Podcast]. October 30. Available at: http://podcastone.com/pg/jsp/program/episode.jsp?programID=436&pid=453680 (accessed July 16, 2015).

Austin, S. (2015). Ep. 192: *WWE COO Triple H*. The Stone Cold Steve Austin Show Unleashed [Podcast]. February 5. Available at: http://podcastone.com/pg/jsp/program/episode.jsp?programID=436&pid=482164 (accessed July 16, 2015).

Foot, John (2011). *Pedalare! Pedalare! A History of Italian Cycling*. London: Bloomsbury Paperbacks.

Hansen, S., and S. Teal (2011). *The Last Outlaw*. Gallatin: Crowbar Press.

Harvey, D. (1996). *Justice, Nature, and the Geography of Difference*. Cambridge, MA: Blackwell Publishers.

Hogan, H., and M. J. Friedman (2002). *Hollywood Hulk Hogan*. New York: Pocket Books.

Jericho, C. (2015). Ep. 107: *Hulk Hogan Pt2*. Talk is Jericho [Podcast]. January 9. Available at: http://podcastone.com/pg/jsp/program/episode.jsp?programID=593&pid=477189 (accessed July 16, 2015).

Legends of Wrestling (2008). Episode 11, *The Territories*. [TV] WWE Network. January 1.

Legends of Wrestling (2009a). Episode 18, *Wrestling with Patriotism*. [TV] WWE Network. July 1.

Legends of Wrestling (2009b). Episode 21, *The Culture of Southern Wrestling*. [TV] WWE Network. December 1.

Legends of Wrestling (2010). Episode 23, *The 1970s*. [TV] WWE Network. June 1.

Legends of Wrestling (2012). Episode 13, *Renegades and Outlaws*. [TV] WWE Network. January 1.

Matysik, L., and B. Goodish (2007). *Brody: The Triumph and Tragedy of Wrestling's Rebel*. Chicago: ECW Press.

Piper, R. (2015a). Ep. 6: *Jake "The Snake" Roberts*. Piper's Pit [Podcast]. July 4. Available at: http://podbay.fm/show/855752234/e/1436041393?autostart=1 (accessed July 16, 2015).

Piper, R. (2015b). Ep. 21: *Hacksaw's Iron Sheik Troubles*. Piper's Pit [Podcast]. July 5. Available at: http://podbay.fm/show/855752234/e/1436043462?autostart=1 (accessed July 16, 2015).

Piper, R. (2015c). Ep. 41: *Vince Russo Part 2*. Piper's Pit [Podcast]. July 5. Available at: http://podbay.fm/show/855752234/e/1436056810?autostart=1 (accessed July 16, 2015).

Ross, J. (2014a). Ep. 29: *Stan "The Lariat" Hansen*. The Ross Report [Podcast]. September 3. Available at: http://podcastone.com/pg/jsp/program/episode.jsp?programID=619&pid=430226 (accessed July 16, 2015).

Ross, J. (2014b). Ep. 31: *Cowboy Bill Watts*. The Ross Report [Podcast]. September 17. Available at: http://podcastone.com/pg/jsp/program/episode.jsp?programID=619&pid=442558 (accessed July 16, 2015).

Ross, J. (2014c). Ep. 45: *Big Van Vader aka Leon White*. The Ross Report [Podcast]. December 24. Available at: http://podcastone.com/pg/jsp/program/episode.jsp?programID=619&pid=474425 (accessed July 16, 2015).

Shoemaker, D. (2014). *The Squared Circle: Life, Death, and Professional Wrestling*. New York: Gotham Books.

The Sheik (2014). *The Sheik* Directed by Igal Hecht. USA: The Orchard.

Zirin, D. (2015). The Absurd, Cowardly, and Morally Bankrupt NLRB Decision Against the Northwestern Football Union. *The Nation*, August 17. Available at: www.thenation.com/article/the-absurd-cowardly-and-morally-bankrupt-nlrb-decision-against-the-northwestern-football-union/ (accessed October 27, 2015).

Chapter 15

In the shadow of mega-events

The value of ethnography in sports geography

Nicholas Wise

Introduction

What do ethnographies tell us about sports geography? A number of academics in sport studies use ethnographic approaches in their research. While research in sports geography is significantly underdeveloped in comparison to sports sociology (Wise 2015b), geographers can productively extend this work by adapting more ethnographic and field-based approaches designed to capture the importance of place and context. Research in sports geography has been heavily influenced by the work of John Bale (2003), who highlighted a number of important analytical themes in his book *Sports Geography*, including landscapes, globalization, diffusion, regional analysis, location, social welfare, place, and geographical imaginaries. Geographers have increasingly taken up these themes to contribute more critically informed studies to the sports geography literature. More recent work has seen scholars looking beyond descriptions of stadia and landscapes to uncover, for example, how sports impact communities (Gaffney 2010), shape contested identities (Conner 2014), aid new conceptual understandings to space and place (Tonts and Atherley 2010), and influence nation-building (Koch 2013).

Contributing to this wider effort to advance a critical approach to sports geography, much of my own research has focused on Haitians in the Dominican Republic (DR) using an ethnographic approach. This methodology has allowed me to better understand how sport adds value to everyday life (Wise 2011, 2014), reinforces a sense of place and community (Wise 2015a; Wise and Harris 2014), and creates social divisions (Wise 2015c). Drawing on my previous research experience in the DR, this chapter outlines the value of ethnographic methods and how these might be applied to future sports geography research in Latin America. More inductive ethnographic research in sports geography is needed. Sport involves experience and takes on multiple local meanings. When focused on these micro-political relationships, ethnographic methods can offer researchers a unique insight into how sports impact people's everyday lives and become implicated in localized power relations. When I began my fieldwork, I had to first gain an understanding of how wider, existing, and often-contested power relations limited control over and access to space(s). Examining sport in the small town of Villa Ascension allowed me to develop this understanding locally, but also to situate it within broader ethnic and racialized geographies of power on the island of Hispaniola.

As I argue in this chapter, a local community-centered focus is essential as Latin America is increasingly coming under the shadow of sporting mega-events. Local voices are often missing in contemporary research – a trend that is productively countered by "slower" ethnographic methods that focus on specific local communities rather than making "quick" generalizations based upon broadly observed impacts. Since investments in sporting mega-events already overshadow local voices, concerns, and needs, it is incumbent upon scholars to directly engage with impacted communities to develop a more inclusive picture of the social impacts of mega-events. Based on my previous research with a rural, underprivileged Haitian community in the DR, I propose a recentering of the scholarship on mega-events around issues of social justice, grounded not just in sensational media reports but in long-term research, to capture the voices of those in underrepresented communities and other places where sports-centered regeneration has occurred. Inductive ethnographic research will be central to future research aimed at investigating and uncovering how communities respond to extensive mega-event developments, as well as the effort to advance a critical sports geography more generally.

The value of ethnography

Ethnographic studies aim to understand everyday interactions by observing, participating, listening to what people say, asking questions, looking at available documents, determining common occurrences, regular events, and collecting memorabilia, materials, or cultural artifacts. In brief, the researcher conducting ethnography is "gathering whatever data are available to throw light on the issues that are the emerging focus of inquiry" (Hammersley and Atkinson 2007: 3). Ethnographies focus on what *emerges*, meaning that, as an inductive method, researchers must first examine all components and surroundings in a locale (even when they may not seem directly related to the study's focus) to develop a detailed sense of social reality. The researcher then needs to make sense of these realities and experiences to critically reflect on how they relate to wider social, political, or economic forces and power relations – all of which shape people's narratives, behaviors, and interactions in and with their surroundings. To inform this analytical work, it is up to the researcher to have a strong base knowledge of history, culture, social conditions, social constructions, local economic situations, and local, regional, or national political situations before entering the field.

Ethnographic research challenges scholars to explore social worlds by living in or working with a particular community. Since ethnographies are observational and participatory, they can only represent a snapshot in time of a community's everyday cultural practices. Ethnographic research can thus pose many challenges with respect to the timing of a study and the researcher's ability to work directly in the field; but in general, the researcher aims to immerse him- or herself in a community to the greatest extent possible. For instance, I volunteered and assisted community programs to get to know members of the community and Haitian soccer players by working alongside them. Living and working with a group of people, or "participant observation," allows researchers to simultaneously engage in and reflect upon daily activities. Participant observation thus offers an intimate portrait of how people interact with their environment, surroundings, encounter socio-political situations, or add meaning to cultural landscapes and everyday spaces – each establishing meaningful insight on place, community, and identity (Cloke *et al.* 2004; Feld and Basso 1996; Hammersley and Atkinson 2007).

Bringing these points together, John Harris (2006: 156) explains that ethnographic "research is best learnt by 'doing'– becoming familiar with the site, and subjects of the inquiry ... where the aim is usually discovery – to find out more about how and why a particular social world is as it is." Therefore, direct immersion, involvement, and observations of daily rituals become the focus for producing data to conceive and reflect on ordinary practices, interactions, and activities common to a particular group of people. Ethnographies represent a rigorous methodology that challenges researchers to avoid assumptions. Researchers need to critically evaluate and write about social phenomena by inquiring about the perspectives of local communities concerning their everyday challenges and situations – and avoiding making assumptions or hypotheses (Cloke *et al.* 2004). Results are thus assessed on their own merit, and not in accordance with any predetermined framework or set of hypotheses. Because ethnographic research does not use any predetermined frameworks, the field becomes a site of discovery for the researcher, who bases initial interpretations on concrete observations. These are then systematically recorded and, as the researcher spends time doing fieldwork, he or she begins to connect them with other data sources and theory to inform the analysis of the study's motivating questions.

Ethnography was pioneered in anthropology (see Malinowski 1922), but "geographers have brought our discipline's theorizations of space, place, scale, landscape, and environment to develop further understandings of spatial processes and concepts in ethnography" (Watson and Till 2010: 122). Ethnographically informed research has contributed a great deal to the discipline since the so-called "critical" turn, which is the focus of this volume. This is largely because ethnography fits well with critical human geography's interest in the micro-politics involved in the production of space and spatial identities, especially at the local scale. Geographers have also long stressed the importance of local histories. To understand events, as well as social constructions of local realities and identities, a strong command of a place's history allows researchers to make sense of observations and interpretations from the field. For instance in political geography, Nick Megoran (2006) notes that much research is based on discourse studies. To avoid repetition across studies, ethnographic approaches challenge geographers to ask new questions in the field and understand what is distinct about a particular research locale and, in turn, how this might raise new research questions for future studies. Because ethnographic methods and approaches contribute greatly to everyday understandings about people and place, in-depth ethnographies typically focus on only one or a small number of case studies. In ethnographically informed research, less is more.

Equally important to critical geography is the principle of reflexivity, whereby researchers interrogate their own truths and political subjectivities as fundamental elements of how knowledge is generated in fieldwork – because of the way this shapes social interactions with research participants and provides or circumscribes a researcher's access to certain experiences in the field (Harris 2006; Megoran 2006; Sands 2002). As Harris (2006: 165) notes, critical reflections are important because researchers "bring [their] own individuality and personality into the text." Moreover, field conversations and ethnographic interviews are key to generating case-specific knowledge and are essential to confirm participant and observational data – allowing the researcher to triangulate and uncover new meanings embedded in a study's emergent themes (Hammersley and Atkinson 2007). As a method particularly attuned to the local scale and open to the dynamic nature of social phenomena, ethnography is well positioned to advance a more critical approach to sports geography research.

Sport ethnography: working with a Haitian community in the Dominican Republic

Since communities create senses of belonging, they are sustained, socially and culturally, through interactions between groups and with individuals. Social scientists focusing on sport have thus used ethnography to develop primary knowledge of sporting communities and social identities. Sports ethnography is a method that has emerged over the past several decades, with studies focusing on, for example, sport training (Klein 1997), surfing (Sands 2002), marathon running (Sugden 2007), local meanings of soccer and baseball (Wise 2014), and watching sporting events in public settings (Weed 2006). Each example noted attempted to achieve similar aims of qualitative analysis – inquiring through immersion to extract cultural knowledge concerning the production of case-specific sporting identities. Sport represents a way of expressing culture through socializations among community members (Walseth 2006). Researchers who directly involve themselves in a community can better assess the role of sport in expressions of a common sense of identity (MacClancy 1996). Yet, sports also divide groups by excluding, deterring participation, or limiting access to space (Wise and Harris 2014; see also Bohland, Nelson, Lee, Conner, Chapters 3, 9, 10, 13 this volume).

As a region characterized by many social fissures, variably resulting from historic inequalities and contemporary wealth gaps, Latin America is an ideal place to ethnographically explore how social inequalities manifest and are both perpetuated and challenged. As a US geographer interested in the daily lives, struggles, and inequalities Haitians face in the DR, I wanted to better understand how soccer contributed to their sense of place and community in a rural, underprivileged community. I therefore spent time in only one community where I was a development volunteer in 2007: Villa Ascension (also referred to as Villa Ascension de Caraballo, adjacent to the community of Caraballo). I had to first build rapport and gain trust from community members. Since sports ethnographers need a common sporting interest with those of their participants to gain acceptance (Sands 2002), for me this meant that I immersed myself by engaging in both soccer with Haitian players and baseball with Dominican players. Each day I would participate in either baseball or soccer, sometimes both, except in the event of torrential downpours, which led participants to just sit around and talk about sports.

Playing soccer and baseball eased my acceptance into both communities. When participating in and observing community sporting activities, I was also conversing with local participants during play and carrying out in-depth interviews informed from participant observations in down time. Much of my fieldwork time, however, was spent participating in various daily activities beyond sport, together with Haitian soccer players. For example, these players would help to administer a children's food program, which was held three times a week in Villa Ascension. I would also assist them because this allowed me to further integrate myself and participate in similar daily activities. Doing so enabled me to understand their role as social contributors who promoted community well-being by helping care for children from the most underprivileged families. To capture other insights like this, I used various qualitative methods, ranging from participant observations, landscape analysis, mental maps, and interviews.

Villa Ascension was an ideal venue to consider the intersections between sport, place, and identity. Having visited the community on several occasions prior to undertaking my primary fieldwork, I realized that community organizers had designated space for soccer by putting metal goal posts at either end. To Haitians, this was a soccer field; kids would play during the day and people would gather to play soccer and socialize when the men played in the evening. Such a space dedicated for soccer is rare in the DR because a major part of the Dominican national identity narrative centers on the sport of baseball. So in a setting where Haitians are regarded as the "other" group, they often struggled to find time and a place to play soccer. Most of the country's accessible sports spaces are baseball fields, regularly controlled and occupied by Dominicans (Wise 2011, 2014). Given this dynamic, and their underrepresented status in the DR, Haitians unite and celebrate their identity and common ideals through soccer.

Although Villa Ascension had a soccer field, it was also common for Haitians in other communities to play soccer on baseball fields. However, in these communities, Haitians can only play soccer when Dominicans were not playing baseball. On weekends, it was typical for another Haitian community to travel to Villa Ascension for a soccer match. It was most common that Haitian men would actively play, while youth and women would spectate and socialize around the soccer field. What also made Villa Ascension's soccer field unique was Haitians would openly share the field with the Dominicans who resided in Villa Ascension and Caraballo. Because two sports were played on one field, the sporting space takes on contrasting "layers of meaning" depending on who is using the space (see Wise 2014).

As this book illustrates, sports spaces have the power to unite and divide groups of people. In Villa Ascension, this was observed each day when Haitians would arrive to play soccer and Dominicans to play baseball. Moreover, as sites of community involvement, sports spaces contribute to a sense of place and a sense of community (Baller 2007; Lee, Chapter 10 this volume; Wise 2011). Ethnographic research allowed me to assess how soccer and baseball were both performed, and, in my field notes, I critically reflected on wider notions of inclusion and exclusion. Exclusion in the DR primarily hinges on social differences of ethnicity and gender, but has important spatial dimensions. Drawing on critical geographic research about space and how local participants perceive place and perform their identity (Cresswell 2004), as well as how one dominant group excludes another, I used an ethnographic approach to put myself in the center of community activities, struggles, and the construction of social binaries – whether Haitian/Dominican or male/female.

Understanding sport in relation to Haitian and Dominican identity is rooted in the politics of a still socially, racially, ethnically, and economically divided Hispaniola. While Haiti controlled Hispaniola for 22 years (1822–44), widespread dispute amidst the global economic recession of the 1930s pushed Haitians to enter the DR or settle along the border.

Dominican President Rafael Trujillo founded the "Dominicanization" (*Dominicanización*) program following the 1936 boundary agreement (Augelli 1980). What followed were mass killings and expulsions of Haitians and anyone with a dark-skin complexion in the border region (Howard 2001). Prejudice persists today from what emerged as struggles over race, said to threaten the DR's "national homogeneity, or national character" (Howard 2001: 156), and sports participation has tended to reinforce this divide.

As MacClancy (1996: 2) notes, sports "are vehicles of identity, providing people with a sense of difference and a way of classifying themselves and others, whether latitudinally or hierarchically." Ethnic "difference" thus complements this imaginary façade of heterogeneous interplays of identity, thereby situating sport as a discourse for accessing socio-cultural semblances of national sporting identity. These interplays are not always immediately visible to outsiders; however, they persist through informal and mundane exchanges, as well as simple contests over access to fields or other sporting spaces (see also Nelson and Cook *et al.*, Chapters 9, 11 this volume). Ethnographic research thus positioned me to grasp the micro-politics of these identity narratives in Villa Ascension by experiencing everyday life and participating in routine activities with local participants. I was challenged to engage and then critically observe, evaluate, and make sense of these experiences and their significance within particular spaces and landscapes.

The sports landscape has long been a focus among geographers, mainly concerning stadia (Bale 1994, 2003; Gaffney 2008). Bale (2003: 131) references sportscapes as "monocultural sites given over solely to sport." While this notion is limited, Villa Ascension's soccer field was initially designated by community organizers. However, local interactions, performances, and competing identity narratives add social value to the making of sports landscapes. Centrally, different groups may ascribe contrasting significance to sporting spaces and practices, as in Villa Ascension, where they took on inherently different meanings between the two groups. To Haitians, playing soccer allowed them to escape everyday struggles (Wise 2015a). Haitians spoke about struggles, such as lack of employment and not having the same socio-economic benefits as Dominicans, but coming together to play soccer allowed them to forget about their daily hardships – at least during that short period of time each day. Forgetting about daily struggles was not only the perspective of those who were actively playing soccer: Haitians gathering at the field to spectate expressed a similar sentiment.

An important finding that stood out when conducting this research was when Haitian soccer players spoke about their lack of possessions. In fact, most Haitians do not have many material belongings. To the Haitians in Villa Ascension, having a soccer field represented an important possession

– the field was of primary importance. Collectively, the Haitians in Villa Ascension sought to maintain their field (Wise 2011, 2014). Soccer players from Villa Ascension often invited other Haitian communities (from across the Puerto Plata region) on weekends, which served to build community and reinforce a sense of distinct Haitian identity in the DR (Wise 2015a). Moreover, the Haitian soccer players in Villa Ascension taught younger Haitians to play soccer, further reinforcing their Haitian culture and ideals. While Haitians constituted the ethnic "other" in the DR, linked to ethnic division, another critical interpretation of this study offered insight into cultures of masculinity among both Haitians and Dominicans – as men excluded women from using the soccer field each evening. The Haitian community-building around soccer thus carried with it important gender-based exclusions. Also congregating in the evenings and weekends to watch soccer matches, women and girls were undoubtedly interested in soccer. However, they were excluded from active participation with the men, despite being integral members of the Dominican–Haitian community (Wise and Harris 2014).

For their part, Dominicans in Villa Ascension and neighboring Cara-ballo often viewed Haitian influences as a threat, and thus established their presence in Villa Ascension's soccer field by using it to play baseball. Dominicans also constantly attempted to teach their Haitian neighbors to play baseball, despite the latter group's preference for soccer. By encouraging Haitians to play baseball, Dominicans were producing and defending an ethnic nationalist identity – which they felt was being intruded upon by the Haitians' nonconformity with local sporting cultures. In this respect, the Dominican effort to influence Haitians to play baseball is linked to historical discourses about the need for official Dominicanization programs to limit Haitian influence. In their efforts to promote baseball (i.e., the locally dominant sporting culture and norms), Dominicans were attempting to defend a particular ethnic vision of their territory and promote their national ideals through sport. It is through such contested notions of sport and the multiple meanings and performances of identity in a sports space that an ethnographic approach assists with gaining insight into such a broad and diffuse effect as nationalism.

Given the geographical complexities concerning contested histories and local interplays of identity between Haitians and Dominicans, Cresswell's (2004) notion of "in place/out of place" added conceptual depth to my interpretations: Haitians were referred to as "others," and therefore out of place in the DR. Because Haitians were seen as being in "another" country, not "their own," a symbolic site such as a designated soccer field represented a stage for collective identity formation. Alternatively, the local setting suggested Dominicans were out of place in Villa Ascension because they were trying to forge their sporting presence in a Haitian soccer field in their own country (Wise 2015c). As I often observed in other towns and villages, Haitians were often excluded from using sports (baseball) fields because Dominicans had priority access. However, in Villa Ascension, the Haitians did share their soccer field and allowed ample time for Dominicans to play baseball each afternoon before they played soccer. When I spoke to the Haitians, they felt it was important the Dominicans were also able to express their sense of sporting identity, despite Dominicans often excluding Haitians.

Informing critical ethnographic research and future directions

As noted above, since sporting mega-events significantly overshadow local voices, it is incumbent upon scholars not to do the same in their research into these transformational events. Moving forward, I am interested in developing a similar ethnographic approach in Manaus, Brazil, the capital of the state of Amazonas, which became home to a new $300-million stadium used in the 2014 FIFA World Cup and slated to host several soccer games for the 2016 Summer Olympic Games. While Manaus is an urban center of two million people, it remains peripheral within the country and is an unlikely place to host sporting mega-events. Nonetheless, neoliberal motives led to these large-scale developments for the event and, perhaps predictably, tangible infrastructural investments do not always reach and/or benefit underprivileged or underrepresented communities in the locale. Although I recognize there are important differences between the DR and Brazil, lessons from my ethnographic research in the DR can inform future research in Brazil – especially as local communities grapple with the effects of sporting mega-events and the neoliberal economic transformations of their cities.

Van Der Merwe's (2007) research addresses how, for policymakers and planners, despite having uncertain benefits, tangible developments for mega-events typically outweigh considerations of intangible impacts on communities. This is because, in so many places around the world, corporate interests are increasingly linked to a country's or city's ability to attract investment (Smith 2012: 27). This much is known – and well covered in the literature on mega-events and neoliberal globalization. But how are local communities actually impacted by mega-event-centered "regeneration" initiatives? By what standards can researchers measure these impacts; and with what tools? Despite the recent proliferation of research on events such as the Olympics or the FIFA World Cup, these remain wholly unanswered questions within the literature. This is a curious omission because academics have spent a great deal of time critiquing neoliberal agendas and social justice themes are central to these criticisms. Going back to Megoran's (2006) argument that too much research in the area of political geography is based on discourse studies, we need to avoid broad generalizing repetition by asking new questions and focusing on specific cases.

By partnering with local communities and specific neighborhoods, scholars can better capture local voices and concerns about the variable and contested impacts of event-led regeneration. When cities regenerate, access to new facilities and amenities is limited and underrepresented groups are sometimes redistributed. Because access to space for sport and recreation may become limited, it is important to understand how people who do not benefit from regeneration adapt and change spaces for sport and recreation to stage and perform their identity for their own well-being. Not only can knowledge gained through ethnographic inquiry help shape awareness to aid critical understandings of social justice, but locally attuned methods may also surprise researchers and force us to rethink preconceived notions of how mega-events impact local communities.

Ethnography will allow us to uncover new perspectives on change and social impacts. For instance, Smith (2012: 28) notes that "neoliberalism is supposed to encourage innovation and progress through healthy competition." Much of the literature on events and regeneration is often based on wider policy initiatives and proposed plans, typically focusing on critiquing corporate interests, globalization, and neoliberal competitiveness trends (e.g., Gaffney 2010; Hall 2006; Spirou 2010). While making an important point, from a methodological standpoint, such studies often lack "on the ground," in-depth research in and with communities to both substantiate and illustrate how events-oriented development policies directly affect local residents. It is the local residents who live through regeneration, and it is therefore imperative to assess their views on how lifestyles and homes have been altered by mega-events, rather than imposing a scholar's preconceived notion of social justice on every community.

Ethnographic research is also needed to uncover and explore some of the "softer," intangible impacts of change in mega-event host cities. Intangible impacts involve a number of social conditions such as local experiences, involvement, educational opportunities, employment and skills training, legacy training, and increased pride in place. For example, policies pertinent to strategic investments for new sporting infrastructures aim to encourage wider participation (Paton et al. 2010; Smith 2012). However, in cases such as Manaus, the use of sporting infrastructures are not only limited, but may not have much practical use in the future. Moreover, sporting infrastructures are a liability because future maintenance costs are also not considered or appropriately accounted for, which can later burden taxpayers (Spirou 2010). But an ethnographic approach does not stop at this simple economic critique. Rather, it would seek to incorporate local voices to trace specific – and potentially unexpected – reactions, needs, and community concerns. Ethnographic research can thus also conceivably inform community policy and put pressure on government officials to enact social policies for the benefit of underrepresented groups rather than further their marginalization. However, it is only through accessing locally informed knowledge that we as academics can better ground critical arguments to advocate for critical and socially just policies.

Furthermore, mega-events can often reinstate dominant discourses about culture and identity (Giardina 2005). These dominant discourses are very broad in scope, however, and, as Andrews and Silk (2012) argue, we must look at different trajectories framed around the context of sport and mega-events to understand how neoliberal practices are at play. But the context needs to be considered locally by scholars working directly in communities – local context needs more local perspective. If, as David Harvey (2005) has argued, power is exerted by the dominant culture in an attempt to enforce individuals' conformity to new practices and ideals, then as researchers we need to slow down our research to incorporate more on-the-ground empirical work that can properly grapple with such cultural transformations and how change is contested. Of course, we may find ourselves in a dilemma because this in-depth research requires longer periods of time in the field to conduct longitudinal impact studies. Scholars also often face language barriers or difficulties communicating and, in some cases, it may be difficult to find acceptance in communities. Yet slowing down our research on mega-events will be essential to advancing new and more critical conceptual understandings of sport, space, identity, and social justice.

As I have suggested, research on these issues is especially timely in Brazil, given ongoing controversies related to hosting the World Cup in 2014 and the Olympics in 2016. So far, the literature on these events has tended to focus on the country's largest cities, but social justice issues are also present in more peripheral communities, such as Manaus – an inland port about 930 miles (1,500 kilometers) from the Atlantic Ocean and a major industrial zone in the state of Amazonas. Alongside environmental challenges from urban expansion in the Amazon, the largest social issue in Manaus is widespread poverty and many urban residents reside in informal housing settlements, or favelas. This, combined with the city's peripheral location, caused much concern and criticism from skeptics about its designation to host matches in 2014 and 2016. Part of the concern was that around $300 million was spent on a 42,000-seat stadium (Arena Amazônia) in a city with no clubs or regular sporting tournaments beyond the local or regional scale. Moreover, only four 2014 World Cup matches were actually played in Arena Amazônia. As preliminary research with urban residents suggests, more work is needed to give voice to the concerns of those communities which are burdened with upkeep expenses of their city's new facilities while paradoxically being denied access to many of the venues (e.g., Andrade and Braga 2014; Malhado and Rothfuss 2013). By working in and with underrepresented communities, academic researchers might amplify their voices and advocate social policies that focus on inclusion and reclaiming sporting spaces for broader use.

To refer back to my previous ethnographic study in the DR, a study of a peripheral place such as Manaus is likely to raise a number of issues connected to the layering of identities or multiple meanings of "us" and "them." As a neoliberalizing country, Brazil's urban spaces are increasingly divided in an exclusionary fashion, with access determined by socio-economic status. Because developments and other regeneration efforts geared toward mega-events are shaped by this neoliberal logic, the themes of inclusion and exclusion or in place/out of place will be central to explaining the unique conjuncture of sport, power, and place in Manaus. Just as in the DR, the notion of staging and performing identities is also expected to take on significant meaning for underrepresented communities' experiences with inclusion and exclusion in Brazil's urban spaces that have recently been transformed for sport and mega-events.

With limited means of access to regenerated spaces, underrepresented groups continually seek alternative ways to transform available spaces for their own well-being and to perform their identity. Ethnographic research is thus needed to uncover how these men and women are mobilizing and responding to the impacts of these regeneration initiatives. It is likewise important to understand how staging recreational space(s) are contested and how altered spaces impact everyday sport and play in communities – especially because this is increasingly a story that cannot be told apart from the effect of standing in the long shadow cast by mega-events. By living in communities and working with residents or activist groups, new insight can be achieved by conducting ethnographies about local struggles to adapt and use space for recreation, again, at a time when public resources are being devoted to more spectacular and centralized venues, events, and infrastructures.

As opposition to mega-event projects continues to rise around the world, geographers also need to rethink the role of sport and social impacts during times of social unrest – as well as the implications for non-democratic polities, which are increasingly winning major sporting event hosting bids (Koch and Valiyev 2015). By expanding ethnographic research, scholars are well positioned to offer new insights into a more critical sports geography of the future. As critical scholars concerned with unsettling hegemonic power relations, our research in this direction might also help to produce bottom-up results to create awareness and inform social policy. The future of critical sports studies thus demands a renewed focus on social justice issues in the shadow of mega-events. Sports ethnography conducted by geographers will frame spatial understandings and offer critical insight on notions of exclusion. The boundary drawing inherent in practices of inclusion and exclusion suggests the importance of geographical perspectives alongside existing sociological debates to add spatially informed understandings of globalization, transnational migrations, and regenerative strategies to inform urban-regional policy and planning.

In sum, ethnographic approaches are not only methodologically appropriate, but essential to the future directions of critical research in sports geography. Especially when working with people in underrepresented communities, there are numerous challenges associated with ethnographic inquiries – making them difficult and rigorous. Researchers are often surprised, or can become frustrated, during ethnographic research – but that is precisely its value. Ethnographic fieldwork requires much time, patience, and ample interpretations, and insight is gained though participation, conversations, and moving beyond one's comfort zone to encounter new ways of seeing and knowing the world.

References

Andrade, R., and S. I. G. Braga (2014). Futebol e Torcedores em Manaus (AM): Breve Digressão e Etnografia Multissituada em "Clima" de Copa do Mundo na Cidade [Soccer and Soccer Fans in Manaus (AM): Brief Digression and Multi-Sited Ethnography in World Cup Mood in the City]. *Ponto Urbe* 14: 2–16.

Andrews, D., and M. Silk (2012). *Sport and Neoliberalism: Politics, Consumption, and Culture*. Philadelphia: Temple University Press.

Augelli, J. P. (1980). Nationalization of Dominican Borderlands. *Geographical Review* 70(1): 19–35.

Bale, J. (1994). *Landscapes of Modern Sport*. London: Leicester University Press.

Bale, J. (2003). *Sports Geography*. London: Routledge.

Baller, S. (2007). Transforming Urban Landscapes: Soccer Fields as Sites of Urban Sociability in the Agglomeration of Dakar. *African Identities* 5(2): 217–30.

Cloke, P., I. Cook, P. Crang, M. Goodwin, J. Painter, and C. Philo (2004). *Practising Human Geography*. London: SAGE.

Conner, N. (2014). Global Cultural Flows and the Routes of Identity: The Imagined Worlds of Celtic FC. *Social & Cultural Geography* 15(5): 525–46.

Cresswell, T. (2004). *Place: A Short Introduction*. Oxford: Blackwell.

Feld, S., and K. H. Basso (1996). *Senses of Place*. Santa Fe: School of American Research Press.

Gaffney, C. (2008). *Temples of the Earthbound Gods*. Austin: University of Texas Press.

Gaffney, C. (2010). Mega-Events and Socio-Spatial Dynamics in Rio de Janeiro, 1919–2016. *Journal of Latin American Geography* 9(1): 7–29.

Giardina, M. (2005). *Sporting Pedagogies: Performing Culture and Identity in the Global Era*. New York: Peter Lang.

Hall, C. (2006). Urban Entrepreneurship, Corporate Interests and Sports Mega-Events: The Thin Policies of Competitiveness within the Hard Outcomes of Neoliberalism. *The Sociological Review* 54(S2): 59–70.

Hammersley, M., and P. Atkinson (2007). *Ethnography: Principles in Practice*. London: Routledge.

Harris, J. (2006). The Science of Research in Sport and Tourism: Some Reflections upon the Promise of the Sociological Imagination. *Journal of Sport & Tourism* 11(2): 153–71.

Harvey, D. (2005). *A Brief History of Neoliberalism*. Oxford: Oxford University Press.

Howard, D. (2001). *Coloring the Nation: Race and Ethnicity in the Dominican Republic*. Oxford: Signal Books.

Klein, A. M. (1997). *Baseball on the Border*. Princeton: Princeton University Press.

Koch, N. (2013). Sport and Soft Authoritarian Nation-Building. *Political Geography* 32: 42–51.

Koch, N., and A. Valiyev (2015). Urban Boosterism in Closed Contexts: Spectacular Urbanization and Second-Tier Mega-Events in Three Caspian Capitals. *Eurasian Geography and Economics* 56(5): 575–98.

MacClancy, J. (1996). *Sport, Identity and Ethnicity*. Oxford: Berg.

Malhado, A. C. M., and R. Rothfuss (2013). Transporting 2014 FIFA World Cup to Sustainability: Exploring Residents' and Tourists' Attitudes and Behaviours. *Journal of Policy Research in Tourism, Leisure and Events* 5(3): 252–69.

Malinowski, B. (1922). *Argonauts of the Western Pacific*. Mt. Prospect: Waveland Press.

Megoran, N. (2006). For Ethnography in Political Geography: Experiencing and Re-Imagining Ferghana Valley Boundary Closures. *Political Geography* 25: 622–40.

Paton, K., G. Mooney, and K. McKee (2010). Class, Citizenship and Regeneration: Glasgow and the Commonwealth Games 2014. *Antipode* 44(4): 1470–89.

Sands, R. R. (2002). *Sport Ethnography*. Champaign: Human Kinetics.

Smith, A. (2012). *Events and Urban Regeneration: The Strategic Use of Events to Revitalise Cities*. London: Routledge.

Spirou, C. (2010). *Urban Tourism and Urban Change*. London: Routledge.

Sugden, J. (2007). Running Havana: Observations on the Political Economy of Sport Tourism in Cuba. *Leisure Studies* 26(2): 235–51.

Tonts, M., and K. Atherley (2010). Competitive Sport and the Construction of Place Identity in Rural Australia. *Sport in Society* 13(3): 381–98.

Van Der Merwe, J. (2007). Political Analysis of South Africa's Hosting of the Rugby and Cricket World Cups: Lessons for the 2010 Football World Cup and Beyond? *Politikon* 34(1): 67–81.

Walseth, K. (2006). Sport and Belonging. *International Review for the Sociology of Sport* 41(3/4): 447–64.

Watson A., and K. Till (2010). Ethnography and Participant Observation. In *The SAGE Handbook of Qualitative Geography* eds. D. DeLyser, S. Herbert, S. Aitken, M. Crang, and L. McDowell. London: SAGE, 121–37.

Weed, M. (2006). The Story of Ethnography: The Experience of Watching the 2002 World Cup in the Pub. *Soccer & Society* 7(1): 76–95.

Wise, N. (2011). Transcending Imaginations through Football Participation and Narratives of the *Other*: Haitian National Identity in the Dominican Republic. *Journal of Sport & Tourism* 16(3): 259–75.

Wise, N. (2014). Layers of the Landscape: Representation and Perceptions of an Ordinary (Shared) Sport Landscape in a Haitian and Dominican Community. *Geographical Research* 52(2): 212–22.

Wise, N. (2015a). Football on the Weekend: Rural Events and the Haitian Imagined Community in the Dominican Republic. In *Exploring Community Festivals and Events* eds. A. Clarke and A. Jepson. London: Routledge, 106–17.

Wise, N. (2015b). Geographical Approaches and the Sociology of Sport. In *Routledge Handbook of the Sociology of Sport* ed. R. Giulianotti. London: Routledge, 142–52.

Wise, N. (2015c). Maintaining Dominican Identity in the Dominican Republic, Forging a Baseball Landscape in Villa Ascension. *International Review for the Sociology of Sport* 50(2): 161–78.

Wise, N., and J. Harris (2014). Finding Football in the Dominican Republic: Haitian Migrants, Space, Place and Notions of Exclusion. In *Football and Migration: Perspectives, Places and Players* eds. R. Elliott and J. Harris. London: Routledge, 180–93.

Conclusion

Chapter 16

Toward a critical geography of sport

Space, power, and social justice

David Jansson and Natalie Koch

Introduction

As post-structural theory started to reach geography in the 1980s, sowing the seeds of what we now consider to be the "critical turn," it seemed to present a major challenge to the discipline's coherence. Michael Dear's (1988) article on the "postmodern challenge" illustrates the anxieties this stimulated among established scholars. In his effort to imagine a research agenda that would hold the field together and accord it more prestige, he took a stab at the geography of sport, categorizing it as a "peripheral" sub-discipline because, he asserted, it "is not central to the structure and explanation of geographical knowledge" (Dear 1988: 271). It has been some time since this dismissal and, while most geographers would now be reticent to publish their value judgments on human geography's various sub-disciplines, the geography of sport remains an unappreciated field and, even today, many intellectuals "overwhelmingly dismiss the sporting world" (Hern 2013: 8).

Yet, in light of the chapters in this volume, and the enormous role sport plays globally in political, social, and economic geographies (Dear's three "priority" fields he claims deserve special status), it is clear that sport is indeed central to geographical knowledge – and should be of keen interest to critical geographers. So, rather than being merely a "fun" diversion from more serious topics, as is still routinely assumed in academia, this volume's focus on power forcefully shows the potential for sport to illuminate, in a most serious manner, a range of questions about space, identity, and social justice. Not only is sport a powerful lens with which to view larger theoretical debates, but a critical geography of sport has the potential to actively shape theory. In this concluding chapter, we build on these arguments to elaborate on how and why sport is an especially promising subject of critical geographical inquiry, and propose further opportunities to advance this scholarship.

In particular, we argue that critical studies in sport can make important contributions to ongoing research and advocacy efforts on issues of social justice. Lawrence Berg (2010: 617) has defined critical geography as "a diverse set of ideas and practices linked by a shared commitment to a broadly conceived emancipatory politics, progressive social change, and the use of a range of critical sociogeographic theories." Putting together sport, emancipatory politics, and social justice in the same sentence may strike many scholars as farfetched, but we hope the diverse contributions to this volume persuasively illustrate that a critical geographic perspective can advance precisely these goals. Not only does sport highlight the workings of power in mundane or everyday ways, it has much to contribute to our understandings of resistance, scale, varying and intersecting axes of difference, and even the Anthropocene.

Sport and spaces of resistance

In studies of the intersections between sport and power, there are two particularly important perspectives. The first relates to how sport can play a role in making and remaking social, cultural, political, and economic space. We can learn a great deal about the way space is constructed in diverse contexts by examining sport. The second perspective builds on this insight, and considers sport as a potential vehicle for creating a more just world. As the chapters in this volume have illustrated, sport can be a primary mechanism through which individuals are socialized as political subjects, as compliant actors obeying dominant spatial logics and hierarchies. But by the same means, sport also allows individuals to challenge spatial socialization and open up possibilities for new social cartographies.

The aggressively hierarchical nature of many sporting activities, both regulated and everyday, can be particularly effective at reinforcing obedience to a singular authority. This is one reason why cross-pollination between sport and a politics of resistance is typically feared and discouraged by sport organizations and other sport authorities – a dynamic that is abundantly clear in Bradley Gardener's chapter on professional wrestling during the "territorial era," when managers systematically worked to suppress all efforts of wrestlers to organize or otherwise demand better pay and working conditions. Given the uneven terrain that divides sports "managers" and sports "laborers," athletes taking public stands and speaking out about politics is often considered deeply controversial: "when the personal becomes political in sports, the cheerleading often comes to an abrupt halt" (Kaufman and Wolff 2010: 156). In the US context, given the relative silence of prominent athletes on the political front today, the political engagement of world-class athletes such as Muhammad Ali and the sprinters Tommie Smith and John Carlos at the 1968 summer Olympics seems to belong to a time long past. But the tide appears to be changing, especially in the case of professional black athletes, who have increasingly taken public stands on controversial political issues, such as police violence against African Americans (Rhoden 2014).

Other recent acts of resistance by professional athletes include a German soccer player's refusal to play an international match against Israel (Bell 2007), and the US National Basketball Association Phoenix Suns team wearing a "Los Suns" jersey to criticize an anti-immigrant law in their home state of Arizona (Agence France Presse 2010). In 2015, we also saw university athletes join anti-racism protests on campuses across the US. At the University of Missouri, for example, African American students began to protest what they perceived to be a hostile racial climate, but were frustrated by the lack of response by the administration. Then, a few black members of the university's football team visited the protesters and afterward enlisted the entire team to support the students by, in effect, going on strike. With the public support of the head coach, the student-athletes refused to play their next regularly scheduled games unless the university president resigned. Within two days of the team's announcement, their demand was met and the president stepped down (Nocera 2015).

While the drama of this particular episode was heightened by the unprecedented actions of a major university football team, resistance and political action in modern sport does have a history, and one that goes beyond Ali, Carlos, and Smith. Even though "athletic activism is non-normative behavior, there is still a long, albeit small, tradition of individuals who have used the playing field to advocate for political and social justice" (Kaufman and Wolff 2010: 158). Indeed, the world of sport provides an environment full of opportunities for the development of a social consciousness and notions of responsible citizenship. As Matt Hern (2013: 21) suggests, "You can't participate in or spectate sports without constantly articulating values, running into difference, talking about what matters and why, and being forced to figure out who you have responsibility for and why." The world of sport opens avenues for athletes, spectators, and the many communities in which they are embedded to pursue agendas toward a better and more socially just future.

Sport and national spaces

One key theme running through many of the chapters in this volume is how identity politics within and across states are often activated in and through sporting activities. Indeed, much of the organizational logic of sport is grounded in the supposed naturalness of competition between teams representing different states. And here it is important to distinguish between the concepts "state" (a political unit representing sovereign control over a clearly defined territory that functions through institutions of governance) and "nation" (a group of people who believe they share a common culture – whether defined in ethnic or civic terms – and history, and who seek or already have control over the political institutions that regulate their lives). International sporting competitions such as the Olympic Games and the FIFA World Cup are essentially competitions between states, while much of the politics behind such competitions relates to the struggle of various "stateless nations" to achieve the right to compete internationally in various sports (Field 2014; Menary 2007).

Furthermore, sport can play a central role in nation-building attempts, and in some cases, as Natalie Koch (2013: 49) has argued, they can "naturalize paternalist state-society relations in which citizens are actively assigned the role of passive spectator," which ultimately legitimates inequalities in power and wealth. In her chapter on "athletic autocrats," she builds on this argument to show how regime-promoted images of a dictator as a sportsman draw on localized tropes of nationalism and masculinity to create the image of a strong, nearly superhuman leader who is in touch with the people and concerned for their health and physical fitness. Especially in the case of personalistic authoritarianism, which revolves around the leader's personal charisma, regimes strategically employ sporting rhetoric to advance their claims to legitimacy and valorize strong-handed, autocratic modes of governing. This is a dynamic that Slavomír Horák further highlights in his chapter on post-Soviet Turkmenistan, where the country's two leaders since 1991 have both used nationalist rhetoric around sport as part of their cult of personality to buttress authoritarian political configurations.

In settings less dominated by a strong-handed authoritarian leader, sport often occupies a central role in the relationship between nation and state. As Webster (2006: 44) puts it, sport can be "used as part of a nation's iconography, or the glue that holds nations together." This is especially clear in Arlene Crampsie's chapter on the Gaelic Athletic Association (GAA), as well as Neil Conner's related study on everyday sports in Ireland, both of which pointed to the importance of nationalistically imagined sports, such as Gaelic football or camogie, to articulate a coherent – and bounded – "Irish" identity. Sport can also be used to literally "stitch" the nation together by arranging linked events throughout the territory of the state, as in the Olympic torch relay (Grant 2014) or country-wide cycling events in Europe such as the Tour de France, Vuelta a España, or Giro d'Italia (Cardoza 2010). Or, as Crampsie shows, the GAA's island-wide mandate meant that it had to bridge both the social and territorial divide between the independent Republic of Ireland and Northern Ireland. As a non-state institution, the GAA is uniquely positioned as a mediator between members that may all identify as "Irish," but "politically inhabit two different colonial spaces." This socially and spatially uneven colonial status also comes out in Magid Shihade's chapter (Chapter 5) on the 1981 conflict in Galilee, Israel, which erupted around a soccer game between teams from two neighboring Palestinian villages, Kafr Yassif and Julis.

As in the Irish case, the conflict did not revolve around a simple axis of colonizer vs. colonized, but rather arose as a result of tensions between those with different subject positions vis-à-vis the colonizing state.

These studies push critical scholars of sport to think beyond simple colonial/post-colonial binaries and grapple with the complexity – and contextuality – of identity narratives as they are contested in particular places at particular moments. Whether it is through sporting institutions, competitions, or discrete venues, sport clearly provides an important sphere for the *performance* of identities (Edensor 2002). So while existing research has highlighted the many ways in which the power of the state is mobilized through sport by certain spatial strategies, Pauliina Raento suggests that this need not be confined to national *human* sports and events. In her chapter on geopolitics and horse sports in Finland, she shows how national identities and geopolitical affinities can be narrated together with certain animals and their sporting talents (see also Koch 2015).

From a political perspective, the imbrication of sport and nationalism is double-edged: sport can be used for jingoistic, nationalistic purposes, entrenching a set of militaristic ideals (Billig 1995). Crampsie also shows how, in the early days of the GAA, the association's ban on foreign games and dances was enforced through policing members by secret vigilance (or "vigilante") committees – resulting in a sort of nationalism by coercion. In his study of Gazprom's sports-oriented "corporate social responsibility" programs in Russia, Veli-Pekka Tynkkynen points to a form of nationalism by enticement – but one that nonetheless promotes a militarized Russian national identity. He shows how the parastatal company, with close ties to President Vladimir Putin's regime, helps to promote the image of an ideal citizen as an able-bodied worker-soldier and to advance Putin's effort to "recover" Russia's lost Great Power status, or *"derzhava."*

In a curiously similar fashion in the US context, the increased "embedding" of nationalism within professional sports performances shows how sport can be a powerful extended arm of the state. In 2015, for example, a Congressional investigative report revealed that the Department of Defense spent nearly US$7 million on displays of "paid patriotism" at professional sports games, indicating a deepening – and worrisome – connection between sports and the country's military-industrial complex (McCain and Flake 2015). When deeply political agendas such as this get written into sporting discourses and performances, sport literally provides an arena for the active contestation of nationalism. Dave Zirin (2005, 2009) has discussed a multitude of examples of athletes challenging the intersection of sport and nationalism at various moments in history, and as scholars who are interested in emancipatory politics, critical geographers should certainly find such stories worthy of further investigation.

With regard to theory, it is also important to ask *why* it is that sport can contribute so powerfully to the reproduction of nationalism.

One fascinating interpretation is offered by Paul Kingsbury (2011) in his study of the psychological aspects of international sporting competitions. Kingsbury asks why nationalist sporting spectacles are so emotionally engaging for so many people. He finds a plausible answer in Slavoj Žižek's concept of "the national Thing," grounded in Lacanian psychoanalysis. Very briefly, Žižek's argument is that a "nation exists only as long as its specific mode of enjoyment continues to be materialized in a set of social practices and transmitted through national myths that structure these practices" (Žižek 1993: 202). The World Cup, according to Kingsbury (2011: 718), is a product of the "critical infrastructure" that provides a vehicle through which citizens can experience a powerful form of national affect that is mobilized through "modes of communal enjoyment, practices of belief, and feelings of anxiety." Kingsbury's analysis indicates that activists who seek to use sport to disrupt nationalism will come face to face with this particular form of *enjoyment*, which may produce intense backlashes against such efforts, because of the deeply rooted psychological dynamics that are exploited by international sporting competitions. This work suggests that critical geographers should find psychological approaches not simply relevant, but also necessary for an emancipatory politics that seeks to engage the world of sport.

Sport and neoliberal spaces

In the area of the economic dynamics of modern sport, we have another example of the potential political and theoretical contributions of a critical geography of sport. From a political perspective, there is much work going on at the grassroots level to resist various elements of the neoliberal, globalized sporting world; critical geographers are well positioned to explain these undesirable aspects of the economics of sport. This is especially important in the wake of the skyrocketing costs of stadiums for megaevents such as the Olympic Games and the FIFA World Cup. In many countries around the world, local communities are "swindled" by the use of public funds to build extremely expensive stadiums for billionaire owners of professional sports teams (Cagan and deMause 2008). Not only do these developments demand an ethnographic lens, as Nicholas Wise argues in his chapter on the value of ethnography "in the shadow of megaevents" in places such as Brazil, but, in considering the case of Turkmenistan's Aziada-2017, Horák suggests the need to look beyond neoliberal economic logics, to see how authoritarian regimes use them to further entrench their legitimacy.

In more liberal contexts, however, community organizers are beginning to agitate against public funds being used to support stadium construction, and other perceived state extravagance in the realm of sport. Such movements tell us something about the ability of "average" people to organize around anti-capitalist values, even if the people involved do not explicitly think of themselves as "anti-capitalist." The anti-stadium movements provide a crucial platform for activists and critical scholars to articulate an alternative economic vision. Furthermore, as Ross (2008) argues, historical studies of sport can illuminate processes of production, commodification, and contradiction within capitalism, and geographers can persuasively show how these processes transform the cultural landscape. Indeed, Jung Woo Lee's chapter illustrates that neoliberal economic logics can be implicated not just in stadium development, but also in their destruction. As urban landscapes become increasingly financialized, sporting landscapes that are deemed insufficiently profitable are increasingly under threat of demolition, as happened with Korea's Dongdaemun Baseball Stadium.

In connection with the financialization of urban space, Lee and Michael Friedman both stress the homogenization of urban landscapes in an era dominated by neoliberal economic logic. David Harvey's (1989) perspective on the shift from managerialism to entrepreneurialism in contemporary cities is relevant here. Cities compete with each other to lure major league professional clubs, building enormous and hugely expensive stadiums, sometimes with only the hope of attracting a tenant. We might link this phenomenon with a more ideological analysis in the sense that city leaders appear to be motivated by an intangible desire to put their cities "on the map" and provide benefits to their residents that are difficult to measure and even define. The prospect of a professional, "major league" sports franchise leaving a city seems to be a nightmare for the leaders of any city. As we see in Friedman's chapter on US "mallparks," stadiums are increasingly the epicenter of power brokering between team owners and city planners, as teams have learned to use the mere threat of departure as a way to leverage more lucrative stadium deals. As it turns out, a new and nicer stadium was precisely what was at heart of the recent announcement that the American football team, the St. Louis Rams, would be moving to Los Angeles (Flamer 2016).

As suggested by all these chapters on stadiums and neoliberalism, and the work upon which they build, a critical geography of sport will need to consider how identity narratives and sporting landscapes come together, not just to reflect political and financial networks, but to actually constitute them. And, in turn, there is potential for critical geographers to contribute to the rethinking of economic relations. Doing so, however, "requires us to imagine, carve out, and create non-market spaces where social and cultural relationships are animated by incommensurability" (Hern 2013: 21). It also requires, as Lee suggests, that local communities learn to value cultural landscapes that may not be as lucrative as a fancy skyscraper, but are nonetheless central to a sense of place. The loss of a cultural icon like the Dongdaemun stadium can thus have highly detrimental impacts on community building. In this case, even when the Seoul

244 D. Jansson and N. Koch

municipal government "replaced" Dongdaemun with a grand new stadium in a different location, this was a failure because that prodigal new venue was simply the equivalent of the fancy skyscraper that resulted in the original's demolition. Homogenized like Friedman's mallparks, it lacked the history and social and cultural value that inhered in Dongdaemun.

The significance of community networks has also been consistently undervalued in the neoliberal push to bigger and better mega-sporting events. As Wise and Horák both note, the displacement of poor communities is a growing problem associated with these events. Capitalism's "creative destruction" occupies a central place in the transformation of cities leading up to the hosting of these mega-events, but not coincidentally it is always the homes of the poor and disenfranchised that are destroyed so that stadiums and other "redevelopment" projects can occupy the land (see also Boykoff 2011; Müller 2011). A clear case of how the "right to the city" in a neoliberal value system becomes reserved largely for the affluent and the powerful, it is also important to note that they are typically those with the biggest climate footprint. Although it was not addressed in this volume, the extent to which sport affects the environment negatively is of clear relevance to critical geography. Given the uneven distribution of costs and benefits from global climate change, it is increasingly important to examine the environmental impact of our sporting activities (DeChano and Hruska 2006). Golf courses, for example, are notorious polluters, using vast amounts of water, pesticides, and fertilizers, and sport stadium construction involves a great deal of energy use as well as the exploitation of other natural resources. Or consider how much air and automobile travel is involved in the world of sport from the professional ranks on down to youth sports. In both cases, sporting activities reveal a mostly hidden form of "ecological privilege" (Nevins 2014).

There are some indications that an environmental awareness in the world of sport is starting to emerge at a range of scales. For example, "sustainability" is now a buzzword even for mega-events such as the Olympic Games, with Olympic organizing committees touting the sustainability of their bids to host the games, and host cities proudly boasting of the latest in sustainable and environmentally sensitive arenas, housing, and transportation projects. However, as some geographers have pointed out, the sustainability agenda tends to suffer various transformations and translations that interfere with the *achievement* of sustainability and thus may represent rather more "green-washing" than true sustainability (Davidson 2013; Holden *et al.* 2008; Müller 2015). While the increasing environmental awareness within sport may be a welcome development at many levels, it is our role as critical geographers to look beyond the rhetoric of sustainability initiatives to fully understand their implications. Only through a critical approach to geography can we hold in focus the dual potential of sport and sporting spaces to either entrench or challenge ecological privilege. In the long run, this would allow us to contribute to changing societal norms in a direction that advances the cause of environmental justice.

Sport and racialized spaces

Racial and ethnic identity politics were also central themes in many of this volume's chapters, and especially those by Jon Bohland, Lise Nelson, Conner, and Wise. In examining how symbolic and structural forces produce racialized spaces of exclusion and belonging, Anthony Kwame Harrison (2013) advances the concept of "racial spatiality" to examine downhill skiing. Noting a similar dynamic as that which unfolds in Nelson's chapter on Latino immigrants not being allowed to play on proper public fields in Rabun County, Georgia, Harrison finds that, on the ski slopes, non-white athletes are perceived as being out of place by many whites. Not only is the sport racialized, but so are the associated sporting spaces, effectively facilitating "the perception that certain racialized bodies are expected to occupy certain social spaces and, complimentarily, that the presence of other bodies creates social disruption, moral unbalance, and/or demands explanation" (Harrison 2013: 317).

With their focus on such racial spatialities, as well as other spatialized identity politics, critical geographers are advantageously positioned to highlight the unequal power dynamics that can be entrenched and perpetuated in sport spaces – and to challenge the "color-blindness" of many white athletes (Brown *et al.* 2003), or of the dominant immigrant-receiving communities at large, as in Rabun County (Nelson) or South Dublin (Conner). As Amanda Coleman (2006) argues, geographers have much to contribute to the study of racialization through sport, and, by extension, challenges to racialization. A critical sports geography would challenge essentialist imaginings of certain sports being the "rightful" domain of only one ethnic, racial, or national group, and instead "elucidate how sporting arenas and playing fields serve as sites in which racialized thinking is manifested, performed, and perpetuated – and perhaps even resisted" (Coleman 2006: 98).

Unfortunately, and in spite of the original plans for the book, Indigenous perspectives are missing from the preceding chapters.[1] In North America in particular, the use of Native American names and nicknames by professional, university, and high school teams remains a major source of contestation. While students, parents, and school officials often argue that the nicknames are a central part of the local place identity, many of these teams have in recent years dropped their previous nicknames and mascots in deference to Native Americans (and others) who found them to be insulting and racist (Coombe 1998; King and Springwood 2000). But some teams are stubbornly holding the line, as in the case of the US

National Football League's Washington Redskins and Major League Base-ball's Cleveland Indians (whose racist logos could hardly be more offensive). Indigenous and other activist groups have protested the continued use of Native American symbols by these teams with mixed results. The US Patent and Trademark Office in 2014 went so far as to strip the Redskins of trade-mark protections, but, in spite of this, the team's owner, Daniel Snyder, has vowed to never change the team's name (Lewis and Tripathis 2014).

Enacted through the institutions and power structures of sport, these conflicts raise questions about who has the right (and ability) to represent and commodify the identity of subaltern groups. But alterity typically takes multiple forms, and a critical approach to the geography of sport would thus highlight the intersectionality of social justice work in sport, especially with regard to gender and sexuality. For example, as Bohland notes, legis-lation known as Title IX in the US was intended to provide more access to sport for girls and women, but in practice, this legislation has had signi-ficant differences for white and black women (see also Rhoden 2012).

Sport and gendered spaces

The gender binary in sport has a long history; women did not participate in the early Olympics and were most likely not even spectators (Mandell 1984: 55). For centuries, women and girls were thought to be too dainty and fragile for sport, and so they were either prohibited from playing or faced drastic rule changes to the sports they were allowed to play. These rule changes sought to minimize sport's supposed danger to the female body and psyche. The exclusions that females face in their participation have continued, as in the case of baseball, which even in recent years has been argued to be "too strenuous" and "too violent" for girls and women (Ring 2009). During the nineteenth century, women were even discouraged from being spectators, as this would involve inhabiting masculine spaces that were considered inappropriate for ladies (Muller and Shelley 2006). Still to this day, men's sport is the (often unspoken) standard, with women's sport imagined as the deviating Other. Men's sports, for example, are not typically labeled by gender – they are framed as just *sports* – whereas female athletics are framed as *women*'s sports. One illustration is seen in comparing the names of the US men's and women's professional basketball leagues: the National Basketball Association (NBA) and the Women's NBA (WNBA). Similarly, in Sweden, the top soccer league for men is called *Allsvenskan* and the women's league is *Damallsvenskan* (*dam* being the adult female gender marker).

A major spatial implication of the fact that competitions are generally organized by gender is that so are the sporting spaces. Female sport spaces are often of lower quality – a situation made abundantly clear in the 2015 FIFA Women's World Cup in Canada, where the women were forced to play on inferior artificial surfaces. The men's competition, by contrast, is always, without exception, played on grass, even if it has to be temporarily installed over an artificial surface. Women also frequently have comparatively limited access to existing venues for play, which both Nelson and Wise note in their chapters, as women were effectively excluded as players on the baseball and soccer fields they analyzed. Also discussing this in Latin American context, Bohland notes that female participation in soccer is locally seen as transgressive. For this reason, many players sought opportunities to play abroad, where they could transcend this stigma and circumscribed access at home, in favor of superior sporting spaces and resources in the United States. Set against Nelson's account of smaller-scale sporting practices among immigrants in rural Georgia, we see that soccer is still understood among her Latino interlocutors as a male domain. In her critical approach to exposing these men's racialized exclusion from ostensibly "public" sports fields in Rabun County, we should thus not lose sight of the important silences about how they themselves exclude others. Struggling to simply find a place to play, these practices ultimately reproduce the idea that Latina women are "out of place" on the soccer field, even in their new home in the United States.

Feminist approaches have been central in setting the foundations for a critical geography of sport (Ross 2008). In today's globalized world, a strict gender binary prevails: "It is hard to even start thinking about sports without thinking of gender binaries: boys play here, girls over there, and the two don't mix" (Hern 2013: 54). This binary has clear spatial implications, but it can also vary geographically. Men and women learn how to "read" and perform masculinity and femininity through sport and sporting discourse, as Koch notes in her chapter on localized valorizations of masculinity and paternal rule, enacted through the widely circulated images of certain autocratic rulers as sportsmen. But pushing far beyond gender performances, the very classification of female and male, a foundation of modern sport, is itself a troublingly political matter. This was revealed by the case of Caster Semenya, the South African runner who won the women's 800-meter race at the 2009 World Championships in track and field. Her gender identity was subsequently questioned by some runners, coaches, and journalists, due to her large margin of victory and her allegedly masculine appearance (Cooky et al. 2013). This controversy raised the question of how officials in a sport can determine the gender of athletes. The scientific answer is that no test that can definitively determine gender, highlighting the arbitrary and socially constructed nature of gender, and (in the Semenya case) the complex collision of the varying histories of sexism, racism, and colonialism.

The complexity of determining which individuals get to participate in female and male competitions is exacerbated by the increasing acknowledgment of transgender people, for whom the sports environment is at best perplexed, at worst hostile and exclusionary (Lovett 2013). But a critical approach to sport geographies would suggest that this need not be. Despite pervasive homophobia in many sports, star athletes are increasingly helping to challenge homophobia in sport and the broader public discourse, as seen recently with the advocacy efforts of English rugby player Ben Cohen and American wrester Hudson Taylor (Branch 2011). In response to the overtly heteronormative culture of ice hockey in Sweden, the club Kiruna IF arranged workshops in LGBTQ issues for its organization (including the players), which led to LGBTQ-certification by a national advocacy and educational organization. The club even adopted a rainbow design for its jersey, a symbol of its commitment to LGBTQ issues (Oldberg 2014). Not limited in its transformative potential to raising public awareness, sport can also be an important site for developing LGBTQ community (Muller 2007a, 2007b; Waitt 2003). In the long run, though, sport may provide an effective platform for the reimagining of the gender binary. By examining the spatial implications of, for example, ungendered sporting competitions, a critical geography of sport is well positioned to imagine more inclusive alternatives.

Drawing on the work of Jackson and Balaji (2011), Koch also stresses that a more global perspective on issues of gender and sexuality is important. For example, Carolyn Prouse (2015) discusses the challenges the hijab poses to the international regulation of sport. The governance bodies portray themselves as looking out for the best interest of female athletes in their determination of whether, and under what conditions, the hijab may be worn. However, these regulatory actions occur within a history of colonial and imperial constitutions of race and gender, and the articulations of these through Orientalism. Likewise, consider the situation of, say, women soccer players in Turkey, where the game is seen as the domain of men (Schleifer 2009). While it would be easy to explain this through resorting to tropes about conservative, Muslim societies, at the same time women have access to thriving professional volleyball and basketball leagues in Turkey, whereas in Western European countries such as Spain and the U.K., where women can still be discouraged from playing a sport like soccer. So a critical geography perspective would have the ability to examine differences between different parts of the world without resorting to essentialist explanations tainted by Orientalism and related spatial prejudices.

Conclusion

Over 20 years ago, Chris Philo (1994: 2) argued that "taking sport seriously does indeed open exciting new windows on a host of issues currently high on the agendas of many contemporary social scientists." As Koch notes in the introduction, the basic assumption running through every chapter in this book is that sport is inherently political. In this sense, taking sport seriously also requires taking *power* seriously. Following the critical turn's focus on power as not only constraining but also enabling, critical scholars of sport are well positioned to critique the negative aspects of modern sport and also contribute to the imagining of a better future through the practice of sport. As noted above, sports and sporting infrastructures open up diverse avenues for scholars, athletes, and the general public to pursue agendas toward a better and more socially just future. The first step in doing so, we believe, is to recognize the way that power dynamics are written into particular sporting spaces, through the ways that they are imagined as "national," "neoliberal," "racialized," or "gendered," and thereby also *naturalized*. Comprising some of the volume's overarching themes, these spatial imaginaries are first and foremost discourses of *power*. Thus, the questions we leave with our readers and critical scholars of sports of the future are: What are our own discourses of power? What spatial discourses can we ourselves advance toward a more just sporting world?

Note

1 In noting this absence, we foremost mourn the loss of our friend and colleague, Doug Foster, to whom this book is dedicated.

References

Agence France Presse (2010). "Los Suns" Back Latinos in Wake of New Immigration Law. *Common Dreams*, May 5. Available at: www.commondreams.org/headline/2010/05/05-3 (accessed January 18, 2016).

Bell, J. (2007). Politics and Sports Clash on German Under-21 Team. *New York Times*, October 10. D6.

Berg, L. (2010). Critical Human Geography. In *Encyclopedia of Geography*, ed. B. Warf. London: Sage, 617–22.

Billig, M. (1995). *Banal Nationalism*. Thousand Oaks: Sage.

Boykoff, J. (2011). Space Matters: The 2010 Winter Olympics and its Discontents. *Human Geography* 4(2): 48–60.

Branch, J. (2011). Two Straight Athletes Combat Homophobia. *New York Times*, May 14. D2.

Brown, T., J. Jackson, K. Brown, R. Sellers, S. Keiper, and W. Manuel (2003). "There's No Race on the Playing Field": Perceptions of Racial Discrimination Among White and Black Athletes. *Journal of Sport and Social Issues* 27(2): 162–83.

Cagan, J., and N. deMause (2008). *Field of Schemes: How the Great Stadium Swindle Turns Public Money into Private Profit*. Lincoln: University of Nebraska Press.

Cardoza, A. (2010). "Making Italians"? Cycling and National Identity in Italy: 1900–1950. *Journal of Modern Italian Studies* 15(3): 354–77.

Coleman, A. (2006). "Race" and Sports: How an Historical Construct Continues to Shape Sports, Space and Society. In *The Geography–Sports Connection: Using Sports to Teach Geography* eds. L. DeChano and F. Shelley. Jacksonville: National Council for Geographic Education, 89–101.

Cooky, C., R. Dycus, and S. Dworkin (2013). "What Makes a Woman a Woman?" Versus "Our First Lady of Sport": A Comparative Analysis of the United States and the South African Media Coverage of Caster Semenya. *Journal of Sport and Social Issues* 37(1): 31–56.

Coombe, R. (1998). *The Cultural Life of Intellectual Properties: Authorship, Appropriations and the Law*. Durham: Duke University Press.

Davidson, M. (2013). The Sustainable and Entrepreneurial Park? *Urban Geography* 34(5): 657–76.

Dear, M. (1988). The Postmodern Challenge: Reconstructing Human Geography. *Transactions of the British Institute of Geographers* 13(3): 262–74.

DeChano, L., and L. Hruska. (2006). The Sport–Physical Environment Relationship. In *The Geography–Sports Connection: Using Sports to Teach Geography* eds. L. DeChano and F. Shelley. Jacksonville: National Council for Geographic Education, 5–16.

Edensor, T. (2002). *National Identity, Popular Culture and Everyday Life*. New York: Berg.

Field, R. (2014). For Kick and Country: The 2010 VIVA World Cup and Sport as a Site for Expressions of Alternate "National" Identities. *National Identities* 16(4): 377–93.

Flamer, K. (2016). NFL Returns to Los Angeles With Rams and Sleek Stadium. *Forbes*, January 15. Available at: www.forbes.com/sites/keithflamer/2016/01/15/future-sleek-stadium-wins-rams-chargers-right-to-move-nfl-back-to-los-angeles/#2715e4857a0b3b6506077ad3 (accessed January 18, 2016).

Grant, A. (2014). Mega-Events and Nationalism: The 2008 Olympic Torch Relay. *Geographical Review* 104(2): 192–208.

Harrison, A. (2013). Black Skiing, Everyday Racism, and the Racial Spatiality of Whiteness. *Journal of Sport and Social Issues* 37(4): 315–39.

Harvey, D. (1989). From Managerialism to Entrepreneurialism: The Transformation in Urban Governance in Late Capitalism. *Geografiska Annaler Series B, Human Geography* 71(1): 3–17.

Hern, M. (2013). *One Game at a Time: Why Sports Matter*. Oakland: AK Press.

Holden, M., J. MacKenzie, and R. Van Wynsberghe (2008). Vancouver's Promise of the World's First Sustainable Olympic Games. *Environment and Planning C: Government and Policy* 26(5): 882–905.

Jackson, R., and M. Balaji (2011). *Global Masculinities and Manhood*. Urbana: University of Illinois Press.

Kaufman, P., and E. Wolff (2010). Playing and Protesting: Sport as a Vehicle for Social Change. *Journal of Sport and Social Issues* 34(2): 154–75.

King, C., and C. Springwood (2000). Fighting Spirits: The Racial Politics of Sports Mascots. *Journal of Sport and Social Issues* 24(3): 282–304.

Kingsbury, P. (2011). The World Cup and the National Thing on Commercial Drive, Vancouver. *Environment and Planning D: Society and Space* 29(4): 716–37.

Koch, N. (2013). Sport and Soft Authoritarian Nation-Building. *Political Geography* 32(1): 42–51.

Koch, N. (2015). Gulf Nationalism and the Geopolitics of Constructing Falconry as a "Heritage Sport." *Studies in Ethnicity and Nationalism* 15(3): 522–39.

Lewis, M., and M. Tripathi (2014). "Redskins" is Bad Business. *New York Times*, June 25, A23.

Lovett, I. (2013). Changing Sex, and Changing Teams. *New York Times*, May 7, A13.

Mandell, R. (1984). *Sport: A Cultural History*. New York: Columbia University Press.

McCain, J., and J. Flake (2015). Tackling Paid Patriotism: A Joint Oversight Report. Available at: www.mccain.senate.gov/public/_cache/files/12de6dcb-d8d8-4a58-8795-562297f948c1/tackling-paid-patriotism-oversight-report.pdf (accessed January 19, 2016).

Menary, S. (2007). When is a National Team not a National Team? *Sport in Society* 10(2): 195–204.

Müller, M. (2011). State Dirigisme in Megaprojects: Governing the 2014 Winter Olympics in Sochi. *Environment and Planning A* 43(9): 2091–108.

Müller, M. (2015). (Im-)Mobile policies: Why Sustainability Went Wrong in the 2014 Olympics in Sochi. *European Urban and Regional Studies* 22(2): 322–38.

Muller, T. (2007a). Liberty for All? Contested Spaces of Women's Basketball. *Gender, Place and Culture* 14(2): 197–213.

Muller, T. (2007b). "Lesbian Community" in Women's National Basketball Association (WNBA) Spaces. *Social and Cultural Geography* 8(1): 9–28.

Muller, T., and F. Shelley (2006). Gender, Sport and Geographic Education. In *The Geography–Sports Connection: Using Sports to Teach Geography* eds. L. DeChano and F. Shelley. Jacksonville: National Council for Geographic Education, 103–13.

Nevins, J. (2014). Academic Jet-Setting in a Time of Climate Destabilization: Ecological Privilege and Professional Geographic Travel. *The Professional Geographer* 66(2): 298–310.

Nocera, J. (2015). Athletes' Potential Realized in Resignations. *New York Times*, November 10, B10.

Oldberg, E. (2014). Hockeyklubb Markerar med Regnbågströja [Hockey Club Takes a Stand with Rainbow Jersey]. *SvD Näringsliv*, July 31, 20.

Philo, C. (1994). In the Same Ballpark? Looking in on the New Sports Geography. In *Community, Landscape and Identity: Horizons in a Geography of Sports* ed. J. Bale. Keele University Department of Geography. Occasional Paper No. 20: 1–18.

Prouse, C. (2015). Harnessing the Hijab: The Emergence of the Muslim Female Footballer Through International Sport Governance. *Gender, Place and Culture* 22(1): 20–36.

Rhoden, W. (2012). Black and White Women Far From Equal Under Title IX. *New York Times*, June 11, D5.

Rhoden, W. (2014). The Emergence of Activist Athletes. *New York Times*, December 4, B14.

Ring, J. (2009). America's Baseball Underground. *Journal of Sport and Social Issues* 33(4): 373–89.

Ross, R. (2008). Contradictions of Cultural Production and the Geographies That (Mostly) Resolve Them: 19th-Century Baseball and the Rise of the 1890 Players' League. *Environment and Planning D: Society and Space* 26(6): 983–1000.

Schleifer, Y. (2009). In Turkey, Women Playing Soccer Vie for Acceptance. *New York Times*, March 4, B10.

Waitt, G. (2003). Gay Games: Performing "Community" Out from the Closet of the Locker Room. *Social and Cultural Geography* 4(2): 167–83.

Webster, G. (2006). Sports, Community, Nationalism and the International State System. In *The Geography–Sports Connection: Using Sports to Teach Geography* eds. L. DeChano and F. Shelley. Jacksonville: National Council for Geographic Education, 33–46.

Zirin, D. (2005). *What's My Name Fool? Sports and Resistance in the United States*. Chicago: Haymarket Books.

Zirin, D. (2009). *A People's History of Sports in the United States*. New York: The New Press.

Žižek, S. (1993). *Tarrying with the Negative: Kant, Hegel, and the Critique of Ideology*. Durham: Duke University Press.

Index